# Indians and Wannabes

UNIVERSITY PRESS OF FLORIDA

Florida A&M University, Tallahassee
Florida Atlantic University, Boca Raton
Florida Gulf Coast University, Ft. Myers
Florida International University, Miami
Florida State University, Tallahassee
New College of Florida, Sarasota
University of Central Florida, Orlando
University of Florida, Gainesville
University of North Florida, Jacksonville
University of South Florida, Tampa
University of West Florida, Pensacola

University Press of Florida
Gainesville
Tallahassee
Tampa
Boca Raton
Pensacola
Orlando
Miami
Jacksonville
Ft. Myers
Sarasota

# Indians and Wannabes

## Native American Powwow Dancing in the Northeast and Beyond

Ann M. Axtmann

*Frontispiece*: Male fancy dancers at the 1995 Schemitzun Feast of the Green Corn and Dance, Mashantucket, Connecticut.


Printed in the United States of America on acid-free paper

This book may be available in an electronic edition.

First cloth printing, 2013
First paperback printing, 2015

Library of Congress Cataloging-in-Publication Data
Axtmann, Ann, author.
Indians and wannabes : Native American powwow dancing in the northeast and beyond / Ann M. Axtmann.
pages cm
Includes bibliographical references and index.
ISBN 978-0-8130-4911-3 (cloth: alk. paper)
ISBN 978-0-8130-6197-9 (pbk.)
1. Powwows—North America. 2. Indian dance—North America. 3. Indians of North America—Ethnic identity. I. Title.
E98.P86A95 2013
970.004'97—dc23 2013029224

The University Press of Florida is the scholarly publishing agency for the State University System of Florida, comprising Florida A&M University, Florida Atlantic University, Florida Gulf Coast University, Florida International University, Florida State University, New College of Florida, University of Central Florida, University of Florida, University of North Florida, University of South Florida, and University of West Florida.

University Press of Florida
15 Northwest 15th Street
Gainesville, FL 32611-2079
http://www.upf.com

# Contents

# Figures

# Acknowledgments

As a ballet dancer, I eventually chose bare feet over pointe shoes for performing, teaching, and choreographing dance theater in Mexico and the United States. Writing followed close behind. There is no doubt that one can dance and write—move and think. This book is the result of a lengthy process of dancing, writing, and creating. From the outset, many people shared my journey.

In the late 1990s when I began my fieldwork, others joined me along the powwow trail: Laurin, Brina, Yuh-jen, Jerry, David, my students at the Gallatin School of Individualized Study at New York University who over the years took my course "Transcultural Performance," and—at that first National Museum of the American Indian powwow at the National Mall in Washington, DC, in 2002—Joanna and Isaac. Later on, Tibor generously drove long distances with me to events in Maine. To all: thank you for coming.

Once I was immersed in the powwow spirit, new friends made me feel at home. I met many people along the way—in New York City, Montana, North Dakota, and New England. I am especially grateful to Cliff Matias (Taíno/Kichwa) and the Redhawk Native American Arts Council, organizers of the Gateway powwows for almost two decades, and the Thunderbird Dancers, who year after year offer their Thunderbird Mid-Summer Pow Wow in Queens, New York. Above all, my respect and admiration go out to the hundreds of powwow dancers I saw perform over the years: each individual contributes in her or his own way to the beauty of the grass, traditional, jingle dress, and fancy dance styles within the powwow circle.

I have many to thank for the realization of this project into print. Early readers include José Esteban Muñoz, who was constant in his belief that a non-Indian could write about Indians as a venture across borders. May Joseph, Brooks McNamara, Barbara Browning, and Randy Martin read the text with keen and discerning eyes. As brilliant scholars who have forged new territory in dance scholarship, Barbara and Randy responded with judicious feedback. My friends and colleagues Kanta Kochhar-Lindgren, Yuh-jen Lu,

Laurie Margot Ross, Brina Coronado, and Ellen Goldman offered astute and useful comments.

Special recognition goes to Harriett Skye (Lakota/Sioux) who carefully read several drafts and offered detailed reflections about the meaning of powwow for herself and her people; she is forever present in these pages as a mentor and friend. I also thank Susanna Sloat, Tara Browner, and the anonymous reviewers whose expert advice helped transform a rather unwieldy manuscript into a book. Special thanks also to Richard Sassaman, who patiently formatted the photo shots from a sundry assortment of pre-digital and digital fieldwork material.

My sincere appreciation to Julie Malnig who, in 2001 as editor of *Dance Research Journal*, supported the publication of "Performative Power in Native American Powwow Dancing." Likewise, Ted Bain invited me to contribute "Space, Time, and Popular Culture: Native American Indian Intertribal Powwows" to the *Mid-Atlantic Almanack* when he was editor in 2000. Many of the ideas in this book were first tested in these articles, in my undergraduate and graduate courses, and at numerous national and international conferences.

While writing this book, I had the good fortune to work with some amazing and supportive people at NYU and the Laban/Bartenieff Institute of Movement Studies in New York. During my archival research I was lucky to have the skillful help of librarians at the Elmer Holmes Bobst Library at NYU, the National Anthropological Archives at the Smithsonian Institution, and the research room at the National Museum of the American Indian in New York. Thank you.

No artistic or scholarly project is possible without family and friends. I am grateful to my uncle, Dr. Philip A. Corfman, who provided me with a lovely, quiet place to work when I first started to write. I thank Tibor J. Pusztai for reminding me that artistic creativity is at the core of it all—and for paprikás chicken and walks with Winston. Thanks also to Herb Rabin, Jean Vitrano, Jessie Greenbaum, Linda Homer, and Mary McLaud, who helped keep my body, mind, and soul intact, and to my dear friends Margot, Patty Wolcott Berger, and Emily Leeser for their wisdom and affection. In travels along life's pathways, my sisters Molly Axtmann and Joanna Axtmann have always been inspirational models of artistry and hard work—Molly in music, Joanna in the visual arts.

My mother, Dr. Annette Axtmann, offered unwavering belief in this project. Her career story serves as an outstanding example that one can make changes in life and move on. This book is dedicated to her and to my father, Elbert Conklin Axtmann, a kind, dynamic, and creative man. Their spirits live on in my son, Thor Axtmann García; his cousins Ariel, Tania, and Isaac; and the little ones, Odin and Gigi. I also thank my daughter-in-law, Maria Pacis García, for her friendship. Gracias, Thor, for rescuing me from many computer glitches and, above all, for just being you.

Finally, I want to thank editors Catherine-Nevil Parker and Kate Babbitt and everyone at the University Press of Florida for their help in so many ways. I am especially grateful to Director Meredith Babb for believing in this project from the beginning. It is with the encouragement and persistent effort of directors such as Meredith that the publishing business is kept alive.

# 1

# Bodies in Motion

## An Introduction

> So the cycle has ever continued, and the way of the Sky World, the *manito aki* or Other World, is always renewed. It could be said that the Sky World is far from the Turtle Island, because understood one way that is true; understood from another perspective, of course, the faraway place is Dream time, the place the initiated enter during *apowa* or *powwaw*—a single person's Dream-Vision or a Dream-Vision shared by a community of initiates—and it is as close as the sky.
>
> PAULA GUNN ALLEN, *POCAHONTAS*

*Scents of burning sage and sizzling venison burgers lift and linger. Piercing voices sing at the Drum. Dancers press, tap, and fly into the arena circle in flashes of blue, yellow, brown, and red, Hwe ya we ya, hwe ya hai—(ya!) It's Schemitzun, it's Indian country.*

Throughout the United States and Canada, thousands of Native American intertribal powwows occur every year. Many of us are familiar with the popular expression "let's have a powwow" to refer to a meeting where important matters will be discussed. Yet in Indian country, a powwow means other things—an intimate tribal gathering, a massive dance competition for large cash prizes, or a memorial for a dead relative celebrated high in the Black Hills. Some see powwows as social affairs where people gather to dance, sing, drum, eat, reestablish family ties, and make new friends. Others confirm the central role of Native spirituality and sacred traditions.

Powwows are typically organized around open spaces outdoors on Indian reservations and college campuses or in parks. In the winter, they are also held indoors at community centers, churches, and schools. Tribal nations, social organizations, families, intertribal communities, or college groups host these events often on holidays such as Labor Day, the Fourth of July, and Veterans Day. Indians and non-Indians attend. Powwows usually begin on Thursday or

Friday and end on Sunday, though they can also last for only a day or two. The most active powwow season is from early spring until fall.

In this book, I examine intertribal powwows primarily in and around New York City, New Jersey, and Connecticut and along the Atlantic coastline into New England. In this area of the Northeast, attendees enjoy a variety of activities: concession stands with food, artwork, and crafts; dance, athletic, and drum exhibitions and contests; and storytelling, hand games, musical entertainment, and Mexican Aztec dancers and other invited performers. Fund-raising events, all-night dancing and singing around a campfire, honoring rituals, and behind-the-scenes political, tribal, and community meetings are also common. In other parts of the country, powwow activities may include automobile, truck, and horse parades; princess pageants; rodeos and horse races; and traditional ceremonies such as giveaways, talking circles, and sweat lodges.

Each region of the United States—in the woodlands, along the shore, on the plains, or in the desert—has its own complex of tribal and intertribal groups. Geography, topography, and traditional ways affect how people live, work, play, worship, celebrate, and perform culture and participate in powwow. Each powwow is distinctive. However, intertribal powwows throughout Indian country share many characteristics and reveal expressions of Native worldviews that offer us revolutionary ways to live in diversity and in peace.

My own interest in powwow began on a hot, dusty June afternoon in Brooklyn, New York. As I watched Native dancers join the Grand Entry of the powwow, tears came to my eyes. Here, I thought, is the very meaning of a dance that is personally, socially, politically, and spiritually relevant. I was fascinated by the dancers' drive and expertise, and several questions came to my mind: Why is this dance so compelling? How do powwow dancers express such meaning and beauty? What do their dances signify for the communities in which they are performed? Later on, the production and diffusion of power became a major concern: in other words, why and how does this compelling performance genre draw us into its circle again and again? These queries coincide with my conviction that the performing arts serve a purpose beyond entertainment or pure artistic beauty. At powwow, this function might include spiritual worship, the affirmation of individual and community identity, social and political change, and the survival of a people and their traditions.

## Powwows Are Everywhere

Inspired by my first experience, I started to go to more powwows. Investigating anything and everything on the subject, I soon noticed powwows persistently cropping up in popular culture and in society at large. Musical examples include Hollywood actor Litefoote's rap songs; the song "Darling, Don't You Cry," by Grammy Award winner Buffy Saint-Marie, and recordings by Jerry Alfred and drum groups such as Mystic River, the Black Lodge Singers, and the Cozad Family. Television dramas on network channels often highlight powwow, as do novels such as Sherman Alexie's *Indian Killer*, Susan Power's *The Grass Dancer*, and Louise Erdrich's *The Bingo Palace* and *The Round House.* Powwow is also present in Ian Frazier's nonfiction study of the Oglala Sioux, *On the Rez*.

Likewise, many articles and informative photo essays have been published in magazines and newspapers, including *Powwow Trails*, *Native Peoples*, *Indian*, and the *New York Times*. Photojournalism uses vivid and colorful photography accompanied by written commentary (Ancona 1993; Contreras and Bernstein 1996; Marra 1996; Roberts 1992, 1998). The testimonies of Native American dancers in these texts bring dance into the discussion in vital ways. Instructional pamphlets can be found at powwow bookstands that explain program order, the role of dance and music, and the behavior expected of all powwow participants (Stephenson 1993; White 1994).

Another way we learn about powwow is by watching videos, DVDs, and films that offer a direct way into the kinetic, auditory, and visual aspects of this unique cultural form. In commercial motion pictures such as *Powwow Highway* and *Thunderheart*, powwow dancing and singing around the drum are depicted as part of Native peoples' daily lives. Documentary films (*I'd Rather be Powwowing*; *Traveling the Distance*) explore this through interviews and footage of powwow activities. In 2003, 4-D Entertainment produced (and screened on network television) a beautiful and informative film on powwow practice, *The World of Native American Dance*. Full Circle Productions has produced several videos on powwow topics, including its history, the songs and dances, the regalia, and other features (*Into the Circle*; *Fancy Dance*; *Jingle Dance*; *Men's and Women's Native American Dance Styles*). Tribal nations often film their own powwows and give away or sell these tapes and DVDs.

Early in the research process I was lucky to attend a performance of the American Indian Dance Theater (AIDT) at the Joyce Theater in New York City, at which Eddie Swimmer's spectacular and moving Hoop Dance made a deep impression on me. AIDT, an innovative dance company founded in 1987, is comprised of Native dancers, scholars, and producers from throughout North America who investigate, compile, and perform the Eagle, Hoop, and San Carlos Apache Dances as well as several powwow dance styles. At the Joyce, Swimmer—who is from both the Eastern Band of the Cherokee of North Carolina and the Chippewa Cree Nation—moved across the stage with over thirty hoops, expressing the beauty, prowess, and force of Indian dance. Keeping his footwork steady, he simultaneously manipulated the hoops into different shapes and images. Gradually lifting them high above his head in an intertwined circle of unity, Swimmer danced freely around the stage. Triumphantly, he ended by facing the audience.

Because of my focus on the dance aspect of powwow, I searched for studies that dealt with the meaning of the movement itself. Within powwow scholarship, lively descriptions, historical tracings, and theoretical research make valuable contributions. Since 1990, at least seven academic texts have been published that explore powwows and powwow dancing. Writing from distinct vantage points, Blackwolf Jones and Gina Jones (1996), Tara Browner (2002), Bryan Burton (1993), Clyde Ellis (2003), Luke Lassiter (1998), and William K. Powers (1990) confirm the complexity of the powwow performance genre. The anthology *Powwow* offers more perspectives (Ellis et al. 2005). Nonetheless, I continued to look for more extensive descriptions and analyses of movement and dance that would help me understand powwow dancing more fully.

In the last few years, powwow has had an ever-increasing presence on the Internet, testament to its overwhelming popularity, proliferation, and presence in the twenty-first century. Today if one Googles "powwow," more than three million links appear in English, German, French and other languages, an indication that powwows are a serious interest for many in the United States, Canada, and beyond. The Web sites contain information about powwow calendars, scholarly articles and books, and specific powwows and tribal nations. Some of them are online stores that sell jewelry, clothing, articles for making tipis, and so forth. Non-Indian powwow aficionados such as hobbyists and Native American spiritualists run some of these; as with all Internet research, some sites are more useful than others. Even so, powwow has definitely joined the information technology age.

Together with the impact of countless powwow events that happen each year across North America and elsewhere, these resources confirm that Native American intertribal powwows are a force to be reckoned with, and they attest to and are proof of the existence of powwow. However, they rarely explore powwow dance styles in detail or in relation to broader theoretical questions. In addition, much of the literature relates powwow to the Plains Indians and to celebrations in the western and southwestern regions of the United States. With only a few exceptions, the Northeast—and even more so the tri-state area of New York City—is, for the most part, ignored.

## Bodies in Motion

Folklorist Barre Toelken suggests that "the powwow phenomenon can be viewed as a decodable kinetic statement about the realities of life for ethnically aware Native Americans, as well as a tableau scene of intense cultural meaning within hostile surroundings" (1991, 138). This embodiment of "intense cultural meaning" through moving, dancing bodies is my primary concern. Specific dance styles—men's grass, men's and women's traditional, women's jingle dress, women's fancy shawl, and men's fancy—further articulate that meaning as they surface time after time as the most common and popular styles in the Northeast and elsewhere.

As sites of knowledge, bodies are rarely studied and moving bodies are studied even less frequently. As Brenda Farnell states in her seminal essay "Moving Bodies, Acting Selves," "Although in the past two decades considerable interdisciplinary attention has been given to 'talk about the body' as a cultural object, and to 'talk of the body' as a phenomenological realm of subjective experience, 'talk from the body' as dynamically embodied action in semantically rich spaces has received comparably little attention" (1999a, 342). Still, how one goes about "talking from the body" is a complex task that can be continually explored, debated, and refined. Dance scholarship and the burgeoning field of "body studies" within such disciplines as anthropology, psychology, sociology, feminist studies, race theory, and art history have made significant progress in examining the body and body movement on many levels.

By pushing moving bodies to the foreground, I join many others in exploring new epistemological approaches that acknowledge the importance of what we viscerally live and express through the body. However, my use of the phrase "moving bodies" does not in any way diminish the fact that these (moving) bodies are, first and foremost, people who move—human beings who feel and think, live and breathe. Both individual and social bodies experience pleasure and pain and ultimately remember and perform those experiences through the senses, through time and space, and through aesthetic choices. And aesthetic choices lead to dance and performance.

In order to study a performance genre such as powwow in which the vitality of moving, dancing bodies is so critical, I was compelled to develop my own methodology, which includes fieldwork, archival research, and analysis. I concur with dance ethnologist Anca Giurchescu's argument that "despite numerous theories, prescriptive texts and technical strategies which can be found on how to conduct fieldwork, the fact remains that the very theory and method of ethnography is dependent upon three factors: socio-cultural and political contexts, the stage in a discipline's development, and the researcher's own scholarly background, ideology and interests" (1999, 41). In this case, I wanted to be attentive to the intricacies of the dance and the meaning and dynamics of Native culture and traditions.

## Fieldwork

*At the Park Slope Native American Dance Festival and Winter Social in Brooklyn, New York, in 1998, I feel, once again, as if I am "coming home." It's a good feeling—being in the right place with the right people. As we chat, my friend and I stroll inside the basement gym of the St. Francis Xavier Lyceum on President Street. Drum beats and song resonate throughout the area as women, men, and children of all ages smile and say hi. Vendors sell anything from dream catchers to Peruvian beaded necklaces, fur tails, and finely crafted wooden sculptures. Visitors from the neighborhood and beyond mingle while organizers from the Redhawk Native American Arts Council keep it going.*

In 1995, I began going to numerous urban, tribal, intertribal, and community Native American powwows in and around New York City. Which ones I attended was largely based on the fact that I lived in Brooklyn at the time. It was only later in the process that I realized how little had been written about powwows in the area. Since that time, more fieldwork has focused on the Northeast region of the United States. Most recently I have been going to powwows in Maine. For an additional perspective on the geopolitical implications of intertribal powwows in other parts of the country, I traveled to Washington, DC, Montana, and North Dakota to attend three important powwows in those areas. A complete list of the powwows used in this book appears in the bibliography.

In doing fieldwork, my intent has been to intersect aesthetic criticism and movement analysis, practices learned from the social sciences, observation of the performer/spectator relationship, and an acute awareness of myself in the process. Initially, I went to events as a visitor, or a "first-timer"—an expression Indians use to identify people from outside the community who are attending powwows for the first time. I thus positioned myself as an audience member, a spectator, in dialogue with others. As performance studies scholar Richard Schechner proposes, the fieldworker "is not a performer and not not a performer, not a spectator and not not a spectator. He is in between two roles just as he is in between two cultures" (1985, 108).

At the beginning, I simply absorbed information through the senses by observing and "moving with" other powwow participants. To hear, see, smell, touch, and taste is a subjective yet effective way to learn about performance, and I surrendered to the experience. Later I took field notes as my attention was drawn to how spectators and performers moved in and organized space, participant interaction, and specific dance styles. Because my focus was bodies in motion, I soon started to notice complex manifestations of everyday movement and dance.

At contemporary powwows, Indians dancing in colorful clothes such as shawls and shirts adorned with feathers, bells, fringe, and intricate beading are an obvious appeal. Powwow regalia consists of the clothes, makeup, and accessories that Indians wear when performing. These are not "costumes," and many people are offended by that term. Each dancer's regalia is distinctive within any given style and is handmade by the dancers or by their relatives or friends. Visitors are often first attracted to the beauty of these outfits. The song of the drum—a steady, forceful sound that is the heart of powwow—also draws them in. In this way, dancers and singers pull everyone present into the powwow spirit. For all powwow attendees, that spirit illuminates and remembers the past while envisioning the future.

I am not Native American, and I am not a powwow dancer. I do not pretend to fully grasp what that means. I am a descendant of ancestors from Alsace Lorraine, Germany, and England. I come from a family of singing ministers, farmers and basket weavers, beer brewers, corporate executives, accountants, homemakers, teachers, scientists, doctors, and visual and performing artists. What motivates me is a deep appreciation for Native dancers who have grown up within the powwow circle and dance the way they do because of their own cultural and spiritual traditions and for personal reasons.

In a lucid moment during fieldwork in North Dakota, I realized that even though I had been going to powwows for over a decade, I would never be more than a temporary visitor. That's okay. As a professional dancer for over thirty years, I feel a strong, visceral connection to powwow dancers, a dancer-to-dancer connection. Likewise, an awareness of my limitations in understanding a performance genre that is not part of my family or cultural heritage, life experience, or expertise sensitizes me about what and how to observe as I "cross borders" into the powwow circle. It also keeps me humble. Ultimately this transcultural task of research and writing about intertribal powwow dancing is a passionate leap of faith. Along the powwow trail, I spoke with many dancers, singers, vendors, powwow organizers, and other Native and non-Native participants. Once the conversation flowed, I rarely felt resistance to my outsider status. Hence, I write about Native Americans—Indians—with the utmost admiration and respect.

## The Means to an End

We move, we dance—these are fundamental human activities. Moreover, body movement has an enormous capacity to communicate without words and offers rich possibilities for understanding the world around us. Movement is life itself, while dance conveys that energy artistically with explicit detail and intensity. Yet how can one best capture the beauty and power of powwow dancing and bridge the chasm between written and nonwritten languages? Often as we delve deeper into the study of moving bodies, we have difficulty as scholars with incorporating meaning into written accounts. Dance anthropologist Drid Williams puts it this way: "The fact is that we are obliged to communicate verbally, even when we talk or write about the other major medium of communication—movement. *We are never free of the problems of language* whether we use it in our attempts to describe, analyze, or explain the dance or whether we want to understand what an author writing from the past means" (2004, 57; Williams's italics). Numerous elements have guided both my fieldwork process and the writing of performance into word: the use of choreographic knowledge, Laban Movement Analysis (LMA), and the notion of performativity. Space and time offer an overarching frame of reference.

Choreographic tools help me organize general information about powwows. My understanding of the layout of performance areas, the spatial patterns that dancers make on the arena floor, diverse rhythmic phrases, and the ways that dancers relate to one other and to their audience informs this study. As a practitioner and teacher of choreography, I constantly grapple with the many aspects that constitute a dance. This practical experience guides me.

LMA sharpens my creative and observational skills. It asks *what*, *how*, *where*, and *why* a person moves. These questions are intrinsic to the notion that movement is the basic language of life. Laban-based theory and methodologies have played a key role in movement and dance studies, and many anthropologists of movement and dance ethnologists incorporate Labanotation, a movement writing system. However, though Labanotation promotes movement literacy, it uses Laban theory differently than LMA does. Dance anthropologist Judy Van Zile explains: "Although LMA and Labanotation . . . both originated from the theories of Rudolf von Laban, Labanotation deals with the structural aspects of movement. Labanotation practitioners often notate entire dances; some qualitative features are inherent in the structural description. LMA practitioners seldom notate an entire dance. Instead, they notate representative qualitative phrases, or add qualitative indications to a Labanotation score" (1999, 95n2). Although I used notation during my research, it is not included here. However,

I do incorporate LMA description and analysis—a form of translating notation and motif writing into (in this case) the English language.

LMA is not limited to human behavior and conceives of movement as part of nature, as anything that embodies lifelike energy—an energy infused with innate expressive qualities. This resonates with Native beliefs that all things in life are interrelated in space and time. Laban established the primacy of movement that is manifest in the tangible and intangible urge to move, in the ability to interact and communicate, and in the performer/spectator relationship. As a choreographer and notator, he developed his theories during the 1920s and 1930s in order to re-create in the street and on the stage particular feelings and ideas as dance theater and massive public performances. In these works, Laban and his dancers expressed elements of nature, emotion, and drama. His creative process resonates with that of Native dancers who through the centuries have danced to commune with nature and a higher spiritual power and to tell stories.

Both individual and group movement must be considered when examining Native American intertribal powwows. As Laban has observed, "Group movements can be brisk and pregnant with the threat of aggression, or soft and sinuous, like the movement of water in a placid lake. People can group themselves as hard, detached rocks on a mountain or as a leisurely flowing stream in a plain. Clouds frequently form most interesting groupings which produce a strangely dramatic effect. Group movements on the stage resemble in a way the shifting clouds from which either thunder rolls, or sunshine breaks" ([1950] 1971, 3). Most powwow dancing performed in groups reveals and reflects a communal meaning. Vanessa Brown (Navajo/Sioux) expresses this beautifully: "When we dance, we experience the rhythms of nature, like our heartbeats, like seasons, like gestation periods. When we dance with other people, we use our bodies like living gestures and symbols in patterns that relate us to those other people who are there, and to all the other people everywhere" (qtd. in Toelken 1991, 151). As I observe a Grand Entry, an intertribal dance, or people dancing together in a grass or fancy dance, it becomes evident that the dancers are individuals in relation to one another as a community of movers.

In addition to my use of choreographic knowledge and LMA, I continually ask myself: How do the terms "performance" and "performativity" relate to Native American intertribal powwows? And how is performance theory relevant to the study of powwow? Several definitions of "performance" offer partial answers. Historian Joseph Roach proposes that performance by consensus might refer to the completion of a purpose, the actualization of potential, and restored behavior related to personal and collective memory (1996, 3). Schechner suggests that "performances exist only as actions, interactions, and relationships" and lists numerous performance types (2002, 24–25).

Each performance genre and the variations within each genre combine their own version of components. Powwow integrates six of the categories Schechner lists: everyday life, the arts, popular entertainment, sacred and secular ritual, and play. Most important, as a performance genre powwow is a lively, reciprocal, and ever-changing dialogue between performers, spectators, and myriad other obvious and not-so-obvious players. During this dialogue, participants interact physically, socially, and spiritually with one another.

Within this ongoing communicative process, a notion of *performativity* emerges. A body action is performative when it articulates an image, feeling, or thought that is understood—consciously or unconsciously—between performer(s) and spectator(s). Bonnie Urciuolu observes that "any activity that coordinates action to create a unity from many selves—dance, ritual, religion, sport, even military actions—can generate performative moments" (2001, 202). My contention is that by identifying body actions as "performative movements," one can distinguish recognizable characteristics of a particular cultural expression, performance genre, or dance style.

In powwow, as actions recur either in the same dance or across dances and are executed repeatedly, they gather strength through the generations—across history. As philosopher Judith Butler asserts, "Performative acts are forms of authoritative speech: most performatives, for instance, are statements that, in the uttering, also perform a certain action and exercise a binding power" (1993, 225). Hence, this power accumulates through repetition and radiates into powwow dance styles as moving bodies transform and are transformed through space and time.

Choreographic tools, LMA, and notions of performance and performativity offer me ways to experience, look at, and write about powwows. They also serve as entrances into the task of prioritizing bodies in motion on many different levels. How do the forms of the dance styles express the content of postcolonial experience? In considering how bodies, transculturation, and power interrelate through movement, the ever-present specter of history and its effect on contemporary Native life must be taken into account.

## History, Genocide, and Dance

The United States continues to be a symbolic and real place of new arrivals and the promise of a better future. Yet centuries ago, before the voluntary and involuntary influx of immigrants from Europe, Latin America, Asia, Africa, the Black Atlantic and elsewhere, the first Americans populated the vast territory now known as the United States. Characterized by infinitely diverse social and cultural practices, languages, and religions, these people "owned," hunted, fished, and worked on a land that included plains, mountains, fertile earth, dense forests, and waterways. When explorers and fur traders arrived in the early 1600s, many Indians welcomed them. But commercial transactions soon developed that would transform Native life forever. Shockingly, in 2013, many members of the general public disregard the fact that this country was originally home to millions of Indian individuals and hundreds of tribal groups and nations.

The intertwined narratives of Indian country, the United States, and Canada have been documented from multiple perspectives, many of which are misguided and misinformed. It was not until the early 1970s that a more Native-focused account began to emerge (Edmunds 1995). Through the decades this viewpoint has strengthened and prevailed, contesting much of what had been written before.

An outstanding example of how information has been misconstrued is the debate about population numbers before the first European explorers came to North America in the late 1400s and early 1500s. In his best-selling book *1491*, Charles C. Mann considers this issue in depth (2006, 33–148). It is now generally accepted that there were approximately 18 million Indians living in what is now the United States of America in the precontact period. Evan T. Pritchard writes that in the Northeast, "there may have been over eighty thousand Algonquian-speaking people in those twenty-eight counties of what is now New York State" in the period 1300 to 1600 CE (2002, 5). Scholars acknowledge that it is likely that in 1400 as many as 20,000 Native people lived in what is now called the state of Maine. These people were predecessors of today's Wabanaki tribes and are part of the Algonquian language family.

Once contact began in earnest, settlers came from many different backgrounds and cultural heritages. Often they considered Native ways of life with trepidation and misunderstanding. As a new nation-state began to formulate its own cultural identity in the late seventeenth and eighteenth centuries, the original inhabitants of the continent were subjected to a long and violent process during which countless tribal nations and individuals were annihilated. Over 400 years of disease and starvation, wars, broken treaties, and the appropriation of land rights are only part of the story. The control and regulation of Indians by the imposition of institutions such as boarding schools, where Indian children were obligated to cut their hair, were prohibited from speaking their indigenous languages, and were indoctrinated into the Christian religion, radically changed Indian lives forever.

The terrible reality is that during the early postcontact years, in the Northeast alone "some tribes were completely wiped out by disease; others lost 50, 75, or 90 percent of their number as one epidemic after another swept through their country" (Calloway [1991] 1999, 53). The eradication of Native peoples in this region was primarily the result of smallpox, bubonic plague, measles, influenza, cholera, typhus, and other infectious illnesses imported from Europe; ongoing wars; and Native peoples' eventual need to "disappear" into the general population in order to survive. Intermarriage with blacks and Europeans, slavery, and what was called the pauper apprenticeship, or the indentured servitude of young Native children, were part of this process (Calloway [1991] 1999; Herndon and Sekatau 2003; Lepore 1998; Newell 2003; Pritchard 2002).

Across the continent, Indians experienced a shrinking land base. Gradually they were confined to increasingly smaller areas of space with minimal means of livelihood. Land boundaries, which had once been nonexistent, were controlled by foreign intruders as greed coupled with a sense of "manifest destiny" repeatedly produced military, cultural, racial, sexual, and biological warfare. Throughout the United States the ultimate plan of the federal government and the U.S. military was to divide and conquer through domination (Jaimes 1992, 123–138; Roberts 1992). Tragically, by the 1930s many Native lifestyles, languages, and religious customs had been destroyed or repressed.

Many scholars, artists, and political activists call this genocide: an American holocaust in which colonizers directly and indirectly attacked the bodies, spirits, and intellects of Native peoples. These attacks transformed the very roots of Native social structures by superimposing organizational hierarchies and alien customs, belief systems, and everyday activities. This process racially and culturally marked and controlled Indian bodies, which were seen as "savage" or "noble," depending on the circumstance. Indians were killed, tortured, infected, raped, displaced, enslaved, and publicly displayed. We must acknowledge and remember the raw physicality of these acts.

Parallel to the physicality of genocide is the physicality of dance. European settlers often regarded Indian dance, a profound and visceral expression of Native spiritual beliefs, as pagan and wild, evil and "uncivilized." This suspicion of Indian bodies, and especially of dancing bodies, was widespread and a key element of the colonization of Native peoples.

In this book, I consider the formation of a collective memory in Indian country that began hundreds of years ago before contact and includes life experiences of genocide and violence that is direct and physical or "passively" covert.

Bodies do not exist in isolation or in a vacuum. Native peoples remember and express all that they and their ancestors have experienced. Poverty, inherited or actual experiences of racism, stereotypical representations in popular media and elsewhere, and the blatant ignoring of the presence of real, flesh-and-blood Indians persist in contemporary times.

In addition, the economic situation in Indian country is dire on reservations, in urban centers, and elsewhere. As Joe Flying Bye (1921–2000), Holy Man of the Hunkpapa tribe of the Lakota/Sioux Nation of the Standing Rock Reservation, says in the film *The Right to Be*: "We are not free today, the buffalo and the humans are not free, we're inside the walls of reservations, buffalo are in the pasture. . . . I'm looking at my people, they have no home, but they have many children, but we have nothing to teach them. All is taken by white people, land is all owned by the government of the United States. All we have is to garden, garden work, get in the car and go someplace, pleasure places, liquor stores, bars. That's all there is on the reservation, other places. How can we train our children, can you tell me how we can train our children, with all this in the wind?" (1995). In their widespread popularity and increasing proliferation, powwows have responded, in part, to this Holy Man's words.

## Book Organization

This text is structured much as an arena program at a typical powwow in the New York City tri-state area, which usually consists of a grass dance, the Grand Entry, intertribal dances, traditional dances, a tiny tots dance, a jingle dress dance, and fancy dances. Within this framework, history, space and time, transcultural exchange, race relations, and power are explored as aspects of powwow meaning. The questions of how and why power operates through the bodies in motion of Native American powwow dancers permeate all the chapters.

In chapters 2 and 3, I examine a "polychronic genealogy" of powwow, a concept that emerges from Native American notions of space and time. In a discussion of early contact dance societies, chapter 2 looks at the Grass Dance of centuries ago and the contemporary grass dance style as two distinct dances. In chapter 3, I continue to trace body actions by looking at the impact of non-Native organized performances on powwow during the nineteenth and early twentieth centuries. Immediately one can observe how intertribal and transcultural exchange influenced powwow development.

Chapter 4, which is based on my fieldwork, revisits the actual experience of powwowing as I take the reader with me along powwow circuits and into performance areas and the arena circle. Powwow circuits or trails refer to the routes that families, friends, tribal leaders and organizers, dancers, drum groups, and vendors follow as they go from one celebration to another in a particular region. Although this diasporic travel, scattering, and gathering has been part of the lifestyle of nomadic Indian tribes for centuries, colonization often made it compulsory. Today, when Indians, non-Indians, and tourists journey along powwow circuits, the result is a kind of taking or retaking of the land. After a glimmer of these "traveling circles," we arrive at the Grand Entry—the first moment of powwow.

In chapters 5, 6, and 7, I grapple with the complex and contentious issue of race. Chapter 5 discusses the meanings of the words "pan-Indian," "tribal" and "intertribal," and "transculturation" and explores powwows as sites of transcultural exchange exemplified in the Grand Entry, the intertribal dance, the tiny tots dance, and the men and women's traditional styles. Chapter 6 looks at racism and its meaning for Native dance. In chapter 7, I examine the flip side of "performing race" by exploring how and why non-Indians—tourists, wannabes, hobbyists, and New Age practitioners—"play Indian." Wannabes is a general term that refers to all non-Indians who dance in the arena circle "as if" they were Indians or "as if" they were performing Native American traditional dances. Both Indians and non-Indians participate at powwows, but the performances of race they engage in have major and significant differences.

The concluding chapter focuses on how the women's jingle dress and the women and men's fancy dance styles exemplify dynamic dance practices that are ancient and modern, traditional and in transformation. This chapter also delves into the role of Native American intertribal powwows in the context of power relations in a postcolonial world.

•

Today Native peoples attain and perform power as tribal and intertribal education, political organizations and activism, and cultural manifestations of many different Indian identities confront hundreds of years of violence and repression. Without a doubt, intertribal powwows and the use of dance as a language of affirmation and unity play a role in these confrontations. Ultimately, intertribal powwows cross and confuse the borders of nations within a nation, places within a space, boundaries within boundaries. Important questions about Indian resilience, fortitude, and solidarity emerge in any consideration of the future of Indian country.

This book is written largely for members of the general public who are attracted to powwows and go to them. It may also appeal to readers who are drawn to the ways that movement theory can inform our understanding of dance, performance, and Native American traditions and to those who study postcolonial power relations and how humans interact with and through their bodies.

Last, this book is not an all-inclusive study of powwow. Many elements of this complex performance genre are not discussed here. Other aspects are mentioned but not analyzed in detail. And though I often draw on fieldwork, I do not offer a comprehensive examination of any specific tribal or intertribal powwow. Furthermore, just as movement and dance are profoundly "in the moment," powwows are forever changing. In this sense, to *write* about powwow dance contradicts its very temporal essence. Given the vast complexity of the subject, the task of studying powwow is a collective venture. Many Indian and non-Indian practitioners and scholars have spoken and written about this spectacular performance genre and will continue to do so in the future.

I wholeheartedly agree with dance scholar Jacqueline Shea Murphy's proposition that "Native dance that continues as a bodily practice, passed from person to person, family to family, generation to generation, that's readable one way inside and another way fifty years outside of its chronological moment, doesn't need to be preserved by hobbyists, or documented by dance scholars, to have the effects it has. It continues to affect its practitioners, its audience members, even the children running around not paying much attention while their parents are practicing what they're going to perform. It has them regardless of whether anyone knows it'll have them, or writes about them" (2007, 26). Hence, this book is a raindrop in the pond, a contribution with a particular focus, no more and no less. My hope is that the enthusiasm, respect, and passion with which it is written will be infectious and will inform and inspire.

## Terminology

How we incorporate terms into our writing is always crucial. This is particularly true when one is writing across borders. "Indian country" is an expression that I use frequently in this book. It refers to anywhere where peoples of Native American descent live and conduct their lives. It can also mean those Indian individuals and tribes who share Native American ancestry and history, traditions, and cultural practices. Indian country also applies to the western regions of the United States where Indians live, although "Indian Territory" is more commonly used in this context.

Native peoples of North America are usually referred to as Native American, Indian, Native, American Indian, and Amerindian. First Nation is an expression common in Canada. Depending on the circumstance, I use Native American, Indian, and Native because they are used interchangeably in Indian country and in powwow scholarship. Indian, once considered derogatory and demeaning, is now commonly used by Native Americans themselves and by others with respect. When writing about a broader mix of Native peoples from the Americas, including people from Mexico, Central, and South America, I use the term indigenous.

In Native American studies, the Northeast points to a large geographical area that reaches from northern Maine and southern Canada into New England, New York State, Pennsylvania, Delaware, and Virginia and across the Midwest and Great Lakes regions as far as Ohio, Indiana, Illinois, Wisconsin, and Michigan. Historically it includes many tribes under the umbrella of the Algonquian, Iroquoian, and Siouan language families (Calloway [1991] 1999, 9; Champagne 1994, 55–91). In this book, my fieldwork focuses on the Atlantic coastline in New England with a concentration on the city of New York and its surrounding states. Hence, here the Northeast refers to this smaller region that has been home to the Algonquian peoples, including the Lenape tribe. Today, however, apart from the Shinnecock Indian Nation on Long Island, the Native population in and around New York City is predominantly intertribal.

Precontact refers to the period before the arrival of Christopher Columbus in 1492 and other early contact European explorers, traders, and settlers. Subsequently the settlement of what is now the United States and Canada by the Spanish, Dutch, Italian, French, English, and Portuguese was sporadic, covered many different areas of the continent, and was full of complex exchanges with Native peoples that were both friendly and violent (Mann 2002).

Finally, colonialism is oftentimes thought of in relation to Africa, Southeast Asia, India, and so forth. In this book, I speak of the colonization of the indigenous peoples of North America and more specifically of the United States. In the mid-1500s, during the early contact years, disease created genocidal losses before European settlers began making laws that can be considered colonization policies. Until the late nineteenth century, Native peoples experienced colonization in many ways as a result of these policies: land was taken away, children were removed from their tribal homes, laws prohibited Indian languages and customs, the federal government broke treaties and agreements, and poverty and disease took a tremendous toll. A postcolonial Indian country began after the end of the Indian wars in the late 1800s. Taking into consideration the indigenous perspective, Native peoples continue to live in the shadow of colonialism.

# 2 

# A Polychronic Genealogy

> The natives of America thought of the cosmos as a unit that was throbbing with the same life-force of which they were conscious within themselves; a force that gave to the rocks and hills their stable, unchanging character; to every living thing on land or water the power of growth and of movement; to man the ability to think, to will and to bring to pass. This universal and permeating life-force was always thought of as sacred, powerful, like a god.
>
> ALICE C. FLETCHER, *INDIAN GAMES AND DANCES WITH NATIVE SONGS*

It's a sunny day in New York City. Under the scorching sun, young men wearing colorful fringe, ankle bells, and hair roaches come into the circle. Hopping, bending, and stamping, they press the dry dirt into the ground. During the contemporary grass dance style, male dancers move side to side and backward in full-bodied, flowing shifts of weight. Their three-dimensional bent-knee twists are supported by a teetering wide stance as they sway and bob in constant, even rhythms.

Historically, grass dancers prepared the ground for camping and for rituals before or after war by stomping down high prairie grass. As Reuben Jess Sandoval Jr. (Yakima) informs us: "There are four or five different stories that go with it. The story I'm most familiar with is that a long time ago, before the Northern Plains tribes would set up a camp, they would call out their grass dancers. The grass dancers would dance down all the grass and bless the ground at the same time. Dancing down the grass would make it easier for people to walk around, to put up their teepees. Also, blessing the ground was so nothing would happen to the people" (qtd. in Contreras and Bernstein 1996, 127–128). Preparing the ground—the earth—through dance is an integrated physical and spiritual act that links contemporary and historical traditions.

The grass dance style described above and performed at powwows today is related to but not to be confused with the Omaha/Hethushka Grass Dance of years ago.

•

In Indian country, dance is a highly significant nonverbal performance text that embodies and transmits narrative across space and time. Here Paul Connerton's (1989) idea that social memory is constructed through commemorative rituals comprised of body actions of posture, patterned movement or lexicons, and verbal and gestural repetition is relevant: today's powwows and powwow dance styles originate from moving bodies. As Brenda Farnell proposes: "If, as history, the past lies behind us, as memory it remains with us, not only in words but also in our neuromuscular patterning and kinesthetic memories—the way in which specific experiences and concepts of time/space are built into our bodily modus operandi" (1999a, 352). Through bodies in motion, this historical process happens in the context of "mythic," cyclical time.

Space and time mesh in a Native American world view. Anthropologist Edward T. Hall's term "polychronic" is a good way to think of this: things happen in a circular way rather than in a chronological, scheduled order (Allen [1986] 1992, 2004; Deloria 1994; Hall 1983, 1989). This is not to exclude the sequential time line that marks human evolution and history. However, polychronicity offers a way to understand how choreographic elements—performative body actions and performance practices—present themselves in ongoing yet complex variations across time. These elements have survived and changed over long periods of time to produce powwow dance styles that carry the force and magnitude of that which endures. They also define powwow as a performance genre.

This chapter examines how actions and practices have emerged from early contact dance societies. The first written records of these societies emerged in the nineteenth century, but oral history tells us that the dances most likely existed in precontact times. Recent scholarship offers versions of powwow history (Browner 2002, 20–32; Ellis 2003, 29–54; Huenemann 1992; Powers 1990; Ridington, Hastings, and Attachie 2005, 124–127; Young 1981). My approach is distinctive in its focus on actual body movement and other performance details. However, tracing movement is a challenge. A body action is never repeated the same way twice. In trying to capture some of these transitory and fleeting moments, one must be humble with the knowledge that dance is an ever-evolving cultural manifestation.

Furthermore, historical records from the distant past are limited by possible fallacies and biases. George Catlin (1796–1872), who made a major contribution to Native American history through written and visual depictions of Indian life, was well aware of its vast diversity even though today his descriptions could be considered offensive:

> The Mandans, like all the other tribes, lead lives of idleness and leisure; and of course devote a great deal of time to their sports and amusements, of which they have a great variety. Of these, dancing is one of the principal, and may be seen in a variety of forms: such as the buffalo dance, the boasting dance, the begging dance, the scalp dance, and a dozen other kinds of dances, all of which have their peculiar characters and meanings or objects.
>
> These exercises are exceedingly grotesque in their appearance, and to the eye of a traveler who knows not their meaning or importance, they are an uncouth and frightful display of starts, and jumps, and yelps, and jarring gutturals, which are sometimes truly terrifying. But when one gives them a little attention, and has been lucky enough to be initiated into their mysterious meaning, they become a subject of the most intense and exciting interest. ([1836] 2002, 23)

Likewise, Clark Wissler's edited anthology *Societies of the Plains Indians* (1916a), which includes his "Discussion on Shamanistic and Dancing Societies"—a source that many powwow scholars refer to (Browner 2002; Ellis 2003; Powers 1990; Young 1981)—is in no way flawless.

Within powwow scholarship, Tara Browner has proposed that much of Wissler's writing is questionable primarily because "in fact, he never saw many of the tribes he wrote about, much less experienced their music and dance" (2002, 26–27). She is concerned with how his written materials have steadily superseded and "pushed aside" Native oral knowledge (2002, 20–21). On the other hand, Clyde Ellis argues that the work of Wissler, James Mooney, and others "formed a bridge between the twilight of the old societies and their dances and the new forms of dance that appeared during and after the reservation era" (2003, 32). As in all historical documentation, how one interprets the data is what is important.

In my examination of the writings of early explorers, settlers, and ethnologists, I want to be mindful of the times in which they wrote. It is also crucial to differentiate between what these people *might* have seen and their oftentimes sweeping conclusions. For the purposes of this project, the nineteenth- and early twentieth-century work of Catlin and Wissler and his colleagues (Robert H. Lowie, Pliny Earle Goddard, Alanson Skinner, and James R. Murie) is particularly evocative in its vivid descriptions of dance rituals. The many oral histories narrated in text and film are also relevant (Browner 2002, 100–144; Roberts 1992; Contreras and Bernstein 1996; and the videos *Into the Circle* [1992], *Schemitzun '94* [1995], and *Native American Men's and Women's Dance Styles*

[1994]). Similarly, any exploration of the connections between today's powwow dances and the dance rituals of earlier times specific to Native peoples in the Northeast must consider several key mid-twentieth-century ethnographies of the Penobscot, Cherokee, and Iroquois tribes (Fenton [1941] 2005; Fenton [1953] 1991; Fletcher [1915] 1994; Kurath [1964] 2000; Speck and Bloom [1951] 1993; and Speck [1940] 1998).

In archival descriptions, eyewitness accounts, and contemporary discussions of powwow history, two factors emerge as constants: the centrality of dance and a phenomenon referred to as Iruska, I-ru-shka, or Eh-Ros-Ka. Broadly speaking, Iruska means a kind of fire power. As James R. Murie explains about the Pawnee or "Chauí": "There was a very powerful medicine society among the Chauí known as the pitararis iruska. . . . The purpose of the dance was to show the power of the members to extinguish the life in the fire, hence the name. Among the Skidi at least, the term iruska has a symbolic or double meaning. The idea is literally 'the fire is in me' and the symbolic meaning is that 'I can extinguish the life in the fire,' or can overcome the power of other medicines" ([1914] 1916, 608). Alice Anne Callahan notes that according to Wissler, the Omaha Grass Dance emerged from an earlier ritual called I-ru-shka in which shamans handled fire and boiling liquids (1990, 25–32).

This coincides with Browner's statement that "the Iruska Dance—generically known as a 'Hot Dance'—had as its focal point the act of drawing meat chunks from a boiling kettle" (2002, 21). Browner adds details about cross-tribal practices:

> Although the Pawnee ceremony did involve snatching chunks of meat from a kettle of boiling water, other tribes performed exactly the same act as part of one or more of their ceremonies—and for entirely different purposes. The practice is not confined to the Plains; northeastern Iroquois perform the same gesture as part of a curing "doing." Pulling boiling hot meat from a kettle, a ritual common to all Hot Dance ceremonies, might to an outsider imply diffusion from a single originating event. Although physically it is the same act, it has different contextual meaning within warrior society ceremonials than it does in dream society rituals and teachings. Moreover, any Plains Indian of the nineteenth century would have been well aware of each warrior society's distinct nature and tribal purpose and of the differences between a warrior society and a dream society such as the Lakota Heyoka. (2002, 23–24)

Thus, though distinct narratives of how, where, and between whom this dance and the notion of Iruska was exchanged can be confusing, a consensus exists that it originated with the Pawnee and was later gifted to the Omaha/Ponca

Nation and other tribes. The act and meaning of "Hot Dance" also varies from tribe to tribe, though the Iruska Dance is most commonly linked to warrior dance societies.

In his documentation of the war dances of the Iowa societies (as recorded by Catlin), Alanson Skinner offers the following:

> The War Dance, which is one of the most exciting and spirited modes of the American Indians, is danced by warriors before starting out on a war excursion, and as often after they have returned. . . . The song in this dance seems to be addressed to the body of an enemy, from its name, Eh-Ros-Ka, meaning the body, the tribe, or war party, rather than an individual, although the beginning of the song is addressed to an individual chief or warrior of the enemies party, thus: O-ta-pa!/Why run you from us when you/Are the most powerful?/But it was not you/O-ta-pa!/It was your body that run,/It was your body, O-ta-pa!/It was your body that run. ([1915] 1916, 696)

In this example, the body as Eh-Ros-Ka is given a kind of autonomy—it was the body "that run"—and is portrayed as individual as well as social.

Murie notes the propelling strength of the Pawnee Iruska as a cross-tribal unity of purpose: "The well-known Omaha, or grass dance, is generally known among the Pawnee as a variation of their own Iruska, though in its present form it was introduced through Oglala influence. . . . In general, from the data at hand, the writer considers it clear that the modern form of this dance lies between the Omaha and the Osaga but that it was derived from an older ceremony which the Omaha, and possibly the Osaga, borrowed of the Pawnee" ([1914] 1916, 624–629). Although Iruska does not have an all-inclusive pan-Indian quality, it surfaces as an underlying and pervasive element of many early rituals. It also hints of the power of the body in relation to numerous grass, warrior, and sacred dances practiced by diverse tribal groups across geographical regions during the early contact years and may relate to the word "powwow" itself.

Most agree that "powwow" first surfaced when French explorers, upon seeing Indian ceremonies in the early seventeenth century, adopted the Algonquian terms *pau pau*, *pauau*, or *pau wau* to refer to meetings of tribal medicine and spiritual leaders or to the shamans themselves. Native American scholar Paula Gunn Allen observes that "men and women alike who were well versed in the traditions of their people and who possessed certain faculties, belonged to certain clans, and were given certain kinds of Dream-Visions occupied the office of priest/priestess or medicine woman/man. . . . Known as the *midewewin*, the Medicine Way or Medicine Dance, it is not necessarily concerned with healing the sick. It might be concerned with interactions between the human sphere and the *manito aki*; it might be concerned with world-renewal ceremonies, or with keeping the community in harmony with cosmic currents as they swirl around the people, whether human, animal, or plant" (2004, 71–72).

Furthermore, many accounts of life in the Northeast during this period attest to the importance and activity of "powwaws" who functioned as powerful shamans among tribes such as the Narragansett, Nipmuck, Pocutuck, Wampanpoag, and other Algonquian groups (Lepore 1998; Rowlandson [1682] 1997). Though settlers considered these shamans to be representatives of Satan, they were actually vital spiritual leaders of their people (Lepore 1998, 97–102). Given this information, connections can be made between how "powwow" first appeared; the ancient and sacred meaning of the *midewewin*, the *manito aki* or "world or land of the spirits; implicit order" (Allen 2004, 334); and the cross-tribal ceremonies of Iruska fire power. In this way, "powwow" has evolved from disparate sources that ultimately combine in close approximation to the meaning of powwow today as a powerful, sacred, and healing entity.

Browner offers yet another etymology of "powwow." She suggests that it emerged when mid-seventeenth-century German settlers came into contact with "various Algonquian-speaking tribes of New England." As she explains, the Germans were attracted to and adopted many of the healing practices of the Indians; subsequently these non-Natives called their folk medicine *pow-wowing* by adopting the Narragansett words *pau wau* from the Algonquian language family (2002, 27–28). Of particular interest here is that while these "pow-wow doctors" traveled widely to practice their medicine and sell herbal and other folk remedies (which often contained large amounts of alcohol and opium), they sometimes included a show of dances. Hence, Indian dancing became associated with the term *pow-wow*.

However the word powwow came to be, powwows are by and large considered to be a Plains Indian phenomenon that did not exist in the Northeast until the mid-twentieth century. The fact that the term itself surfaced in the northeast region points not only to the importance of powwow as it was linked to sacred, spiritual practices and the Algonquian *powwaws* but also to the possibility that some Algonquian, Iroquois, and Cherokee dance rituals may relate to powwow dances today. It also reveals the many ways that Native peoples created vast exchange networks among themselves that extended and continue to extend across the continent.

It is readily apparent that multiple forces have influenced the development of contemporary powwow dance styles over a period that extends from the 1500s (and most likely earlier) through to contemporary times. Oral history across generations of Native peoples, the accounts of first explorers and ethnologists who observed and recorded events during early contact, and the work of scholars and artists such Caitlin and Wissler during the nineteenth and early twentieth centuries all contribute to one of the most extended histories of a dance genre in the Americas. Therefore, imagining powwow dance history as a polychronic genealogy allows one to acknowledge the enduring presence and power of Iruska alongside the polychronic actions and practices that can be traced from early contact dance societies, non-Native influences during the late nineteenth and early twentieth centuries, and contemporary influences and changes. Powwow history began long ago and is ongoing.

## Dance Societies

Many scholars affirm that powwow dance styles evolved from the Omaha Hethushka/Grass Dance Society's styles, which were eventually shared across Indian country. As Boye Ladd (Winnebago) relays: "An old story that goes back to a great-great-great-grandfather says that powwow dancing originated from four Omaha brothers who were warriors. They had returned from an exhibition and performed a war dance in celebration of their success. This was way before the coming of the white man. They were not necessarily celebrating the taking of life but pride in their good medicine. The dance they performed was a celebration of their good fortune as members of a family, a society, a clan, and a tribe. It was a dance based in pride. We still see that pride today" (qtd. in Roberts 1992, 17). Ladd's explanation affirms the significance of the Omaha Hethushka/Grass Dance Society in powwow history. Later I'll say more about this society in relationship to the grass dance and other powwow styles of today. Meanwhile, let's look at how actions and practices first came about.

Dance societies, which are sometimes referred to as feasts, associations, or sodalities, were practiced primarily (though not exclusively) by the Plains Indians. As Wissler and others have documented, many such societies existed during the nineteenth century and earlier. These can be grouped in several ways: the military or *akicita* societies for men that had animal, war, and hierarchical implications; feast and dance societies; dream cults that include animals, berdaches, and *heyokas*; and women's groups. English speakers gave the dances in these categories names such as Thunder Dance, Mocking Dance, Hot Dance, Kissing Dance, and Begging Dance. Ellis states that the societies that practiced these dances were military, social, and religious (2003, 29–54). Their sheer numbers confirm that we have only scratched the surface of their vast diversity.

Though it is widely accepted that powwow dancing is derived from the Plains

Indians, my research confirms that because of the customary gifting, trading, and borrowing of dances in general, actions were also exchanged across other regional areas. Likewise, early-twentieth-century accounts of Algonquian, Iroquois, and Cherokee (in the Southeast) dance rituals forecast much of what we see in the powwow circle today. As the derivation of the word "powwow" suggests, links exist between the rituals of Plains societies and the Algonquian medicine way in the Northeast.

In recognition of this transnational process, powwow scholar Gloria Young groups seven early influential dances into a loosely woven complex that included the war dance (before war), the scalp dance (after war), the calumet or pipe dance (to greet), the grass or Omaha dance, the dream or drum dance, the stomp dance, and the "gift dance," if gift-giving was the most important aspect of any of the above (1981, 103–118). Chris Roberts writes that Plains Indian dancing was of three types: "dream-cult dancing like the ill-fated Ghost Dance, vow fulfillment dances like the Sundance, and warrior society dancing" (1992, 17). However one groups these dances, strong ties exist between early societies and contemporary powwows that can be highlighted by identifying body movements.

## Actions and Practices

The circular spatial form predominates at powwows, and the incorporation of animal and bird movements and sounds into the dances links Indians with the natural world. War and hunting narratives underscore the importance of traditional and spiritual belief systems. Subtle associations also exist between how dancers moved and move in space. Examples include how and why dancers enter the space in a parade-like formation, the circular movement around the dance arena, and the sometimes diffuse yet connected ways that dancers relate to one another.

Within the ever-recurring practice of the circle, several actions can be detected from the following account of the Blackfeet Pigeon Society:

> At the beginning of the ceremony everybody is seated. . . . When they sit in their places and sing, the pigeons beat time by striking arrows on their bows. At the proper moment all, except the bear shirts, rise and dance in a circle, each with a drawn bow, the arrow pointed downward. The four yellow pigeons dance in the center and as the ring of dancers threatens to close in, they threaten them and pretend to drive them back to their seats. Then after an interval of singing the two bear shirts take a hand. On the ground before them they rest their bows. They lean forward holding their heads out like bears. As those in the circle rise to dance, the spectators throw buffalo chips at the bear shirts, at which they raise their

> heads, holding their closed fists at their cheeks and growling like bears. This is repeated once. They rise, take up their bows and dance into the circle, driving the dancers back, then dance outside and drive them to the middle again. This is repeated four times in all. When food is brought in the bear shirts growl and take it; the others wait and eat what remains. The signal for closing the ceremonies is given by this unique pair, they discharging their blunt arrows at the sky. (Wissler 1916c, 374–375)

In this description, a mobile circle actively moves inward and opens outward as the bear shirts "rise, take up their bows and dance into the circle, driving the dancers back, then dance outside and drive them to the middle again" four times. Moreover, the "throwing of buffalo chips" coincides with contemporary powwow practice, albeit differently; today spectators honor a dancer by throwing money on a blanket as he or she moves around the arena. The act of throwing something *at* the dancers (as in the Pigeon Society) or *for* the dancers (as at present-day powwows) resonate with one another as similar moments with distinctive meanings.

Another shared aspect of the Blackfeet Pigeon Dance (and the dances of many other early dance societies) and today's powwows is the integration of feasting and dancing. Food preparation and the sharing of food have always formed an integral part of Native ceremonies and powwows. Likewise, the use of a "drawn bow" and the "discharging of the arrows into the sky" marks a circular beginning and end while the active, taut strength of drawing an arrow indicates a readiness to hunt or to fight. The embodiment of animal movement, as when the dancers "lean forward holding their heads like bears," points to an intimacy between Native peoples, animals, birds, and nature that prevails today.

A later description of another dance called the Pigeon Dance that is assigned to the Cherokee tribe suggests that this practice continued: "Timid, frail, defenseless, the pigeons live in mortal fear of the eagle. Tremblingly the flock stops and scans the sky [lest] the frightful one be coming. When at last he swoops upon them they cringe helplessly and huddle together. The eagle selects a young and tender one and carries him away. Deep in despair, with feathers drooping, the pigeons depart. Such is the Pigeon Dance, typically Cherokee in mood and pattern" (Mason 1944, 162). Archives are replete with narratives of dancers executing animal, bird, and even insect-like body movements and confirm this type of activity in many Plains societies and in rituals practiced by eastern tribes. In contemporary Native dance, dancers often use regalia and body actions to create the visual and kinetic impression of an eagle, a butterfly, a wolf, a coyote, or a bear, and some of these animal movements are embodied in powwow styles.

Many origin stories of dances relate to animals and birds. For example, Skinner describes his version of the genesis of the Bouncing Dance of the Iowa as "started by a man who came upon a coyote performing it, and received the ritual from him. It was a foggy, showery day, and the coyote found a fine fat buffalo which had died. He gorged himself on fat meat until he felt so good that he began to dance and sing. . . . The peculiar actions of the dancer were in imitation of the dancing of the happy coyote" ([1915] 1916, 703–704). This kind of "imitation of the dancing happy coyote" and embodiments of bears, pigeons, and eagles in dance illustrate how present-day dancers relate to and depict the natural world.

Contemporary traditional male dancers depict startled deer or foxes with stop-and-go movements of quick wariness. In an example of insect embodiment, young fancy shawl dancers—as seen in figure 14—produce a lively mirage of butterflies in a field full of colorful wildflowers as each girl or woman, holding a flowing fringed shawl, opens, closes, and tips her body as she lightly skims the floor.

The animal, bird, or insect depicted determines the kind of outfit a dancer wears:

> The tokala seems to be the kit-fox and the society is so named because its members are supposed to be as active and wily on the warpath as this little animal is known to be in his native state. . . . The members wear a kit-fox skin around the neck, the head before, the tail behind. To the nose part some small bags of medicine are attached. The edges, feet, and ears may be worked in porcupine quills and hung with bells according to the tastes of the individual owners. They take the jaw bones of the tokala, paint them red or blue (the old native colors), fasten them on a strip of otterskin or some similar material, and wear the bones on the forehead. On the back of the head is fastened a bunch of crow tail-feathers sidewise, and sticking up are two eagle feathers. All the members used this head regalia. Some roached their hair about 1 1/4 in. wide from the middle of the forehead to the back of the head, leaving hair about 1 1/2 in. long, sticking up. Those who have their hair cut have a band of porcupine work around their heads with ornaments on the sides of the face hanging down. The members are painted yellow, with red over the mouths. When participating in a dance, the officers paint their bodies yellow. (Wissler 1916a, 14–17)

Here we see that a century ago or even earlier, the men of the Oglala Kit-Fox Society wore hair roaches similar to those used by male powwow dancers in present time. The term "I-ru-shka" was used in the nineteenth century to refer to these head ornaments, but, as seen above, it also means "the fire is in me" (Callahan 1990, 25). Contemporary hair roaches are usually constructed using porcupine guard hairs and hair from the tail of a deer.

Through the years, dancers have always put their regalia together with the same elaborate care. As educator and filmmaker Harriett Skye (Lakota/Sioux) writes, "Costumes are based on the individual's conception of humans and animals and this is what they are interpreting when they dance. It's all interpretive and varies from dancer to dancer" (personal communication, 1999).

Frequently, the dances of these early societies combined animal or bird movement (with regalia) with the movements of a warrior or hunter to tell a conquest story. A Dog Society dance attributed to the Hidasta and Mandan tribal groups incorporated many body movements that are used in present time:

> All members wore long whistles, and carried in their left arm some weapon, while the hoof rattle was held in the right hand. A circle was formed. In the center there was a large drum, which was beaten by five poorly clad musicians; in addition to these men, who were seated, two drummers stood on the side, beating hand-drums. After whistling in their places in accompaniment to the rapid and violent beats of the drum, the Dogs suddenly began to dance, dropping their robes to the ground. Several of them danced in the middle of the circle, leaning their bodies forward, jumping up some distance with both feet and coming down firmly on the ground. The other Indians danced without any attention to orderly arrangement, crowding one another, turning their faces towards the circle, and occasionally joining in lowering the head and upper part of the body. (Lowie [1913] 1916b, 318)

The circle, the carrying of rattles and weapons, the large drum and hand drums, and the actual movements of "leaning forward," "turning their faces towards the circle," and "occasionally . . . lowering the head and upper part of the body" are elements of men's traditional dance styles today.

The narration of individual dancers' stories is more explicit in the following Bull Society dance of the Eastern Dakota:

> During the dance the Bulls carried shields, guns, and lances. Some wore war bonnets. Those members who had executed some noble deed recounted it and went through a mock performance of it. Thus, a man who struck a coup would count coup on one of the spectators. Those who had been wounded in battle approached the audience and went through the motion of being shot. Many of the dancers discharged their guns. . . . All the dancers pretended to be bulls. Some tried to frighten the women and children. Boys looking on would sharpen sticks and prod the Bulls with them, who would

> jump and snort like real bulls. Sometimes they would jump up with both feet, sometimes with each foot alternately. (Lowie [1913] 1916c, 190–191)

The Bull Society dance is another illustration of how actions and practices—such as dancers who recounted "some noble deed" and made "a mock performance of it" and dancers who "pretended to be bulls"—emerge through dancing bodies. Note also that the interaction between performers and spectators sets a precedent for audience participation at contemporary powwows.

Warrior, military, and hunting themes were also represented in the way dancers entered the arena. For instance, in the Brave Men's Society—also called the Black Mouths—of the Hidasta and Mandan, dancers organized themselves by societal functions: "While dancing, the Black Mouths lift their circle open at one side. The order in which they marched was: one spear officer, one rattler, the rank and file, the pipe bearers, the rank and file, the second rattler, the second spear officer" (Lowie [1913] 1916b, 314).

The notion of a performative entrance appears repeatedly in archival reports, suggesting that earlier practices serve as antecedents for the contemporary circling procession at powwows or Grand Entry. However, contradictions exist in the historical record. For example, Robin Ridington, Dennis Hastings, and Tommy Attachie write that Rufus White from the Dane-zaa in northeastern British Columbia remembers powwows in this way: "In them days, they never had a grand entry. There was no such thing as grand entry. When the dancers came to the door, and the arena director brought them in and set them on the seats, then they start dancing from there. In later years, these and other tribes started having the grand entry, they kind of copied out from them and started having grand entry here" (qtd. in Ridington, Hastings, and Attachie 2005, 115). It is imperative to consider information from oral traditional records and to be wary of generalized conclusions.

## Women's, Berdache, and *Heyoka* Societies

Other significant aspects of powwow history relate to women's, berdache, and *heyoka*, or Heyo'ka, societies. Spirituality, sex, and humor are key elements of many early dance societies, Native culture in general, and contemporary powwows. Since the early contact period, sexuality has always been a critical site of misunderstanding, repression, and negotiation between Indians and non-Indians. Euro-American settlers exoticized Native bodies as both noble and savage, and fundamental differences existed between how the colonizer and the colonized approached sexual issues. As Allen points out, from an Indian perspective, "sexual openness at an early age was usual and accepted—one of the many reasons the English Christians labeled the locals 'savage'—although pregnancy either didn't occur as a result of these adventures or, if it did, somehow doesn't make it into the record" (2004, 184). These differing world views are evident in how early ethnologists documented women's societies and berdache societies.

Many historical records confirm women's participation in dance societies. Murie describes how Pawnee women openly expressed their sexuality as they performed across gender during the One Horn Dance in celebrations after war: "Men came in singing victory songs and told of daring deeds. . . . Women dances, scalp dances, and victory dances were held for many days. The last dance was one by the women acting as men. Women were at liberty to go with any man and men with any woman" ([1914] 1916, 622). This offers just a glimpse of women's participation in these societies. Wissler identifies many dances specific to women within the Oglala societies, some of which are identified by English-speakers as the Shield-Bearers, Praiseworthy Women, Owns Alone, the Prairie Chicken Dance, and the Scalp Dance (1916a, 75–80). Hundreds of women's dance societies were recorded during these years.

Berdache societies paired the sexual, including homosexuality, with the sacred and embodied spiritual endowment (Allen [1986] 1992, 198–200, 245–261; Williams [1986] 1992). As historian Walter L. Williams points out, "The holiness of the berdache has to do with Indian views that everything that exists is a reflection of the spiritual" ([1986] 1992, 32). The term berdache—originally an Arabic word meaning a boy who was a sex slave—is broadly used to identify a particular type of dance society as well as contemporary peoples who are homosexual or transsexual and are endowed with spiritual gifts. Today such individuals often refer to themselves as Two-Spirit People, identify as "gay and indigenous," and have their own powwow gatherings and dance activities (Gilley 2005).

Humor relates to the notion of the trickster, the contrary one, the clown, and the dreamer. These elements are present in *heyoka* societies. In general, *heyoka* refers to people, often performers, who act as clowns or "lunatics" who do things contrary to nature and expectation. As Browner explains, the Lakota Heyo'ka—in contrast to warrior groups—were dream societies and were "open to all who dreamed of Thunderbeings, regardless of gender (although women were rare)" (2002, 24). A link can be made between both berdache and *heyoka* and today's "contraries"—powwow dancers who often move counterclockwise through the Grand Entry and intertribal dances against the flow of other dancers. Many *heyoka* societies existed in the early contact period and into the nineteenth century, and often Indians used humor to cope with oppression. Joke telling is an integral component of contemporary powwows, particularly on the part of the emcee. These kinds of historical connections are also evident in what might be called self-contained rituals that are often performed at powwows but also elsewhere and are repeatedly executed time after time through history.

## Self-Contained Rituals: An Example

As performances within performances, self-contained rituals can be seen as crystallized performance practices. For instance, in his writing about the Iowa societies, Skinner refers to a ritual practiced by members of the Tukala Society: "When they went to war they might never flee but were obliged to fight to the end. If they dropped anything they had to hire a brave to pick it up for them, and if they were thrown from their horses or fell, they had to wait until someone, preferably a brave, raised them" ([1915] 1916, 698).

The practice of picking something up from the ground such as an eagle feather was recorded during a Wild West show at Madison Square Garden in New York City in 1886: "At noon . . . the Pawnee, Sioux, and Comanche Indians who had been with the show all summer were eating their last dinner before leaving for their home reservations. All were decked out in new boots, pants, vests, and broad-brimmed felt hats. The night before they had performed a Medicine Dance in honor of their friend, Buffalo Bill. They had planted an eagle feather in the center of the great tent and danced around it. No man dared touch the feather unless he had killed a man in battle and could prove it by someone present" (Yost 1980, 174). These two examples resonate with aspects of today's Eagle Dance ritual in which veterans recover fallen eagle feathers from the powwow arena.

In the East, both the Iroquois and the Cherokee tribes practiced an Eagle Dance that is rarely mentioned in powwow scholarship and shares its name and certain ritualistic aspects with the ceremony discussed here (Fenton [1953] 1991; Kurath [1964] 2000; Speck and Bloom [1951] 1993). Moreover, although the Eagle Dance that William N. Fenton, Gertrude P. Kurath, and Frank G. Speak and Leonard Bloom write about is distinctly different, a few correlations can be made in terms of reverence for the majestic eagle. More broadly, the dance's core meaning of reconciliation and peace resonates with the sense of powwow as a unifying force.

Fenton argues that the Iroquois Eagle Dance is related to the Calumet Dance, an exhibit dance that is included at contemporary Schemitzun and Shinnecock powwows in the New York City tri-state area. However, the Iroquois Calumet Dance was not actually a dance but a ceremony in which strangers greeted and formed pacts with one another (Fenton [1953] 1991). These connections might be too vague for some. Even so, they offer hints of the complexity of powwow history and the possibility that many "origin stories" have yet to be uncovered.

At contemporary intertribal powwows, the Eagle Dance ceremony expresses spirituality, but it also signifies the respect that Indians feel for their warriors and veterans. Lisa Stephenson writes that "during an eagle feather ceremony, regardless of the tradition in which it's performed, spectators should stand and remove caps or hats. PICTURE TAKING—with still or video cameras—IS NOT PERMISSIBLE" (1993, 21). Because the eagle is considered a special messenger of the Great Spirit, its feathers are sacred. When a feather falls from a dancer's regalia, some believe that it is a fallen enemy and could turn against the person who dropped it. Thus, the feather is "captured" and a prayer is said to ask it for forgiveness. The ceremony is often "performed by four traditional dancers, veterans (warriors who have earned the privilege) who dance around the feather. At a certain point in the song, they approach the feather from the four directions and attack the feather, usually four times. . . . When the feather is retrieved, a prayer is said" (Stephenson 1993, 21).

As Skye further explains: "The Eagle Dance is an extremely sacred dance for most tribes, particularly in the Southwest. It is done for religious ceremonies and is usually not recognized as such by non-Indians. Within the structure of some tribal groups everyone must stand during the Eagle Dance out of respect for the sky, the earth, and the great messenger the Eagle" (personal communication, 1999). During my fieldwork I caught a rare glimpse of this ceremony at a Thunderbird powwow in Queens, New York. Five veterans put a white cowboy hat on the ground near a feather that had fallen from a dancer's regalia. The men sprinkled tobacco around it. They then faced inward and danced clockwise, circling the feather and the hat about three times.

The descriptions of the Iowa Tukala Society, the event in 1886, and other versions of the Eagle Dance illustrate how a self-contained ritual can happen in different times and places and continue to be used today. Given the severity of colonization in the United States, the fact that this kind of "mini-performance" survives attests to the power of Native ritual through time. There are many other examples: honoring and naming ceremonies, hand games, and the giveaways that are usually based on specific tribal and regional practices.

•

Self-contained rituals and body actions and practices such as dancing in a circle; embodying animals, birds, and insects; wearing regalia; and telling stories are always in a state of transformation. To recap, this transformation is largely attributable to exchanges between tribal groups. Iruska and dance are always present in one form or another. Even in precontact times, the seeds of powwow dance styles were most likely already planted. Young tells us that "the grass or Omaha warrior societies which developed out of the old Iruska met the Algonquian shamanism and Medicine Lodge among the easternmost Siouan tribes and created the environment out of which emerged the Drum Dance. Then, in the 1880s, the grass and Drum dance met and intermingled in the variety of tribes in Indian Territory" (Young 1981, 153). Thus, within a process of transnational meetings of east and west, many tribes engaged in peaceful interaction with one another, and "each meeting led to the exchange of ideas and accoutrements and caused change in the dances of each tribe" (Young 1981, 153).

Likewise, Ashworth (1986, 38), Browner (2002, 27), Kavanagh (1992, 109–111), Kracht (1994, 328–330), Roberts (1992, 17), Rynkiewich (1980, 34–37), and the early ethnologists link contemporary powwow dancing to the Ghost Dance, other dream cults, and shamanistic dance societies. In 1916, Wissler reported that

> our data for the first time make it clear that the ghost dance was but one of a group of modern ceremonies which have since become conspicuous because of their diffusion. Among the best known of these are the peyote, the hand game ceremonies, and the grass dance we are now discussing. Dr. Kroeber seems to have been the first to offer specific evidence of ghost dance influence in the grass dance and hand game ceremonies of the Arapaho and Gros Ventre. Quite recently Dr. Barrett described the Central Algonkin form of the grass dance, the "dream dance," and sought to connect it with the ghost dance. It is however, due to the work of Mr. Murie, that we get sight of the common elements in all these ceremonies. (Wissler 1916b, 868)

The connections that Kroeber made and Wissler restated reinforce the notion that powwow dance styles emerged from actions and practices that transferred meaning and power across tribal and geographical boundaries.

Young proposes that "among the Pawnee, the war dance was modified slowly into a dance of peace, and the Iruska was transformed into a Ghost-type tribal ceremonial. Both merged again into a new war dance which honored veterans, the character it still holds today" (1981, 249). For many, the War Dance came to signify intertribal powwow dancing in general (Powers 1990). In addition, although there are records of women's dance societies from the nineteenth century onward, war dances and the Omaha/Hethushka Grass Dance had less influence on women's styles than they did on men's styles. I will deal more with this in discussing the women's traditional, jingle dress, and fancy shawl dances in later chapters.

## The Omaha/Hethushka Grass Dance and the Contemporary Grass Dance Style

Contemporary intertribal powwows have evolved from many types of body movement, music, and regalia while body actions are interwoven into warrior, hunter, and spiritual narratives. Yet the Iruska fire power of the Omaha/Hethushka Grass Dance and other dance societies predominates as a force through history. Today's powwow dance styles are often called dances or dance categories. In this book they are referred to as styles. The contemporary grass dance that I described at the beginning of the chapter is a full-bodied male dance style that echoes the older dance in some ways.

The connection with today's grass dance style is unmistakable in de Smet's 1867 description of a Grass Dance as performed by the Yankton Sioux: "At the ceremonial dances each member carries a long bunch of grass, which is among them emblem of abundance and charity. It is the grass that nourishes their horses and domestic animals, and fattens the buffalo, the deer, the elk, the bighorn and the antelope of the plains and mountains. . . . It is especially in the spring, when the grass is tender and sweet, that their ceremonial dances take place. The badge or distinctive mark of the society is the bunch of grass braided and attached to the waist of each member in the form and appearance of a long tail" (Laubin and Laubin 1976, 445). Though today's grass dancers use yarn and chainette fringe instead of grass, the notion of grass as abundance and charity prevails.

Many agree that the Omaha/Hethushka Grass Dance was the first powwow dance (Ladd in Roberts 1992, 17; Powers 1990, 136–137; White 1994, 12). Boye Ladd claims that "the grass dance is a dance that goes back to the beginning of the origins of powwow. The Omahas used sweet grass braids as a fringe on their dance clothes. It is said that these represented scalps. Then the Omahas started using feathers as decorations." He describes how the older Grass Dance evolved into the fancy dance style, noting that it began with "feathered arm bustles, knee bustles, back bustles, and big feathered headdresses. This became known as the Omaha dance and then the fancy dance" (qtd. in Roberts 1992, 20). Most important, the Grass Dance of early contact and postcontact times relates to the contemporary dance of the same name and shares actions and practices with other dance styles such as the men's fancy and traditional styles. Browner explains that the older Grass Dance is "rather the ancestral form of what are now called the Northern Traditional styles" (2002, 26). For sure, sorting out the distinctions between the Omaha/Hethushka Grass Dance and the more "modern" grass dance style can be complicated and even perplexing.

Young proposes that the Grass Dance of the nineteenth century was disseminated in the following way:

> At the same time [around 1800, during a simultaneous diffusion of the Sun Dance] the Grass Dance was spreading among the Pawnee, Omaha, Iowa, Oto, Dakota, and Ponca. The Grass Dance probably started as a curing society dance, perhaps the Pawnee Iruska, which was said to have originated from the vision of a man named Crowfeather. Sometime after 1860, the Omaha introduced it to the Sioux and, sometimes called the Omaha Dance, it spread to other tribes. . . . By 1880, most of the Plains tribes from Oklahoma Territory to Canada had adopted the Grass Dance. . . . The Ponca Grass Dance, the He-thus-ka, was said to have taken on "a religious flavor" and admitted women. This Ponca version was given to the Kansa, and the two tribes passed it on to the three bands of the Osage in 1885. The Osage chose to make it their major annual tribal ceremony (the In'lon-shka), abandoning other dances. (1994, 11–13)

Young's statement reconfirms not only the intricate intertribal exchanges that took place between dance societies but also the "religious flavor" of the Grass Dance.

The Lakota referred to a war dance ritual as "Omaha'ha Kai'yotag, Oma'ha Wacipi, or Peji Mignaka Wacipi—Omaha Society, Omaha Dance, or Grass Bustle Dance." This is sometimes called the Omaha Hethushka ceremony (Laubin and Laubin 1976, 438). Anthropologist Mark Awakuni-Swetland concurs: "A principal dance form of the Plains powwow is the *Hethu'shka* (War Dance). . . . The Omahas are generally acknowledged by other tribes as the originators of this dance. This legacy is preserved by the practice of many Plains tribes referring to their war dance as the 'Omaha' dance" (2008, 44).

Awakuni-Swetland also makes the important point that the Hethushka/Omaha Grass Dance emerged during a period of great upheaval in Indian country and "is clearly an example of Native perseverance and ingenuity" (2008, 91). Today the men's grass, traditional, and fancy dance styles share characteristics with this older dance, even though each one embodies its own distinctive style and meaning. One of the most intricate and stunning styles is the contemporary grass dance seen in figure 1.

The contemporary grass dance style, which is executed either before the Grand Entry or after an intertribal or the men's traditional dances, produces a vivid kinetic image. The roach headdresses of grass dancers have either "a pair of plumes . . . attached with a strong, flexible wire such as a car choke cable or piano wire or a spreader with two tail feathers attached to spinners" (*Native American Men's and Women's Dance Styles*). Other features may include "a shirt, pants, and aprons decorated with long yarn and ribbon fringe. A matched beadwork set includes headband, extra long harnesses, and a belt with side drops, arm bands and cuffs. Bells are worn around the ankle above fur anklets. Hard-soled beaded moccasins are traditional but many dancers now wear beaded or painted sneakers or aqua socks. Dancers can also add a choker, a loop necklace or bone breastplate and many carry a fan, scarf, dream catcher, coup stick, mirror board, or fur-wrapped hoop" (*Native American Men's and Women's Dance Styles*).

The fringe, roach headdresses, and bells distinguish the young, physically fit grass dancer as he performs, hopping on one foot while the other taps front, back, front, back, lifting with the same leg that taps, and turning in place. The headdress spins and bells jingle in time with the drum while the colorful fringe, hanging from the shoulders, waist, and apron, moves with hypnotic lightness. Stephenson explains that "dancers should keep either up or down with the beat of the drum, nodding quickly, several times to each beat—or moving from side to side; the purpose of this action is to keep the roach crest feathers spinning" (1993, 11). As dancers coordinate roach, bells, fringe, and body movement, they exude an intense visceral dexterity that is demonstrated by how they integrate movement, music, and regalia while performing repetitive movements on the right and the left.

Wade Baker (Hidasta Cree) says, "The grass dance . . . as I was taught by the older people, is that I have to repeat what I do on the left side on the right side" (*Schemitzun '94*). As fringe moves side to side, lateral shifts coupled with openings and closings of the torso produce a mesmerizing effect. With open legs firmly planted on the ground, dancers reach diagonally across their bodies on several levels of the vertical while lowering the pelvis downward by twists and bounces. Strength travels up through the dancers' feet, which are in intimate contact with the earth. Grass dancers also use the space behind themselves as they bend their elbows backward and wag or shake their lower backs, replicating animal movement. This unusual use of the space behind the body illustrates the concept that the past, present, and future interrelate. Reinforcing this circular sense of time, many powwow dances move clockwise around the arena. In the grass dance style, however, the floor patterns between dancers seem haphazard, not systematic. Cohesiveness is expressed in the swaying fringe and in each dancer's rhythmic coordination with the drum.

As we look backward to look ahead, dancing bodies of the societies of the early contact years and into the nineteenth and early twentieth centuries gave impetus to myriad dance styles. In the late 1800s the influences on Native American intertribal powwows continued to evolve as outsiders and Native peoples mutually influenced one another's lives and cultural practices.

# 3

## Inner and Outer Influences

This chapter continues to trace powwow history. I examine the juxtaposition of Native American dance activities during the nineteenth and early twentieth centuries with events organized by outsiders in which Indians participated and were frequently a major attraction. Although colonialism devastated the lifestyles and much of the traditional culture of Native Americans, these did not vanish. On the contrary, the force of Iruska and the actions and practices discussed in chapter 2 were kept alive and evolved in a multitude of ways. Years later some of these would reappear in the powwow dances we know today.

From the mid-1800s into the twentieth century, massive numbers of non-Native people began to move from east to west. During this period, when the early contact dance societies were first recorded in earnest, Indians realized how valuable their dance and music performances could be in their interactions with the newcomers. As Native American scholar Philip J. Deloria notes: "Indian people of all tribes of course had performance traditions built around dance and religious practice, but these were meant for Indian audiences. First performances for non-Indians most likely came as part of diplomatic protocols. As contact zones became busier and more widely spread, non-Indian visitors increasingly took Native ceremonies as entertaining spectacles" (2004, 57). In addition, "Indian people on diplomatic visits to Washington D.C. would often be asked to perform songs and dances" (Deloria 2004, 57).

Euro-Americans have always been intrigued by the dance of Native Americans and were drawn to their performances for a multitude of reasons that included curiosity and a kind of voyeurism about difference. Indians knew this and used it to their advantage by inviting non-Indians to many of their ceremonies. As a result, "By the mid-nineteenth century, Iroquois, Penobscot, and others had started offering Indian-show performances designed for urban audiences; these would expand in the later nineteenth century and the early twentieth to encompass performers from numerous tribes. Midcentury Indian performers—particularly those who devised and managed their own performances—surely set and reinforced white expectations concerning Indian gesture, custom, and appearance, but, by and large, their material seems to have emerged from Native cultural practice rather than the fictions of the Indian play" (Deloria 2004, 57–58). When Indians organized "picnics," Indian fairs and expositions, and summer encampments to revive many of the pre-reservation traditions, they welcomed non-Native people (Deloria 2004, Ellis 2003).

Later, during the time when Indians voluntarily and involuntarily participated in performances organized by non-Indians, they continued to dance and produce their own events. This practice demonstrates that dance did not disappear from Indian culture. As one of a variety of Indian performance forms, dance continued to flourish.

The fact that dance survived is attributable to the determination of Native peoples to retain their culture in the face of the threats posed to it. By the mid-nineteenth century, Christian missionaries, U.S. government officials, and the general settler population had mounted concerted attacks on Native dance. Many of these people feared and mistrusted gatherings such as the dance societies, the Ghost Dance religion, and the Sun Dance, and they perceived gatherings of Natives to worship in non-Christian ways as a threat to the successful colonization of the continent. As a result, Indian dance became a focus of government officials:

> For many years missionaries, educators, and even the government frowned upon Indian dancing. The great Sun Dance of the Sioux and other Plains tribes was forcibly suppressed, at the point of arms, in the early 1880s. All Indian dancing was feared as "war dancing." Even better-informed people who realized something of its real significance recommended its suppression because thus, at one blow, the entire social, political, and religious life of a tribe could be crushed. Dancing was the most Indian thing about Indians. The government wanted to destroy all tribal organization, everything Indian, and so struck the dancing first of all. (Laubin and Laubin 1976, 81)

Although this negative and destructive attitude had existed from early contact days, in the late nineteenth century it took the form of an official battle as non-Indians responded to Native dancing with misunderstanding, disgust, and much worse. Tara Browner (2002), Clyde Ellis (2003), Jacqueline Shea Murphy (2007), Gloria Young (1981), and others have already written a great deal about this disturbing period in U.S. history. Here I focus on how the situation affected the development of today's powwow.

From the late 1800s until the 1930s officials prohibited Indian dance. In

March 1883 the federal government published *Rules Governing the Court of Indian Offenses*, also known as the Code of Indian Defenses, a set of legal rules for Native peoples living on most Indian reservations. This list of rules was prefaced by a letter written by Henry M. Teller, secretary of the Department of the Interior, that clearly stated what federal officials thought of Indian dance as well as other traditions related to marriage, medicine men, and property:

> I desire to call your attention to what I regard as a great hindrance to the civilization of the Indians, viz, the continuance of the old heathenish dances, such as the sun-dance, scalp-dance, & c. These dances, or feasts, as they are sometimes called, ought, in my judgment, to be discontinued, and if the Indians now supported by the Government are not willing to discontinue them, the agents should be instructed to compel such discontinuance. These feasts or dances are not social gatherings for the amusement of these people, but, on the contrary, are intended and calculated to stimulate the warlike passions of the young warriors of the tribe. At such feasts the warrior recounts his deeds of daring, boasts of his inhumanity in the destruction of his enemies, and his treatment of the female captives, in language that ought to shock even a savage ear. (Teller 1883, 1)

The Code of Indian Defenses remained in place until 1933. Non-Indians throughout North America were distrustful and ambivalent about Native dance in general—wherever it was performed. This had a great deal to do with the needs and desires of non-Indians during this time. Murphy observes that "dance practices and gatherings threatened assimilation policies based on classroom education and literacy, as they affirmed the importance of history told not in writing or even in words, but rather bodily. Praying through bodily movement and ritual practice rather than through sitting, reading, and believing threatened colonizers' notions of how spirituality is manifested" (2007, 31).

After the rules of the Court of Indian Offenses were put in place, government agents often sent written accounts to the Commissioner of Indian Affairs about events they had never actually seen. One letter written from Fort Yates, North Dakota, by agent E. E. Mossman in May 1923 to Commissioner of Indian Affairs Charles Burke illustrates the prejudiced and shallow way non-Indians viewed Indian culture: "The screaming and ki-yi-ing of the squaws, the barbaric tomtom, the savage dress, and the fantastic motions have nothing to do and are not an expression of anything in any way elevating" (qtd. in Murphy 2007, 88). On the reservations, dancing Indians were threatened with imprisonment and the withholding of rations, and they were prohibited from traveling (Ellis 2003, 68–69; Murphy 2007, 37–38). Despite these obstacles, Indians defended their right to dance in brilliant ways by refusing to obey these bans and continuing to organize and practice their own rituals and dances by accommodating to circumstances and going underground (Ellis 2003, 76–77, Murphy 2007, 43–52).

Simultaneously, world's fairs, non-Indian organized arts and crafts festivals (sometimes called ceremonials in the Southwest) and Wild West shows began to emerge. Native performers had little or no control over the circumstances of their participation in such events. Nonetheless, as Simon Brascoupé (Kitigan Zibi Anisinabeb) notes, these performances "fulfilled the even more important task of maintaining the continuity of culture right under the noses of the people who were repressing them. . . . Such opportunities provided needed income and became an act of resistance during a time when Native American culture was under its greatest threat" (1994, 95). Consequently, while these "showcases" exploited Indians for commercial entertainment throughout the United States, Canada, and in Europe, they also provided alternative spaces where dance and a sense of being Indian were kept alive.

The practice of exhibiting Native peoples from around the world can be identified as far back as 1493, when Columbus took an Arawak to the Caribbean and put him on display for two years until he died "of sadness," according to performance scholar Coco Fusco (1995, 41). Fusco notes how persistent the practice of exhibiting Indians and other ethnic and national groups has been: "Over the last 500 years, Australian Aborigines, Tahitians, Aztecs, Iroquois, Cherokee, Ojibways, Iowas, Mohawks, Botocudos, Guianese, Hottentots, Kaffirs, Nubians, Somalians, Singhalese, Patagonians, Tierra del Fuegans, Kahucks, Anapondans, Zulus, Bushmen, Japanese, East Indians, and Laplanders have been exhibited in the taverns, theaters, gardens, museums, zoos, circuses, and world's fairs of Europe and the freak shows of the United States" (1995, 41) . She dates this practice of taking Indians to Europe from the late fifteenth century. Charles M. Hinsley suggests that displays of live indigenous peoples began in the 1870s, when "Johan Adrian Jacobsen was hired by Carl Hagenbeck, a German animal trainer and zoo master, to travel around Europe with a family of six Greenland Eskimos" (1992, 344).

Wolfgang Haberland discusses a tour of nine Bella Coola dancers that took place in 1885–1886 and was also led by Jacobsen. He writes: "Jacobsen was obviously trying to show 'original' dances, i.e. such dances and activities as were common among the Bella Coolas or on the Northwest Coast. . . . The performances had obviously been changed and expanded in the course of time, perhaps also in an attempt to meet the expectations of the public" (1987, 345–346). In exhibitions such as those Jacobsen mounted, there was likely a balancing act between real Native dance and dances that fulfilled audiences' expectations of what "Indian dance" should be.

In another record of Sioux Indians in Budapest, Hungary, in 1886, one gets a sense of what such exhibits looked like.

> Between the different productions, the Indians presented their "national dances." The musical accompaniment came from the rhythmic sound of rattles tied beneath the knees of the men and the monotone drumming of one of the older members of the group. A source of particular joy for the audience was that on one occasion "the dance was accompanied by loud howling, similar to the howl of a dog or jackal, a dance in which the feet were lifted in a way similar to the Hungarian czardas with rapid foot movement. They bend forward repeatedly as though seeking an invisible enemy, attentively anchor their faces towards the earth and wave their horrible weapons to the left and right." At other times the dance seemed to be "but a waddling to a monotonous drumming," in which the Indians "simper about in one place, at most shaking their elbows a bit to the music." (Letay 1987, 378)

One can read through the stereotypical language of the sources Letay quoted to see glimpses of the movement one sees at present-day men's powwow dances, particularly the description of the foot movements and the "bend[ing] forward repeatedly as though seeking an invisible enemy." Public displays like these later evolved into more complex and more theatrical performance genres.

During the nineteenth and early twentieth centuries, non-Indian performance genres in which Native Americans were portrayed developed from representations of life in the western United States. Sources that portrayed these representations included personal correspondence, guide books, emigration newspapers, information from land speculators, dime novels of the 1870s, and plays based on characters and particular events (Blackstone 1986, 3–7). In the Northeast in the early to mid-1800s one of the more successful theater productions was John Augustus Stone's *Metamora; or, The Last of the Wampanoags*, in which Edwin Forrest portrayed King Philip (Lepore 1998, 194–204). Likewise, nineteenth-century medicine shows included Native dancers (McNamara 1976).

In the mid-nineteenth century, world's fairs and exhibitions developed that included representations of ethnic groups from around the world. In the latter part of the century, arts and crafts festivals and Wild West shows became popular forms of entertainment. None of these were developed or controlled by Indians. Native Americans were depicted in each of these genres in ways that complicate powwow history. Fusco notes that these events were "a critical component of a burgeoning mass culture whose development coincided with the growth of urban centers and populations, European colonialism, and American expansionism" (1995, 40).

## World's Fairs

World's fairs began with the Great Exposition of the Works of Industry of All Nations in London in 1851. This was followed two years later by a World's Fair in New York City. Over seven decades, from the mid-1800s until 1916, many international exhibitions were held in cities in Europe and the United States (Greenhalgh 1988; Hinsley 1992; Rydell 1984). Deloria explains how Native Americans were used in U.S. expositions and fairs: "At Chicago, fair officials imported some Native leaders for opening ceremonies; others were recruited for ethnological exhibits in the Anthropology Building and for more commercial enterprises on the midway. At the Louisiana Purchase Exhibition in 1904, Indian students would be brought as demonstrations of Indian education" (2004, 252n15).

Most of these fairs included two components: "displays of industrial achievement and promise for the regional or national metropolis, and exhibits of primitive 'others' collected from peripheral territories or colonies" (Hinsley 1992, 345). World's fair historian Robert W. Rydell writes that "exposition promoters drew upon and shaped such sources of entertainment as the zoological garden, the minstrel show, the circus, the museum of curiosities, the dime novel, and the Wild West show." He adds, "World's fairs existed as part of a broader universe of white supremacist entertainments; what distinguished them were their scientific, artistic, and political underpinnings" (1984, 6).

At some world's fairs in the United States, Indians performed in "ethnographic villages." This type of exhibit was introduced in 1889. Organizers marketed these villages as either authentic representations or as circus-like freak shows (Hinsley 1992). The exhibits and the fairs affected Native Americans in three ways: as sites where Indians could exchange ideas, as opportunities for Indians to travel abroad, and as ways for Indians to gain access to non-Indian performance practices that would later affect Native dance. All of these had an influence on contemporary powwows.

Few records reveal specific body actions and performance practices that might link the dances performed at these fairs with contemporary powwow dance styles. However, documentation of a parade at the Trans-Mississippi and International Exposition in Omaha, Nebraska, in 1898 reveals an opening act much like the Grand Entry of today:

> This procession along the Midway avenues and across the Bluff Tract—but evidently not through the White city proper—represented one of the high points of the exposition. Thousands of spectators lined the streets as exposition police led the way from encampment onto the Midway, followed by Indian musicians and hundreds of men and women on foot. Mercer, astride a horse, came next in the procession at the head of "150 reads [*sic*] mounted upon horses and dressed in war costumes." Many of the Indians on horseback "waved with great satisfaction great bunches of flesh, to which was attached hair, not human flesh and hair, but flesh and hair torn from a beef that had been slaughtered during the morning hours." When the parade eventually concluded back at the encampment, visitors, for a twenty-five cent admissions fee, could see the Indians "amuse and entertain" through athletic events, music, and dance. (Rydell 1984, 114)

Despite the overt racism of such displays, we can see here the components of a Grand Entry. One can only imagine how Native peoples felt about these kinds of enactments and the complex meaning these activities must have had for them.

At the fairs Indians were not passive onlookers but active participants who had a lot to say about the places they visited and the people they met (Napier 1987, 383). Geronimo, the renowned chief of the Chiricahua Apache people, went to the Trans-Mississippi and International Exposition at Omaha in 1898, along with twenty-one other Apache prisoners from Fort Sill. The experience crystallized his understanding of his people's colonized position. He is recorded as saying, "right here at the exposition are enough people coming in every day to put an end to every Indian in the world if they saw fit to do so. Besides this, the white men have all the guns, powder and bullets" (Rydell 1984, 117–118). Gloria Young suggests that the participation of Indians at the fair in Omaha was "the starting place of many friendships which led to interactions like the transfer of the drum from the Kickapoos to the Iowas" (1981, 187). The Native American perspective has yet to be fully integrated into a comprehensive understanding of Indian and non-Indian relations at this time, though recent studies by Deloria (2004, 52–80) and Murphy (2007, 57–78) add much to the discussion by looking at Native experience at the Wild West shows that were often performed at world's fairs.

## Arts and Crafts Festivals and Tours Organized by Non-Indians

As railroad networks developed in the West and Southwest in the early 1900s, towns began to compete for tourist trade. Cultural display became commonplace and developed in ways that would eventually affect today's powwows. While the U.S. government banned Native rituals, it promoted other types of arts and crafts festivals and "Indian detours," which were part of the emerging tourist industry in the West. Thus continued a kind of love/hate relationship with Indians in which their dance was officially prohibited but at the same time glorified and used by event organizers to attract tourists looking for a "real" experience of the Southwest. As Murphy proposes, while dance was promoted as "art" and "amusement," it was largely "disconnected from Indian understandings of dance as integral to religious practice" (2007, 83). By the 1920s, "Tourists could visit a Tewa village as part of a packaged 'Indian Detour' sponsored by the Santa Fe Railroad and the Fred Harvey Company, a hotel and restaurant developer expanding in the Southwest" (Sweet 1985, 45). People traveled west to take these tours so they could catch a glimpse of an exciting and "exotic" region. The Indians they encountered in these tours were often marketed as "noble but dangerous primitives." Moreover, Indian detours included dance displays.

During the same period, anthropologists began "reviving" festivals such as the Santa Fe Fiesta in New Mexico, which was organized in 1919 by Edgar Hewett, director of the School of American Research and the Museum of New Mexico. Jill D. Sweet notes that "Hewett, genuinely concerned for the survival of Indian culture, was not directly interested in tourist dollars, but he received much financial support for the event from local merchants primarily interested in tourism" (1985, 50). At these festivals, which were produced in the 1920s, there might be "Navajo sand painting demonstrations, parades, baseball games, foot races, horse races, rodeo events, and arts and crafts exhibits" (Sweet 1985, 46). The first, the Inter-Tribal Indian Ceremonial in Gallup, New Mexico, was organized in 1922 by Mike Kirk, owner of a trading post (Sweet 1985, 46).

These theatrical events for tourists included elements of ritual and secular entertainment. They featured dance, music, a display of traditional outfits, and booths that sold arts and crafts. Native American performances were advertised as "tributes to the American Indian." However, the dances were used to entice people to spend money, and the only ones who benefited from this commercialization were the organizers and their affiliates (Sweet 1985, 10–11).

During this time, state and federal authorities exhibited a profoundly patronizing attitude toward Native peoples. Murphy records that "while non-Indian artists and tourists flocked to Southwest Indian dances in pursuit of their own enrichment, federal officials, seeing themselves as responsible for the well-being of their wards, focused on the harm they saw the dances causing Native peoples themselves. In dance restrictions newly reissued in the 1920s, government officials stressed what they saw as the ceremonial dances' waste of time, energy, and resources; the immorality of sexuality the dances enabled; and ways the dances were barbaric and degrading" (Murphy 2007, 84). In light of the paternalism of government officials and new restrictions on Native ritual practices, Indians began to retreat from the public eye in order to practice their traditional culture. The 1920s were thus characterized by a context of both secrecy and openness. What non-Indians saw at the arts and crafts festivals for tourists became more than ever a type of dance that was geared toward a non-Indian audience. It was only at home that Native dancing reaffirmed its full spiritual and sacred meaning.

Many elements of the format of contemporary powwows emerged during this period, such as the Grand Entry, the circle, and the inclusion of tourists at Native American dance events. The powwow is truly a mix of peoples, both Indian and non-Indian, and the roots of that cultural exchange lie in the performance venues Native Americans participated in during the early decades of the twentieth century. Other elements of contemporary powwows can be traced to this time period. For example, non-Indian organizers emphasized sports, arts and crafts, and dance competitions; these were usually judged by non-Indians. Present-day powwow competitions possibly evolved from this practice. During these events it became evident to many Indians that one could dance for money, even though the pay was minimal.

## Wild West Shows

Repeatedly I have been told that the Grand Entry was influenced by the opening procession of the Wild West shows that were popular during the late nineteenth and early twentieth centuries. Yet, as mentioned above, grand entry–like rituals were also performed at world's fairs and festivals and as part of many early contact dance societies. The following description of the opening parade of a Buffalo Bill exhibition accentuates theatrical display:

> At the head of the line on a white horse rode Buffalo Bill, raising his hat to the cheering multitude that thronged the sidewalks. Next came the band wagon, pulled by six white horses almost dancing to the tunes played by the musicians. Then came the Indians, feathered and painted, shrieking war whoops—Pawnees, Sioux and Wichitas riding their bare-backed, painted ponies—warriors and chiefs together. Following the red men came a contingent of Mexican vaqueros in bright serapes—oversized sombreros almost hiding their dark faces. Annie Oakley, straight and regal, looking like a frontier queen, rode by herself with cowboys

> and scouts, on horse and afoot, herding along steers, buffaloes, mules and horses—filling the air with a cacophony of yells, whip lashes, neighs, brays, bellows, creaks of saddle leather and beat of hoofs on the pavement. Bringing up the rear was the Deadwood Mail Coach (bullet riddled by Black Hills bandits) pulled by six mules and driven by bearded John Nelson. (Leonard and Goodman 1955, 239–240)

In this parade, Native Americans were clearly performing "Indianness," but they were doing so within the paradigm of the American frontier, or the "Wild West." As Native American scholar Rayna Green (Cherokee) states: "These warriors, Lords of the Plains, forever mounted on their ponies, forever attacking wagon trains and hunting buffalo, become *the* Indian in the American imagination" (1988, 38).

Nonetheless, the act of taking and owning space in an initial entrance into the arena marks dance societies, world's fairs, arts and crafts festivals, Wild West shows, and present-day powwows. As performance practices, they are similarly executed yet embody different meanings. While dance societies and the contemporary Grand Entry perform introspection and community, the Wild West shows expressed an exaggerated, stereotypical view of Indianness.

Buffalo Bill's Wild West, the touring exhibition of U.S. Army Indian scout, colonel, and entertainer William F. Cody, was the best known and most widely traveled of more than eighty companies of Wild West shows. Others include Pawnee Bill's Historic Wild West, Dr. W. F. Carver's Wild America, and the Miller Brothers 101 Ranch Wild West Show (Blackstone 1986, 8). These shows featured Indians from many different tribal groups alongside non-Indian performers. For example, Pawnee Bill's Historical Wild West Indian Museum and Encampment Show included "eighty-four Pawnee, Kaw, Wichita, Comanche and Kiowa performers, fifty cowboys and Mexican vaqueros, thirty trappers, hunters and scouts and one hundred sixty-five horses, mules and buffalo" (Young 1981, 175).

The Wild West show, which included parades, dramatic enactments of "life in the west," and rodeos, shared its "business methods, advertising techniques, and general structure" with the circus, but "it blended the excitement and surprise of the circus with demonstrations of Western skills and the narrative of Western melodramas" (Blackstone 1986, 8). These shows depicted Indians as noble savages, and Indian actors participated as warriors, "squaws," dancers, and singers.

In order to recruit Indians for his productions, Cody sometimes held large auditions on reservations: "Often five or six hundred people would show up in full regalia and of course not everybody could be hired. The government required that the Indians be well fed and sent back home with a new suit of clothes. During the late nineteenth century these 'try-outs' were annual affairs during the spring season" (Yost 1980, 143). Cody consistently defended his treatment of his recruits, as the following account illustrates: "During their stay in New York City in the winter of 1886–1887, for example, he informed federal authorities that his Indian employees attended church twice each Sunday for two months, had visited city hall, a newspaper office, Central Park, Bellevue Hospital, and 'all the principle places of legitimate public entertainment in New York.' . . . And as Cody liked to remind his detractors, Indians with his show were earning good money, paying their own way, and learning to live like whites" (Ellis 2003, 90).

Hundreds of Indians joined the shows for a wide range of reasons related to the harsh reality of colonization and as a way to make money. Each individual's story was different. As Harriett Skye (Lakota/Sioux) explains:

> The wild west shows were the big attraction of the times. As for how Indians felt, I believe the word was powerless. Cody exploited Sitting Bull and I believe Sitting Bull allowed it. He knew that his life was essentially over. The great life of the Indian people would never be the same again because the buffalo were gone as well as our hunting grounds. The Black Hills were invaded by the gold rush and as an old man the assault, genocide—both cultural and physical—was well on its way. Before Sitting Bull was killed in 1898 his greatest fear was [that he would] become a reservation Indian, but that too was inevitable. (personal communication, March 13, 1996)

Indian prisoners of war were also forced to participate. For instance, the army placed 100 Sioux prisoners in Cody's custody to become actors in his 1891–1892 tour of Europe (Napier 1987, 385).

Travel across geographical regions was an important component of Wild West shows. Because of this many Indians signed up for the adventure and as an opportunity to find out more about the "white man's" world (Blackstone 1986; Napier 1987; Yost 1980; Young 1981). Indian performers often performed twice a day for decades, trekking constantly from place to place. In a reversal of the westward trend, Indians would often "go east" to New York City—as seen in the above description—and perhaps such travelers tangentially influenced the development of powwows in the Northeast. From 1887 to 1906, these arduous tours included venues overseas, in Great Britain and elsewhere.

In Europe, Indians were tourists as well as entertainers. They expressed little awe when they met such dignitaries as Queen Victoria, King Edward VII, the Kaiser of Germany, and the pope (Napier 1987). Historian Rita G. Napier analyzes a meeting of some Indian performers and Pope Leo XIII in 1890: "Power was a central preoccupation in Plains Indian societies, but their definition of it differed dramatically from that of the followers of the Pope. Little was more significant in an individual's or a tribe's life. Without power a person was insignificant; with power he or she could do almost anything. Most important of all, seeking power was seeking 'the eyes to see and the strength to understand' that a Lakota might be like the Great Spirit, Wakan Tanka. This power, this understanding, this oneness with everything else was sought through dreams or visions" (1987, 399).

Indian performers who traveled abroad encountered many Western-based concepts of political and spiritual power. In the United States, they had already learned the enormous differences between themselves and non-Indians. Now the parameters extended across the Atlantic Ocean. These experiences would have consequences that lasted well into the twentieth century. For example, Luther Standing Bear, a prolific performer in Wild West shows who appeared in the United States and abroad, later in life became "a significant figure in American Indian intellectual history" (Deloria 2004, 76). Standing Bear worked as an actor, a translator, and an author and appeared in films. Deloria theorizes about what the effect of his experiences with Wild West shows might have been on his consciousness:

> In 1906, Standing Bear, his brother Henry, and one hundred Pine Ridge Oglalas traveled to New York City to appear at the Hippodrome, in an international show that ran through the winter season. On trips like these, outside the confines of the Wild West, Native performers like Standing Bear came to see that they were part of a national cohort of Indian people working, not just in Wild West Shows, but in circuses, traveling medicine shows, urban revues, lecture circuits, and sideshows. (Deloria 2004, 75)

Although events organized by non-Natives where Indians performed influenced the development of powwows, the spiritual and social aspects of the early contact dance societies were not lost. Instead, they were transformed through moving, dancing bodies. The Indians who traveled outside the United States, especially those who went to Europe, experienced the cosmopolitanism of European cities and broadened their understanding of the world beyond tribal life and the United States. It is possible that awareness of an international global culture led in part to the ease and cordiality that Native peoples often exhibit toward the vast numbers of "foreigners" from the Americas, Asia, and Europe who today attend powwow. For example, Schemitzun, the powwow hosted by the Mashantucket Pequot Tribal Nation in Connecticut, the Annual Crow Fair

Celebration in Montana, and the Annual United Tribes International Powwow in Bismarck, North Dakota, are international as well as national events.

A unique element of the Wild West shows was the popular "wild war dances," performed in a style that relates directly to the contemporary men's fancy dance and emphasizes quick and complicated footwork. These "show-stopping" dances attracted non-Indian audiences and contributed to the commercial success of Wild West shows. In 1930, Julia M. Buttree analyzed the commercial cynicism of one organizer: "When a certain Wild West showman was putting on Indian dancers, doing weird barbaric hopping, yelling, and brandishing of spears, he was asked by one who knew how false such a demonstration was: 'Why do you do that? You know that that is not the real Indian dancing.' He replied: 'Sure, I know. But that's what the public thinks is Indian dancing, so I must give it to them'" (1930, 7).

The spatial configuration of Wild West shows and non-Indian fairs and arts and crafts festivals also may have contributed to practices in today's powwows. All of these performance venues had a main arena surrounded by concession stands. Today, Indian powwows are often organized in this way.

The coexistence of dance societies and Indian "picnics," Indian fairs and expositions, and summer encampments during the late nineteenth and early twentieth centuries with events that portrayed Indian culture but were organized by non-Indians presents us with a complex picture of Indian dance during this period. It also invites questions about how Native dancing might have been affected.

An almost eerie contradiction exists between Indian participation in the performances organized by non-Indians and the genocide that was happening throughout the continent. Joseph Roach analyzes this complexity: "The polarity machine of the Wild West 'Exhibition'—Cody never allowed it to be called a 'show'—was sanctified as a historical simulation of catastrophic expenditure. Steeped in the violence of gunfire, it certainly enacted the theme of machismo in the face of race war. Buffalo Bill also dramatized the despoliation of the West, the wanton slaughter of the buffalo, in a way that exemplifies my definition of violence as the performance of waste" (1996, 206). It is painfully ironic that so many Native individuals performed their own destruction in this and other obvious "performances of waste." Particularly in the Wild West shows, Native Americans enacted devastating battles such as the Wounded Knee Massacre of 1890 in which Native American men, women, and children were brutally and unjustly killed.

How Indian performers felt about this is largely unknown, although when they played the roles of "bad" Indians, one can postulate that they fully understood what they were doing. Murphy proposes that "while their bodies conformed to audience expectations of how an Indian is and danced like disciplined Indian bodies do, their dancing nonetheless continued to invoke and enact cultural, political, and spiritual agency." For Murphy, this suggests that "the performers, somewhat paradoxically, saw more of a connection between the stage and their own worldviews and ways of life than audience members—supposedly titillated by the performers' status as 'real Indians' on stage—did" (2007, 69–70).

All of these performance genres can be seen as a series of complex intertribal and transcultural experiences and influences between Indians and non-Indians, and all of them affected today's powwow dancing. Gloria Young elaborates: "Exhibitions, wild west shows and dances for local whites provided opportunities to dance the new war dance. In traveling shows, Oklahoma Indians interacted with Sioux from South Dakota who retained the Grass dance as a secular dance and, at home, individuals from many tribes had the opportunity to observe or participate in the Osage Elonska. Both helped to encourage war dancing. By the end of World War I, the slow or straight war dance of modern powwows had assumed its present form" (1981, 249).

Throughout history, Indians have demonstrated their astute ability to invent, improvise, and survive. They have also confirmed the power of dance for themselves and others. Dance continued, even during the worst moments of prohibition when those who subscribed to Christian ideologies looked down on what some considered the "waste and lack of productivity in Indian dancing" (Murphy 2007, 86). During the second half of the nineteenth and the early twentieth centuries, it was often the case that the only legal performances of Indian dance were those that took place at commercial theatrical events. As Young points out, Indians made do: "In dealings with other Indian people and with the Commissioner of Indian Affairs, agents, missionaries and townspeople, Indian leaders negotiated in such a manner that they were often able to modify and keep a dance rather than abandon it or accept a totally new product in its place. Many instances have been documented of the combining of new dances with the old, or of non-Indian elements with old Indian dances" (1981, 301–302).

This process of "combining new dances with the old" and exchanging actions and practices originally emerged as a coping strategy in a time of legal and cultural oppression, and it persists today in powwow practices and in the everyday lives of Indian dancers. A *New York Times* article on the American Indian Dance Theater quotes a young fancy shawl dancer, Dawn Russell: "When we go to clubs, sometimes I'll catch myself doing a fancy-shawl step to urban music. . . . And sometimes I'll take a step I learned at a club and work it into my fancy-shawl routine. We do that with life every day. We take a little bit from both worlds and combine it to survive" (qtd. in Reardon 1998, 24). This ability to integrate elements of Native and non-Native culture was particularly prevalent as Indians resisted and accommodated to the invasion of people and "progress."

## The First Powwows

When John Collier became Commissioner of Indian Affairs in 1934, he overturned the Code of Indian Offenses, and Indian dance was once again permitted. Subsequently, the complexity of power relations, mutual appropriation, and tourism created a "new" form. This became, as Philip Paul (Flathead) tells us, a "new way of demonstrating our pride" (qtd. in Roberts 1992, 22). As male and female Indian soldiers who had served in World War II and earlier wars returned home (Browner 2002; Ellis 2003; Howard 1955, 1976; Powers 1990; Roberts 1992), powwows as we know them today began to appear, possibly during the 1930s and 1940s, though there are accounts of powwows occurring much earlier on.

At first small local events, often called fairs or picnics, were scheduled on commemorative days such as the Fourth of July, Memorial Day, and Christmas. These events gradually grew in size and reputation. At these celebrations, veterans were welcomed home and honored. In his work on powwow history in the Southwest, Ellis offers an analysis of the simultaneous existence of dance societies and the emergence of powwow: "On the one hand, pre-reservation warrior societies and their dance rituals maintained some of the power and utility that had previously made them so important. On the other hand, as dance traditions responded to new realities, the momentum that was helping to revive warrior society dances also produced a new kind of secular event increasingly referred to during the post-World War II years as the powwow" (2003, 20). The combination of dancing, singing at the drum, other rituals, and concession stands became part of what are now called intertribal powwows.

The many origin stories in Indian country about powwows demonstrate how difficult it is to determine exactly when powwows first appeared. Each tribe has its own account. This multiplicity of narratives adds richness and beauty to a performance genre that has evolved as a process of sharing across borders rather than within a specific tribal group or nation. This sharing has produced powwows that are intertribal and transcultural, urban and rural, taking place on and off the reservation.

Some say that in 1870 when the U.S. military forced the Ponca to leave their homes in the northern plains of Nebraska and move to Oklahoma, they brought their dances with them as "celebration . . . because they had made that trip" (Abe Conklin, Ponca/Osage, *Into the Circle*). Although narrators such as Conklin are aware of the many narratives that exist, he feels certain that his story is the real one: "You're going to hear a lot of different stories, you're going to get a lot of stories and a lot of different stories. I've been in places where I've told stories to different people and they don't even use it. They'd rather use somebody else's stories but they don't want to use actually where it comes from, and where it originated from, and how it originated. The beginning of the Oklahoma powwow started right here at White Eagle about 1887" (*Into the Circle*).

In the same way, Leonard Cozad describes how his people, the Kiowa, began a kind of powwow in the 1890s near Rainy Mountain, where they performed the War Dance. George "Woogee" Watchmaker (Comanche) says that the first powwows were picnics with a few friends and relatives who came together informally by word of mouth (*Into the Circle*). Yet another story says that the Omaha hosted the first intertribal powwow in 1879. For that event, many tribes—Omaha, Comanche, Kiowa, Cheyenne, and others—traveled over 300 miles to attend (*The World of American Indian Dance*).

Within powwow scholarship, Young suggests that powwows began in 1926 at the Haskell Indian School in Lawrence, Kansas, at an intertribal event that included dance contests, a tipi, a parade, and a play by students from the school (1981, 270–271). Susan A. Krouse and other scholars cite dance contests as the origin of the modern powwow (1991, 38). If we accept William K. Power's assertion that war dances were first performed in competition on the northern plains around 1955, that date marks the "beginning" of current powwow practice (Powers 1990, 50–60; Howard 1955). Even though the oral narratives of Abe Conklin (Ponca/Osage), Leonard Cozad (Kiowa), George "Woogee" Watchmaker (Comanche), and others attest to much earlier events, these might not have included competition and were most likely more tribal than intertribal.

In the Northeast, especially in the New York City area, origin stories began in more recent times. For instance, on March 16, 1941, the *New York Times* published an article titled "Indian Tribes Hold Powwow in Hotel." This powwow, which was held under the auspices of the American Indian Federation, attracted 1,500 dancers and attendees. The article quotes Chief Wappapenna of the Sac and Fox tribe of Iowa: "You see we have a fight all our own. . . . Hitler took our sign of peace and twisted it out of shape. He also took our "How" sign and made a "Heil" sign. We don't like that." At the end of this intriguing article, the journalist states that the event "followed the pattern of early powwows that took place in the Fall of every year to give thanks to the success of crops" (*New York Times* 1941).

On September 27, 1953, two powwows were held in New York, one in Manhattan and one in Brooklyn: "At the powwow Father Knickerbocker (James O'Brian), representing the Mayor, doffed a three-cornered hat and was inducted into the Iroquois confederacy by Sachem Clinton (Loud Voice) Rickard of the Tuscarora tribe. Father Knickerbocker then donned a head-dress and joined reluctantly in a brief tribal dance. . . . In Brooklyn another New Yorker was inducted into a tribe. With seventy Indians of fifteen tribes attending, Borough President John Cashmore was welcomed to the Choctaw tribe by Chief Earl Two Bears. Dances and rituals were performed by Indians of the United Association for the Advancement of American Indians, Inc." (*New York Times* 1953). These accounts testify to the presence of intertribal gatherings in New York City and illustrate the kind of "adoptions" that are common within tribal groups in general and particularly those located in the mid-Atlantic region and in New England.

In the New York City tri-state area, powwows are re-created each year, in the same place and usually on the same date. At these events, contemporary narratives evolve as powwow continues to grow and change. Since 1994, the Gateway to the Nations Pow Wow has been held almost every year in June at Floyd Bennett Field in Brooklyn, a former municipal airfield that became a Navy air station and is now a park. Similarly, the Thunderbird Pow Wow has been held at Queens County Farm Museum each July since 1982. In 2011, the Shinnecock tribe on the eastern shore of Long Island celebrated its 65th Labor Day powwow on their reservation, located between Southampton Beach and Montauk Highway, where they have lived since 1848.

In and around New York City, which was once home to thousands of Indians of the Lenape tribe, when a powwow event happens there is a sense of coming home. The act of returning every year to the same general area and date helps us link powwow history, geography, and place. It also reinforces the circularity of time and space in Indian country.

James Watt (Blackfeet), a traditional dancer, notes the continuities: "The place we powwow now used to be the place we'd meet and have our Sundance. Everybody would come together and camp. They'd dance the Sundance and after that they would just go into dancing and having a good time" (qtd. in Roberts 1992, 17). Similarly, in Connecticut the Mohegan and Mashantucket Pequot tribes continue to hold their Green Corn Festivals at the end of August or the beginning of September. These festivals have been held in the same place for years. For the Pequot, the festival coincides with or joins with their powwow. Thus, memory often relates to specific land sites and moments in time that hold ancient and sacred meaning.

# 4

# Traveling Circles

> I was still on my bay horse, and once more I felt the riders of the west, the north, the east, the south, behind me in formation, as before, and we were going east. I looked ahead and saw the mountains there with rocks and forests on them, and from the mountains flashed all colors upward to the heavens. Then I was standing on the highest mountain of them all, and round about beneath me was the whole hoop of the world. . . . And I saw that the sacred hoop of my people was one of many hoops that made one circle, wide as daylight and as starlight, and in the center grew one mighty flowering tree to shelter all the children of one mother and one father. And I saw that it was holy.
>
> BLACK ELK, HOLY MAN OF THE OGLALA SIOUX,
> IN BLACK ELK AND NEIHARDT, *BLACK ELK SPEAKS*

Space and time contextualize and permeate Native American intertribal powwows, where individuals and groups of people, moving bodies, activate and organize spatial formations. Just as historically performative actions and performance practices embodied power, movement—as sensory experience, as spatial and temporal practices, and in the dance itself—contributes to the power of today's powwow. In this chapter I invite the reader to join me as we metaphorically travel across the land on our way to "the powwow." I also examine the spatial organization of powwow performance areas and the centrality of the arena circle where powwow dancers perform.

Native world views incorporate a circular sense of space and time (Allen [1986] 1992, 2004; Collier [1949] 1995; Momaday 1987; Sarris 1993). Paula Gunn Allen argues for a politics of continuance instead of nostalgia, proposing that time flows around and through life, not backward or forward. She reminds us that the Indian universe constantly moves in a circular flux, in contrast to the linear, static, and exact idea of western time ([1986] 1992, 59). Nonetheless, the linearity of historical progression is visible in the persistence of Iruska through centuries of performance practices and in the orderly sequencing of the powwow's arena program, which "officially" begins with a Grand Entry and ends with a closing ceremony. Circularity is present at powwows in spatial configurations, the way these events recur year after year, and in many performance elements. At powwow, this sense of space and time, which is both sequential and circular, creates a place where movement has no end or beginning, a place where a plane of time "composed of moments, *ad infinitum*, in perpetual motion" is enacted (Momaday 1987, 158).

Some Native perceptions of space and time, the circle, and the hoop are specific to particular tribes. For instance, Tara Browner notes that "Northern-style pow-wow uses two indigenous metaphors: the Sacred Hoop and the Sacred Fire. The former is from the Lakota people (including Nakota and Dakota), and the latter from the Anishnaabeg Three Fires Confederacy (Ojibwe, Odawa, and Bodewaadmi). For the Lakota, the Sacred Hoop symbolizes a protective spiritual force that surrounds them. The Anishnaabeg Sacred Fire serves as a central focal point, bringing together the 'Three Fires'—the three nations making up the Anishnaabeg Confederacy" (Browner 2002, 3). The Cherokee Medicine Wheel, which is round like the earth, the moon, and the sun, is based on the interrelationship between the four cardinal directions and the four sacred colors: east (red); north (blue); west (black); and south (white). Each of these has particular meaning. The Wabanaki, or people of the dawn (a generic term for all Maine Indians since the 1700s), visualize their history as a circle that is repeated over and over in the thousands of baskets woven by the Penobscot, Passamaquoddy, Micmac, Maliseet, and Abenaki tribes.

Most Algonquian belief systems also emphasize the centrality of the circle: "The first thing the elders teach is the importance of the 'hoop,' or circle. Nature is full of circles—the sun, the full moon, the iris and pupil of the eye, a pond, a bird's nest. When sitting in council, the Algonquian people sit in a circle, which is a symbol of equality as every person has an equal chance to be heard. The fire in the center burns a circle in the grass and leaves a circle of ashes behind. The gourd bowl they pass clockwise around the circle is round" (Pritchard 2002, 68). These are only a few examples of the differences and similarities in how tribal groups conceptualize space and the circle.

Just as Indian concepts of space and time relate to a sense of harmony and of being at one with others and with the world, powwow hoops strengthen Native ways of life in a process of empowerment. Hoop shapes are seen everywhere in the arena circle: as part of the dance styles and the dance regalia, in how the singers circle the drum, and when the drum groups surround the arena or sit at its center. The general organization of the performance area is also hoop-like.

Powwow hoops lead us to the land and to the sky, important aspects of Indian life and of financial, social, and spiritual survival (Churchill 1992; Churchill and LaDuke 1992; Deloria Jr. 1994, [1970] 1988; Jaimes 1992). Ward Churchill explains: "The liberation of Native North America, liberation of the land first and foremost, is *the* key to fundamental and positive changes of many other sorts" (1992, 177). The memory of land as a place of endless struggle between Indians and Euro-Americans is fully present at powwows as Native people move, interact, and organize their lives in space. This is true in the Plains of the West, in the deserts of the Southwest, on the farmlands of the Midwest, and in the woodlands and often-crowded urban areas of the Northeast.

Throughout North America, Native American powwows can be visualized as geographical, physical, and human hoops that engage in overlapping, often simultaneous diasporic productions of space. This chapter's title, "Traveling Circles," refers to the totality of powwow performance sites across the continent and to individuals who journey from one event to another. In producing space, these sites become "imagined communities" (Anderson 1983) in which postcolonial relations are negotiated and performed. As anthropologist Arjun Appadurai reminds us, "Many persons on the globe live in such imagined worlds (and not just imagined communities) and thus are able to contest and sometimes even subvert the imagined worlds of the official mind and of entrepreneurial mentality that surrounds them" (1996, 33). It is this subversion of the official manifest at powwows that interests me. One goal here is to reveal how powwow performances of space maintain and nurture particularly Indian ways of being and points of view. As "imagined worlds," powwows reflect local, national, and global realities that question and contest Anglo-American hegemony with their prolific and ever-increasing presence.

## The Arena Circle

> You have noticed that everything an Indian does is in a circle, and that is because the Power of the World always works in circles, and everything tries to be round. . . . The life of a man is a circle from childhood to childhood, and so it is in everything where power moves. Our teepees were round like the nests of birds, and these were always set in a circle, the nation's hoop, a nest of many nests, where the Great Spirit meant for us to hatch our children.
>
> BLACK ELK, HOLY MAN OF THE OGLALA SIOUX,
> IN BLACK ELK AND NEIHARDT, *BLACK ELK SPEAKS*

The power of the "nation's hoop" Black Elk speaks of is evident in the circular area where powwow dancers perform. This central space, where most performance activities take place, is the key to what defines powwows as sacred events. Historian and philosopher of religion Mircea Eliade proposes that "revelation of sacred space makes it possible to obtain a fixed point and hence to acquire orientation in the chaos of homogeneity, to 'found a world' and to live in a real sense" (1961, 23, 63). In the powwow arena, the sacred "fixed point" is a circle.

This circle is not flat or one-dimensional; it marks the four cardinal directions of east, west, north, and south, but it also contains the sky, the earth, and the heart. In his description of the formation of the Omaha dance lodges where sacred dances were held, Mark Awakuni-Swetland emphasizes that "the circular arrangement reinforced the cosmic symbolism of the two great clan divisions, of earth and sky, male and female, creating a single dwelling for the entire tribe" (2008, 12). This cosmic symbolism exists at powwows today. It is present in the shape of the arena, in how dancers sometimes move in that space in circular fashion, in how the four cardinals directions frame particular powwow rituals and entrances and exits to and from the arena, and in the way that all powwow activity focuses toward the center of the arena.

The powwow arena is where both first-timers and seasoned powwowers quicken their senses through their bodies. The physical sensations one experiences at powwows include listening to music, announcements, conversation, and babies crying; seeing a wide variety of dances, arts, and crafts; seeing people dressed in elaborate and colorful regalia made of beads, feathers, and buckskin or simple T-shirts and blue jeans; touching other people in a Round Dance; sitting next to one another on the bleachers; handling the many items at the vendor stands; tasting everything from Indian tacos (fry bread with a meat or bean sauce and lettuce, tomato, and cheese) to mint tea, corn soup, and hotdogs; and smelling food and burning sage and sweet grass. One shares this environment with others—family, friends, and strangers.

The openness of powwow activities to the sky is in itself a statement. This is the case whether that sky is gray and stormy or deep blue or even imagined in an enclosed stadium, church gymnasium, or community center. Kenyan author Ngũgĩ wa Thiong'o maintains that "the more open the performance space, the more it seems to terrify those in possession of repressive power":

> Colonial conquests resulted in clear-cut boundaries that defined the dominated space with controlled points of exit and entrance and the formation of a colonial state to run the occupied territory. And right from the beginning the colonial state was very wary of the open air. It was not sure of what was being done, out there, in the open spaces, in the plains, in the

> forested valleys and mountains. It was even less sure of people dancing in the streets, in market squares, in churchyards and burial places. And what did those drumbeats in the dark of the night really mean? What did they portend?
>
> The postcolonial state has the same fear of the uncontrolled space, a fear which long ago Euripides dramatized in a confrontation between maenads and the state in the play *The Bacchae*. (1998, 63–64)

Powwow arenas are distinguished by the combined forces of circularity and exposed space, whether they are inside or outside.

Eliade explains that "all forms of cosmos—universe, temple, house, human body—have an 'opening' above. The meaning of this symbolism now becomes clearer; the opening makes possible passage from one mode of being to another, from one existential situation to another" (1961, 180). In his discussion of powwow space and time, anthropologist Daniel J. Gelo proposes that "the arena itself consists of more concentric circles" and that "the placement of the drum in the center of the dance ring marks the consecration of the area" (2005, 135–139). Powwow dancing is a form of prayer, a sacred passage to a higher power, to other people who are with us, and to others who have passed on. When someone dances outside, particularly in a place of natural beauty, that individual is closer to the sky and consequently to the Great Spirit, as are all who are present as fellow dancers or as witnesses.

Dance, music, and regalia intensify and magnify these spaces. The exact shape and orientation of each arena in the larger powwow performance area is different. Before activities begin at intertribal powwows, the bare arena speaks of unlimited possibility. When it is alive with dancers, it is a vibrant display of postcolonial relations, a performative challenge to centuries of genocide.

At the Crow Fair Celebration in Montana in 1997, the arena, a grassy field, was surrounded by a permanent wooden structure with a roof over the bleachers. In the early morning when it was empty it stood as a promise of things to come. At one end, a raised platform was reserved for the arena directors and dignitaries. In the middle, loudspeakers hung from a solitary pole. Along the edge, four floodlights shed bright light into the center of the arena twenty-four hours a day, suggesting the intensity of the space and of the powwow. Similarly, lights were lit for four days during Schemitzun in Connecticut in 1997. The powwow was held inside the Hartford civic center, which is surrounded by restaurants, stores, and offices. Three tiers of seats reached so high that the immense distance between the performers and the spectators produced an alienating effect. Nevertheless, even from a distance, the arena of this urban civic center radiated unity and vigor. In the middle of Hartford, the arena of this Native American powwow seemed to say, "Here we are and don't forget it."

The Schemitzun arena in 1995, which was set up under an enormous tent, was organized with a small stage on the east side and three sides of bleachers reaching up as high as thirty benches. The space was completely filled with thousands of dancers and the people who came to watch them. On the stage, where the emcee and the Mashantucket Pequot tribal leaders sat, a special place was reserved for elders and invited guests. In front of the bleachers on the ground, circles of chairs were placed in which more than fifty drum groups sat; each group had from five to twenty singers. The drum groups are circles around the circle.

At the United Tribes International Powwow in Bismarck, North Dakota, in 2009, the Lone Star arena was similar to the Crow Fair arena. The center was accentuated by a tall pole with loudspeakers, floodlights turned toward the middle of the arena, and the arena was surrounded by bleachers. In contrast, in 2006 at the Mawiomi of Tribes Aroostook Band of Micmacs Annual Powwow in Caribou, Maine, the central space was looser, more casual. The arena was in a large, dry grassy field in which the singers sat at a drum in the middle of the space and dancers moved around them.

Each arena has its own unique spirit that is created by the arrangement of elements and the people that gather in it. And each participant and attendee experiences this spirit and feels a sense of belonging. Although no powwow is the same, all arena circles simultaneously generate centripetal *and* centrifugal force. The magnetism that ties each powwow together pulls it inward but also radiates the powwow spirit upward and outward.

## Traveling through Space

Powwow experience begins long before the actual powwow is set up and before the arena program begins as Indians and non-Indians exert the necessary energy and raise the resources they will need to travel from one event to another. As a diasporic practice, these powwow circuits—pathways that spread horizontally throughout the continent—reaffirm the connection between space and land.

Traveling to the powwow may include lengthy trips by car, van, trailer, bus, train, or plane. Attending a powwow may mean pitching a tent and camping out on the powwow grounds, staying in homes with friends or family, or staying in motels. It will probably involve eating whatever is available and affordable on the run. These trips can be expensive and can be a financial burden for those with limited funds, and sleeping in a tent is not an option for everyone. I have spoken to Native people who can no longer go to powwows for one or both of these reasons.

Wherever powwows are celebrated, many people trek great distances to meet between individual, tribal, and community borders. Border crossing is an important aspect of powwowing. Philip J. Deloria examines how "*auto* and *mobility* that made up the word *automobile* pointed exactly to the ways in which mobility helped Indian people preserve and reimagine their own *auto*nomy in the face of the reservation system." Thus, "Automotive mobility helped Indian people evade supervision and take possession of the landscape, helping make reservations into distinctly tribal spaces" (2004, 153). Cars and other vehicles facilitate a reinforcement of reservations as Indian communities and nations. They also make possible a breaking out, a crossing over of borders. Lisa Brooks (Abenaki) writes of an "intertwining of psychological, social, and physical travel within the layered geographies of Native space" (2008, 229).

At the Thunderbird Grand Midsummer Pow Wow in 2000, just observing and thinking about dance was a challenge because of the intense July heat. During my long bus ride to Queens, New York, I noticed two fellow powwowers. One man was already wearing part of his regalia, a round feathered bustle ornament, while his companion, another male, carried a large duffel bag with the words "Lenape Indian" on it, a reminder of the original inhabitants of the now hectic and crowded city of New York. Within the diasporic space of powwowing, travelers frequently meet and interact.

When Native individuals from many different tribal communities and nations go from powwow to powwow, identity can be abstruse. These groups now include indigenous peoples from Mexico, Ecuador, and elsewhere in the Americas who participate in powwows. A tribal leader, organizer, or prize-winning dancer might be a valued member of Indian country, while in the outside world that same person could be underemployed or "undereducated." The capacity Indians have to execute diverse social roles is one illustration of the many ways they have learned to cope with colonization. This ability to operate openly or subversively as circumstances dictate has been crucial to their survival.

People who travel to powwows commonly drive hundreds of miles or more in a single day. This activity is key to understanding how individuals produce, use, and generate power by demanding of their moving bodies that extra physical effort as they travel along powwow circuits. Boye Ladd (Winnebago) analyzes powwow space in geographical terms: "Powwows take place in geographic circuits which are roughly a half day's drive in diameter. These circuits overlap.

I've been able to identify about sixteen in the U.S. and Canada. The two primary circuits are the Northern and Southern. The more formal southern plains influence is centered in Oklahoma and the looser Northern style is centered in the Dakotas, Montana, and the Canadian provinces of Alberta and Saskatchewan" (qtd. in Roberts 1992, 33). Many such circuits exist in the Northeast. A drum group might play at a powwow in Rhode Island on Friday evening and be expected for another event on Saturday morning in Bar Harbor, Maine. As powwowers make journeys that are often long and arduous, they move along myriad overlapping pathways.

In the film *Traveling the Distance*, Dr. Dale Brooks (Seneca) explains the shared desire that is in evidence along powwow circuits: "Most powwows today in the United States are intertribal, and it's the coming together of all tribes for the same purpose—to be together, to share." It is not accidental that both *Traveling the Distance* and *I'd Rather be Powwowing* begin with shots from inside a moving vehicle along an interstate highway. In 1995, the program notes for the Shinnecock Powwow noted the distances people travel and the hospitality with which they are received:

> "Hakame," said our Ancient Ones in greeting friends from far and near. We the Shinnecock people, welcome you today as we host Native American friends from all over the United States, Canada, Mexico, and Central America who bring with them their uniquely beautiful cultures. Go back in time with us during our annual Pow Wow, the gathering of the Native people of this land, listen to ancient songs, hear the drums echo through Shinnecock Hills as they did 3,000 years ago and remember the Creator who made all things in harmony with each other. In the words of Chief Thunder Bird (1907–1989): "Come sit with us in peace on Good Mother Earth."

This convocation invites the public to gather at the Shinnecock Reservation "from all over the United States, Canada, Mexico, and Central America." Some people come to powwows from as far away as Europe and points farther east. At the Crow Fair in 1997, I noticed Germans, Japanese, and Koreans.

## The Performance Area—Entrance Ways, Topography, and Spatial Organization

After traveling, one arrives. Many of the New Jersey and New York State powwows are held on farms, in parks, or even on military bases. Whether the powwow venue is surrounded by skyscrapers or towering mountains, a sprawling reservation or a tree-lined main street in a small New England town, one is exposed to the vicinity beyond.

The entrance ways and spatial organization of these performance areas are alike yet different at each event and include not only the arena but anywhere and everywhere powwow activities take place. In celebration after celebration, one walks through parking lots and then along a path lined with tipis or booths. The powwow is almost always down a road or around the bend from one's arrival point. Schemitzun offers us an excellent example of a performance area.

For years, Schemitzun, the largest powwow on the East Coast, has been organized by the Mashantucket Pequot Tribal Nation, the owners of the lucrative Foxwoods Casino and Resort near Ledyard, Connecticut. For the 1995 powwow, the host tribal nation gave money for gas, food, and lodging to many invited dignitaries, arena directors, drum groups, and dancers. A sea of dancers floods the Pequot arena each year. Many participate in Schemitzun largely because of the prize money that is awarded for competing dancers and drum groups. Each individual and tribal nation experiences powwow and powwow dancing differently; while some have criticized the commercial aspects of Schemitzun, others do not.

For me, entering the performance area of Schemitzun in 1995 was an experience in contrasts. As I traveled along the highway to the powwow, even before I entered the reservation, I saw a prominent building towering high in the hills. As I approached the grounds, this postmodern white structure with turquoise ribbing loomed larger and larger. This was the Grand Pequot Tower of Foxwoods Casino. As I continued into the woods, I saw houses of all sizes nestled among the trees, almost hidden, out of sight. At the main entrance to Foxwoods, a golden statue of an Indian shoots an arrow into the sky in a moment of triumph, power, and independence, a performative, symbolic gesture signifying freedom. On the day I visited, much of the casino was still under construction.

When I reached my destination at 9:30 a.m. the parking lots of the casino were already filled to capacity. After many meandering attempts to locate the powwow, I finally found a simple, lettered sign that said "Schemitzun '95" and told me where to turn. At that point, I realized that the crowds had come for the powwow *and* the casino.

Foxwoods hovered above the Schemitzun '95 performance area. Down the hill from the casino's main building, at the powwow entrance, tickets were sold for $10—twice the usual $5 fee of that time. Food stalls were situated along a path that curved down from the casino into an open space with several large tents, a huge tipi (said to be the "biggest in the world"), and portable toilets.

The enormous performance area included the space inside the arena and the space outside the arena—-the surrounding tents, the casino, and the area beyond the casino. In the early morning, people were just getting organized, but already venison burgers, fry bread, and tea were being sold.

The spatial layout of the Schemitzun 1995 powwow and its environs—the casino on top of the hill and the powwow below—serves as a reminder that we live in the United States, a capitalist country where financial wealth is synonymous with power and control. Matt Cohen reminds us that "how people live in a space, their social experience of it, affects the way they represent that space to others." In the United States, "taking seriously the place from which a certain notion of space is articulated, then, has ongoing implications for property and sovereignty claims" (2010, 21–23). How one thinks about space and power in Indian country is different than how most people think about those issues in the mainstream, capitalist United States. In the performance area of Schemitzun '95, the lower, more open area of the powwow—where hundreds of people constantly moved in and out—could be considered the more dominant, for it was closer to the ground, to the earth.

As powwow attendees moved in and around the powwow, they shifted easily between the central arena where the powwow dance and music program was performed and the entire performance area in which performers and spectators engaged in socializing, eating at the food stalls, shopping at the vendor stands, and so forth. Moving bodies actively consumed, disrupted, and produced space as they interacted with one another. In this way, all participants were involved in what sociologist Erving Goffman describes as an encounter of "reciprocal influence" (1959, 15–16). Today's powwows are also spaces of transcultural exchange and negotiation as all attendees enjoy and share in powwow activities. This phenomenon of mediation between Indians and non-Indians was first seen at world's fairs, arts and craft festivals, and Wild West shows.

To a large extent, those who create performance define it—both performers and spectators. Ngũgĩ wa Thiong'o's comments on African performance pertain here:

> The pre-colonial African performance area was often the open space in a courtyard or in an arena surrounded by wood and natural hedge. It could also be inside buildings, as when stories are told in the evening around the fireside. But the open space was more dominant, and even in the intimate circle around the fireside, it is the openness of the performance area that is marked: the story-teller and the interactive listeners are in the same area. Visitors could come into the scene at any time, for the main

> door was not barred to would-be guests. In addition, any of the observers could go in and out at will. Any space could be turned into a performance area as long as there were people around. Thus the performance space was defined by the presence or absence of people. (1998, 63)

At powwows, as visitors, performers, spectators, and organizers move freely within the performance area, they express the personality of each event through their relations with each other. A powwow would not be a powwow without the individuals who make it so.

Examining the vendors' tables is one activity that all individuals enjoy at powwows. In two immense tented rooms at Schemitzun '95, attendees looked at, bought, and sold crafts and traditional articles from the United States, Canada, Mexico, Ecuador, Peru, and Chile. Many contemporary artists displayed their artwork, which included paintings, stone carvings, sculptures created with driftwood, and gigantic dream catchers. Pamphlets and books on Native cultures, tapes, CDs, T-shirts, sweatshirts, musical instruments, jewelry, fur, and leather articles were also for sale. Because of the crowds of men, women, and children, there was an hour-long wait to buy food. Two years later, at Schemitzun '97, there were many more concession stands and food lines were shorter.

People are drawn to annual powwows in urban centers such as Hartford, Connecticut, and New York City, and in small towns throughout the New York City tri-state area such as Sayerville or Belvidere, New Jersey. These performance areas have many similar physical characteristics, and often the same participants attend the same events. The Shinnecock Indian Nation has an especially strong presence along the powwow circuit, not only with their own Labor Day powwow but also as dancers, vendors, singers, and spectators at other celebrations. In Maine, New Hampshire, and Vermont powwowers travel a circuit that is specific to New England. In the West, most of the champion dancers from the years before 2009 came from the Dakotas, according to the Web site for the United Tribes International Powwow. A population of Indian and non-Indian powwow participants lives in each geographical area that is supplemented by those who travel great distances, especially the emcees, the champion dancers, and drum groups.

At all the powwows I attended, regardless of how big or small they were or whether they took place in Brooklyn, Long Island, Caribou, Northampton, or Bismarck, the performance areas had a comforting similarity. This reinforces an overlapping simultaneity in time.

Powwow performances in Indian country include not only the dancers, the singers at the drum, the Indian and non-Indian vendors, and the organizers but also the millions of people who attend as spectators. Dance scholar Adrienne L. Kaeppler makes the following evocative statement about the vital presence of the audience: "I want to emphasize the importance of the audience to fieldwork on human movement systems. Audiences do not have the same role from culture to culture and the audience-performer relationship may be a continuum rather than two distinct categories. Performances require viewers, but who are these viewers and what do the viewers see and understand? Viewers may be the gods, engaged audience members, spectators who have little understanding of a performance, or, perhaps, only the performers viewing themselves" (1999, 22). Powwow would not be powwow without its spectators. These can take the form of a Great Spirit who presides over these events, ancestors who may be "watching on," and the Indians and non-Indians who participate and mobilize in the performance areas time after time.

One kind of audience member at powwows is the non-Indian who has been given permission by powwow organizers to sell his or her wares alongside Native-run vendor tables. I talked with one of these individuals at the Return to Beaver Creek Native American Powwow in Belvidere, New Jersey. The woman, who was wearing a Mexican huipil, or traditional embroidered top, told me that she lives during the winter months in Mexico with the Huichol in a small, remote village in Oaxaca. In the spring and summer she works at powwows in order to sell folk art and clothing to "support the needs of the village." The woman was Caucasian, blonde, and middle aged.

Booths set up by people from all over the Americas encircled the arena at the Shinnecock Labor Day Powwow in Southampton, New York, in 1995. The performance area was a wide-open space with a proscenium stage (see figure 6). The stage, a cement structure with drum-like designs along its curved front, was built high off the ground. The audience sat in front in a semi-circle on the ground or on folding lawn chairs. This spatial arrangement produced a considerable distance between performers and spectators—an unusual presentational mode for powwows. Nevertheless, a cordial atmosphere prevailed: people walked around the grounds visiting with one another, and friends and strangers often shared a meal. People frequently shook hands. The energetic flow of body movement contrasted with the hierarchical spatial positioning of the "drum stage."

At the outermost perimeter of the performance area, the Shinnecock Reservation stretched into the topography as a reminder that national and global public spheres are always present as outer, mobile edges beyond the powwow proper. At Shinnecock these "outer edges" were the wet marshes of Long Island Sound, while at events in the urban settings of Hartford, Connecticut, and Manhattan, Brooklyn, and Queens in New York City, concrete surrounded the powwow setting. In New York City, the Redhawk Native American Arts Council, the American Indian Community House (AICH), and the Thunderbird Dancers generally use interior performance venues, although they also organize their powwows in nearby outdoor settings. All three of these groups are dominant forces in regional Indian affairs.

The newest of the three organizations, the Redhawk Native American Arts Council, holds several powwows each year. Cliff Matias (Taíno/Kichwa), the coordinator for many years, explains: "This is a way for those of us who live in the cities to come together. That's the idea of the urban powwow" (personal communication, 1995). Even in cities, participants and attendees at powwows engage in complex productions of space in which people act and interact.

An example of a venue where these types of exchanges take place is Floyd Bennett Field in Brooklyn, the site of the Gateway to the Nations PowWow for many years. The performance area at Gateway powwows typically has concession stands around the perimeter and a central arena. Around the arena wooden benches, hay bales, and folding garden chairs for the dancers and for some spectators circle an open, dry, and dusty area. Several invited drum groups gather inside the organizers' tent, from which the emcee speaks. Extra seating or bleachers for the audience is located outside the arena circle to one side. Concession stands dispersed throughout the perimeter sell the usual items: food, jewelry, masks, dolls, trinkets of all kinds, drums, feathers, beads, candles, leather medicine bags, and many other things. Peruvian and Mexican stands display articles that are well suited to tourist trade. Most of the objects for sale are popular with powwow visitors, but Indians also buy them for their own use; these include buckskin clothing, T-shirts, and hair ornaments. The regalia dancers wear is often decorated with these items. At the powwow, one is engulfed by sensory experiences. The entire performance area at a Gateway powwow vibrates with the booming sound of the drum. The smell of sage incense fills the vicinity. On sunny summer days, sweltering heat warms the body. From inside the arena, the dancers emit intense energy.

Powwow is a performance genre that is always in transformation. I observed several changes during the ten years I attended Gateway powwows. In 1995, giant tipis lined the entrance way. Later, there was only one tipi and food vendors were located on one side of the performance area outside the arena in an enclosed picnic area. In addition, in 2002, the organizers placed themselves, the emcee, the drum groups, the dancers, elders, and the disabled in special designated sections around the arena. Visitors sat on the wooden benches and hay bales that in previous years had been reserved for the dancers. Newcomers often don't understand that the innermost space around the circle is for the dancers and singers, not the audience. Organizers thus maintained control of the space by sectioning off specific areas. At Schemitzun in 1995 and 1997, the Crow Fair in 1997, and the United Tribes International Powwow in 2009, the drum groups sat between the bleachers and the performance space because the bleachers were permanently positioned around the arena. At most powwows Indian and non-Indian attendees circle the arena with chairs they bring from home. The bleachers, the singers at the drum, and chairs of audience members form a tight layer around the arena circle. This tightening gives a sense of cohesion to the innermost center of the performance space.

In contrast to the venue for the Gateway powwows, the topography at the Queens County Farm Museum, the venue for the Thunderbird Mid-Summer Pow-Wow, is not as open. Fruit trees are scattered throughout the area and obstruct the view. The arena is centrally located and is surrounded with concession stands. However, non-Indian food vendors are located outside the performance area, next to the museum store. About one-third of the vendors at Thunderbird powwows are indigenous people from Ecuador, Peru, and perhaps other Latin American countries, who sell clothing, small trinkets, and jewelry. The presence of many Latino/a run concession stands attests to the exchanges between global public spheres and this urban powwow. Although the Thunderbird event is located at a farm museum, individuals who participate live and work in the greater New York region. In the years I attended, the Native American booths at the Thunderbird powwows included a Shinnecock stand, a station where fur pelts were sold, and an AICH table with books, newspapers, and information about HIV. Very little artwork was displayed except for some exquisite dream catchers.

The more dispersed arrangements of vendors, dancers, and attendees at Thunderbird resonate with Goffman's concept of front and back regions. He suggests that "performers appear in the front and back regions; the audience appears only in the front region; the outsiders are excluded from both regions" (1959, 144–145). Likewise, reiterating Ngũgĩ wa Thiong'o's assertion that people make the space, a kind of multilayered counterpoint materializes as people interact. As a result, an informal, dialectical sense of order and disorder moves between the more obvious front regions and "behind the scenes" in the back regions, which include camping tents, tipis, and vans as well as places where private tribal ceremonies and political meetings take place.

At powwows, front and back regions reveal the underpinnings of intertribal, interracial, and transcultural exchange. Issues such as obtaining permits to hold powwows in parks, civic centers, churches and so forth; sources of funding; and policing at powwows illustrate the complexity of relations between Native organizers and the nation-state. These relations are constantly being negotiated. Even determining who has the right to dance, sing and drum, or work as a vendor is an ongoing aspect of powwow life.

Many intertribal groups in the New York City area organize their powwows indoors. These spaces affect the powwow experience. For example, at the civic center where Schemitzun '97 was held, the performance area was not intimate. Some vendors were located off to one side in a colossal warehouse-like room, while other concession stands were on the first and second floors of the building.

In 1998, I attended another urban powwow in Brooklyn, the Park Slope Native American Dance Festival and Winter Social, organized by Redhawk in conjunction with the Action Youth Council of St. Francis Xavier Lyceum, a church group. Activities were held in the church gymnasium, a rectangular space with basketball nets, barred windows, a wooden floor, a small kitchen, and an overhanging balcony. A drum group sat at one end of the gym next to the emcee and the organizers' table. There was a small dance area located between the organizers' table and the wooden benches and chairs for the audience. Stalls with information about Redhawk, music tapes and CDs, and artwork and crafts were located along the walls. Although the focus of this event was the drum and the dancing, proportionally more space was given to public seating and concession stands than is customary at powwows. This suggests an emphasis on performing *for others* and selling to them. If the dance arena had been larger and more drum groups had been present, where would the audience have sat? And where would the vendors' tables have been placed? The spatial organization can determine how inviting any given powwow is for outsiders and can distribute power relations between everyone—performers, spectators, vendors, Indians, and non-Indians.

The 4th Annual UNITY Spring Pow-Wow organized by the Youth Council of the American Indian Community House was also an urban event that took place indoors. It started off the powwow season in New York City in 1997. This smaller powwow took place in a confined area at the AICH in which the slow, easy intermixing of individuals created a cross-cultural audience that included regular powwow attendees, Indians from the area, scholars from the National Museum of the American Indian and elsewhere, and many families and young people. A kind of crowded intimacy was produced. A few concession stands were arranged in an adjacent room, while in the common room several tables were set up for fry bread and tea. People moved in and out of the surrounding areas. As the afternoon progressed, the arena filled with dancers—Indians and non-Indians, some in regalia and others in street clothes. Subsequently, in 1998, UNITY held its powwow in a larger room in a midtown YMCA, but there was no seating for the public. In contrast to Redhawk's practice of making space for the audience, this AICH event seemed to forget about the spectators.

At the Park Slope powwow in 1998, those who were present, especially the spectators, represented a mix of class, age, race, ethnicity, and gender. People at the concession stands and in the kitchen were friendly, and audience members engaged in conversation with one another, perhaps because most of them were residents of the immediate neighborhood. The general communal feeling was consistent with Matias's announcement at the beginning: "This is a social gathering, a kind of party."

Likewise, the intertribal and interracial audience at the Thunderbird PowWow in 1997 was rich with diversity. Indigenous peoples from the Americas mingled with people from India and Europe, and the Shinnecock Indian Nation was well represented. At the Gateway to the Nations PowWow that same year, families predominated but no particular ethnic group was more represented than other groups. In recent years this powwow has included an increasing number of people of African descent, a change that most likely reflects a change in the demographics of the area of Brooklyn where the powwow is held. It may also be that members of the Shinnecock Nation, whose ancestors intermarried with African Americans in the seventeenth century, now participate at Gateway in greater numbers.

As dancers drum, singers dance, and people in colorful regalia stand in line for food, dancers and spectators, insiders and outsiders, engage in complex, fluid relationships that differ radically from the typical dichotomy of performer and spectator. As a result, individuals often participate in different powwow activities. At one moment, a Native American dancer might dance or sing at the drum, at another he or she might watch someone else dance. Usually non-Indians are curious bystanders though at times when invited they join an intertribal or a Round Dance. Indians who are not dancing often watch their family members perform. Insiders and outsiders, Indians and non-Indians, dancers and audience members share a meal together and join in friendly, informal conversation. In other words, a performer is not just a performer and a spectator is not just a spectator. The kind of audience interaction that so many experimental theater and dance troupes try to incorporate into their work is already an integral part of powwow.

Even when the performance arena is surrounded by towering bleachers (as at Schemitzun '97), slightly disrupted by a proscenium stage (as at Shinnecock in 1995), off to one side (as at Beaver Creek in 1997), or held indoors in an enclosed space, people continue to circulate behind, around, and toward a powerful center. Before the program officially begins, the emcee reminds dancers to register, and Indians and non-Indians flow freely throughout the area, greeting one another, looking at the concession stands, and eating. Little by little they congregate toward the arena.

## Pre-Performance Waiting

A fascinating aspect of the pre-performance lull is how the singers take their places around the drum for the warm-up. At powwows, the musicians who sit, sing, and play around a large, round drum are referred to as "the singers." The term used to refer to both the singers and the instrument, and the music that is played is called the drum. At Park Slope in 1998, the Mystic River Singers from Connecticut sat around the drum in silence as they waited for the Grand Entry. Dressed in blue jeans, baseball caps, T-shirts, and lumber jackets, they seemed to own the space, to mark it, as they silently gathered themselves. Time and again, I have seen drum groups sit for long periods of time in stillness as they reinforce, almost protect, the circle while conversing quietly or practicing. At Schemitzun '95, as people filtered toward the arena for the Saturday afternoon Grand Entry, there was a stark contrast between the singers as they came in, sat down, and waited and the "tourists" who entered chatting and fluttering about.

Anticipation is high before the Grand Entry. All powwowers continue to move around the performance area as the emcee controls time (usually using a loudspeaker) as it transitions from polychronic organization into the more chronological order of the program. At Park Slope in 1998, as performers prepared for the arena program and others leisurely moved about, an invited emcee from the Crow Tribal Nation stood in front and quietly began to speak. With calm authority, he talked about the history of powwow, the dances, and many other details of Native culture. There was a lot of activity in the room and it was noisy, but he kept going, seemingly oblivious to the racket. Eventually people took notice. He also spoke about how wearing feathers brings Indians closer to the birds while buckskin joins them to the animals. He talked about how "the authenticity of our culture is kept in our hearts." Later, this man had such command over the audience that he no longer needed to stand; he sat at the table as he spoke. Another emcee at Beaver Creek in 1997 repeatedly spoke of sobriety and called for Indians to "bring our people back" into the community and traditional ways. He also made a lot of self-referential Indian jokes.

## Entertainment

During the waiting periods before the morning program and again before the afternoon program, activities and performances occur that regulate time in a more linear fashion. This is when gourd dancing is often done. I have also seen flute performances, Aztec dancers, hand drum contests, storytelling, folk singers, and, even some dancers from Soweto, South Africa, who participated at the United Tribes International Powwow in 2009. At a powwow in Sayerville, New Jersey, in 1997, Kevin Locke (Lakota/Sioux), a world-renowned flautist and hoop dancer, provided the entertainment. As Locke began, he noted a hawk flying overhead. During his presentation, he talked about seven directions: east, west, south, north, earth, heaven, and in the heart—the dimensions of the sacred space of the arena circle.

Locke danced with about twenty hoops using first one, then two, and so forth. Hopping inside them while keeping beat with the drum, he raised the hoops over his head, making geometric shapes and wings around his body. In constant motion, he performed yet another manifestation of powerfully intertwined circles. As he concluded, Locke invited people into the arena to try out the hoops. The people of Sayerville joined in immediately. This activity served as a catalyst in which Indians and non-Indians of the town and elsewhere could participate in a transcultural exchange that was organized and directed by Indians.

At the United Tribes International Powwow in 2009, Ricky Bird, another hoop dancer, singer, and fashion designer, led the audience in songs during a special children's event in the morning before the first arena program. She also demonstrated her clothing line. Young high school–age women and three Indian men modeled. Afterward, Bird performed a Hoop Dance in which she involved the children. Locke was in the audience with his daughter, and Bird acknowledged him as her mentor. It was wonderful to see him there in his "home" powwow ten years after that New Jersey performance. Later in the day he danced in some intertribal dances and the men's traditional dances carrying a few hoops.

In general, entertainment happens twice a day, once in the morning before the midday Grand Entry and again in the evening. It may include the hand game, basketball, hand drum competitions, pop and folk singers, comedians, golf tournaments, and storytellers. Comedian Charlie Hill, ventriloquist puppeteer Buddy Big Mountain, and Native American country singer Susan Whipple—all well known in Indian country—were on the Schemitzun program in

1995 and 1997. Some of the other performers in 1997 were rap artists Lite-Foot and Haida, political activist and singer John Trudell, and the Ximalli Aztec Dancers.

The entertainment program and the arena program serve different purposes. Powwow entertainers earn their living as actors, comedians, and musicians at resorts, in theaters, and on film. Their performances are presentational. They embody what it means to "go professional" as an Indian entertainer. Native Americans are proud of these people who have made a name for themselves. Whether it is a rap singer, a champion fancy dancer, or a 92-year-old elder marking his steps in the Grand Entry, these individuals execute a sense of being Indian that takes into account and emphasizes the presence of Native peoples in North America and the world, albeit in different ways.

•

Finally, everyone who is present prepares for the arena program with the first performative moment: the roll call of drum groups. This is an event that happens at larger powwows such as Schemitzun. At smaller powwows, where there are fewer drum groups, a role call is not part of the program.

At Schemitzun in 1995 and 1997, during a very special drum roll call, the emcee named the groups—Porcupine Singers from South Dakota, Mystic River from Connecticut, Whitefish Jr. from Saskatchewan, Northern Wind from Ontario, and so on. Each one responded by drumming. Then all the drum groups performed together in what is called the power of thunder. The impressive sound, made by over fifty groups, was very much like the sound of an impending thunderstorm. Literally making the heart beat faster, the drum roll call and the warm-up songs reverberated with loud and energetic rumblings and the first piercing vocals of the day. At the larger powwows I attended in Montana and North Dakota, the experience of the drum roll call was equally thrilling, though only at Schemitzun was there that moment when all the drum groups played at once.

After a pre-performance waiting period, the Grand Entry initiates the program. Whether the powwow is being held in a wide-open field, a church gymnasium, or a park, people gather around the circle. The drum beats, singers sing, and the performance begins.

1. Grass dancer Daniel Francis Dana (Penobscot) at the 2006 Annual Native American Festival, Bar Harbor, Maine.

2. Grand Entry at the 1997 Annual Crow Fair Celebration, Crow Agency, Montana.

3. The drum at the 1995 Schemitzun Feast of Green Corn and Dance, Mashantucket, Connecticut.

4. Intertribal dance at the 2009 Annual United Tribes International Powwow, Bismarck, North Dakota.

5. Non-Indian spectators at the 1995 Gateway to the Nations PowWow, Brooklyn, New York.

6. The proscenium stage at the 1995 Annual Shinnecock Labor Day Powwow, Southampton, New York.

7. Mexican Aztec dancers from the Americas at the 2005 Gateway to the Nations PowWow, Brooklyn, New York.

8. Male traditional dancer at the 2009 Annual United Tribes International Powwow, Bismarck, North Dakota.

9. Male traditional dancer at the 1995 Annual Shinnecock Labor Day Powwow, Southampton, New York.

10. Female traditional dancer at the 2009 United Tribes International Powwow, Bismarck, North Dakota.

1. Playing Indian at Oberlin College in 1915. Anita Tritschler and Stanley A. Corfman, he author's maternal grandparents, sitting next to the banister—Anita in the top row nd Stanley directly below her. (Collection of the author)

12. Chris Butterfly, a non-Indian dancer at the Native American Pow-Wow at Wells Harbor Community Park, Wells, Maine, 2009.

13. Young jingle dress dancers at the 2009 Annual United Tribes International Powwow, Bismarck, North Dakota.

14. A woman dancing in the fancy shawl style at the 2009 Annual United Tribes International Powwow, Bismarck, North Dakota.

15. A man dancing in the fancy dance style at the 2009 Annual United Tribes International Powwow, Bismarck, North Dakota.

# 5

## Transcultural Beginnings

> We dance with pride and think about how we have survived
> and are still here, especially when we see the children dancing.
>
> HARRIETT SKYE (LAKOTA/SIOUX)

As they circle around the arena in the Grand Entry, participants produce a light up-and-down movement that draws us in. Moving with the drum, some dancers advance with two steps on the left foot, two on the right while others take one small short step to the right and then another to the left. Some emphasize a side-to-side motion, while others stress a more forward-going movement. Many of those taking part in the Grand Entry simply walk casually along in the crowd. In an oceanic, wavelike motion, moving bodies perform numerous dance styles—grass, traditional, jingle dress, fancy, and so forth. Often a performer will dance his or her style throughout. Many individuals who represent tribal nations and various communities in the United States and Canada execute full-bodied movement as their regalia accentuates the complexity of their dance.

Indigenous peoples from throughout the Americas participate at powwows, and sometimes we see them in the Grand Entry. Vendors come from countries such as Mexico, Peru, Colombia, Ecuador, and Bolivia, but the performers in the arena from Latin America are primarily Mexican Aztec dancers and Puerto Rican Taíno at urban powwows in New York City. Aztec dancers, who sometimes join the Grand Entry and dance specialty numbers, wear theatrical outfits and perform a series of pieces presented as Mexican dances and rituals (see figure 7). They also contribute to the entertainment part of the arena program.

The intertribal powwows examined in this book are diverse and inclusive. For example, at Schemitzun in 1995 and 1997, the tribal elders impressed me. In northern Maine at Caribou, the Mawiomi in 2006 resembled an extended family picnic. At the 6th Annual Honor the Earth Powwow in Northampton, Massachusetts, many non-Indians attended a celebration that was characterized by an overall tone of sobriety and spiritualism. The myriad dances performed at powwows, the transformative quality of these events, and the many relationships among participants lead to the notion of transcultural performance, a concept that emerges from a process basic to powwow: transculturation.

Anthropologist Fernando Ortiz introduced the idea of transculturation in the mid-twentieth century in his detailed analysis of the history of Cuba seen through sugar and tobacco production (Ortiz [1947] 1995). Ortiz demonstrated how the complexity of two very different elements contributed to a fluid, multi-layered, and complex Cuban culture that affected immigration, music and dance, and political movements, among other things. Bronislaw Malinowski explains Ortiz's notion of transculturation as "a process in which both parts of the equation are modified, a process from which a new reality emerges, transformed and complex, a reality that is not a mechanical agglomeration of traits, nor even a mosaic, but a new phenomenon, original and independent" (Malinowski [1947] 1995, xi). The transformation that Malinowski describes is at the core of powwow in numerous ways. As a transcultural performance genre, powwow embodies motion, sensory experience, and interactions between performers and spectators that produce multiple perspectives and mediation. Bodies in motion are key to understanding powwow as a transcultural performance.

At powwow, motion is present in the dance but also in the ways that travel is a key element in powwowing. Shared sensory experience at powwows is full and inviting. In addition, people who attend powwows represent a broad array of categories that make up society in terms of race, ethnicity, age, gender, and class. Hundreds of tribal groups are represented, as are, in lesser numbers, non-Indians from North America, Europe, Asia, and other parts of the world. Powwow is a profoundly intergenerational and family affair that includes the very young and the very old. Males and females of all ages form part of the powwow circle and persons of different socioeconomic classes join in. It is important to conceive of cultural exchange at powwows as a process of mediation between individuals in all these categories. We tend to focus on race and ethnicity when thinking cross-culturally. Although race and ethnicity are important, powwow offers us a broader and more comprehensive way of thinking about transculturation.

Powwow attendees participate in and bring many different viewpoints to powwow. Even the casual visitor or tourist engages in exchanges with other powwow participants. And all powwowers act, interact, and give and take while together producing a "new phenomenon, original and independent" in Indian country and the United States. In this chapter, I look at the initial components of the arena program. The Grand Entry, the intertribal dances, and the "tiny tots," or children's dance category, are prime examples of how transculturation is experienced and performed. I then examine the traditional men's and women's dance styles.

## The Grand Entry

As the momentous spectacle of the Grand Entry begins, the emcee asks the audience to stand and men to remove their hats. Entering from the east in parade formation, the procession moves around the arena circle. Many dancers are in full regalia, and sometimes dancers move in lines of four or five abreast. Julia White describes this moment: "All dancers enter the arena from the East as the place on the Medicine Wheel of new beginnings, of new birth and rebirth, and of awakenings. . . . Leading the Grand Entry is the Eagle Staff, followed by the American Flag, the Canadian Flag, the POW-MIA Flag, and the Tribal Flag of the Pow Wow host" (1994, 9). Each community or tribal nation establishes its own order of flag bearers, lead dancers, veterans, princesses, honored guests and tribal leaders, and performers within various dance categories. At Gateway to the Nations PowWow in 1995, two lead dancers, invited veterans, and flag bearers led the Grand Entry. The male lead dancer who was about seventy years old, warmed up beforehand. Moving with the drum, sensing the rhythm, and swaying from side to side, he was deeply involved in a visceral kinetic experience. Seven years later, in 2002, this same dancer was still vibrantly present.

The Grand Entry accentuates the arena circle as a powerful center of activity and purpose, or, as Erving Goffman and Dean MacCannell might say, an obvious and seductive "front region." As the powwow comes alive, dancing bodies join together in an infinite display of body actions. Although the Grand Entry varies from powwow to powwow, people seem to be comfortable with the differences as they travel the powwow circuits. The Grand Entry at Shinnecock in 1995 seemed to "take the land" in a path that moved from the main gate through the reservation, around the audience, and then behind and onto the stage. Dancers at the Crow Fair in 1997 moved in single file, creating a snakelike sinuous curve around the arena (see figure 2, *bottom*).

The Grand Entry usually happens around midday and again in the evening, though this can vary, as can the actual start time of the powwow: "Grand Entry begins when it is ready to begin. Indian Time is circular. Past, present and future are cycles of reality, with no beginning and no end. Time is indivisible. You cannot cut liquid water with a knife and you cannot separate time with a second hand. Time is fluid. You are never late nor early within Indian Time, because you cannot divide it. Things begin when things are ready to begin" (Jones and Jones 1996, 38). Yet many emcees will repeatedly say, "Today we're going to be on time, white people's time, not Indian time." Temporal practices become more linear while the circularity of the arena is reinforced as people execute the physical and metaphysical act of entering the community circle. First walking, then dancing, the participants in the Grand Entry enter and move around the arena with measured informal grace.

The eagle staff, the American flag, and the powwow flag are prominent features of the Grand Entry. Flags in Indian country symbolize the land as nation. Thus, the color guards, lead dancers, and veterans who carry the flags honor both the land and the United States (see figure 2, *top*). Many Native Americans have served in the military, and history is replete with stories of their bravery and ingenuity. The Navajo code breakers during World War II and the many veterans of the Vietnam War are only two examples. Veterans play a key role at powwows, and the flag bearers are usually men and women in military uniform. Thus, in the Grand Entry, Native peoples—the first inhabitants of our land—affirm a unique and multifaceted view of what it means to be a citizen of the United States.

During the Grand Entry, the emcee thanks the audience for coming. This is a continual refrain at many powwows. He also keeps the entrance parade going with an ongoing narrative during which he invites Indians and sometimes non-Indians to join in. He also makes other comments. For example, at a Gateway to the Nations PowWow event, an emcee repeatedly declared: "This is a special day, a beautiful day, all days are beautiful, it's just that some days the clouds come to hide the beauty, and that when we have a bad day we can remember this day of coming together, of sharing, and of memory."

At Schemitzun in 1995, the Grand Entry took more than an hour because of the many dancers who participated that year. In 1997, performers emerged from under the emcee's platform almost as if from an enormous cave. At night the stage lights gave another entry a particularly staged look. The arena directors at Schemitzun in 1995 and 1997 did an impressive job of organizing the dancers: hundreds of them filled the space, circling again and again in a layered spiral. The order of the Grand Entry at Schemitzun in 1997 was flag bearers, elders (or goldens) from the Mashantucket Pequot Tribal Nation and other nations, color guards, royalty, men, women, juniors, and little tots, all in dance categories that included traditional, grass, jingle dress, and fancy.

During the Grand Entry at Schemitzun in 1995, the goldens caught my attention. Most of these men and women wore traditional regalia. Though the grass dancers might come into the arena first to prepare the ground, the traditional dancers, usually the most mature members of the community, lead the dance categories in the Grand Entry. Years of living deeply etched onto their strongly lined faces, the elders step, stomp, turn, and circle together as if they have been dancing forever. They combine concentrated inner focus with a dignified, forward vision of the far future. The goldens make calm and steady contact with the ground with gentle, light stamps of the feet. Their participation in the Grand Entry is a powerful performance of ancient memory, and it is incredibly moving. Some of them are quite old, yet they continue to come together in dance.

At the same event, a small boy about three or four years old also danced. In contrast to the elders, he did not direct his gaze in any distinguishable way or execute clearly defined moves. Drawn into the circular movement around the arena, this tiny person danced with his whole body in free-flowing motion for over an hour. As the Grand Entry continued, he joined the others, bobbing up and down, blurring into myriad colors and scattered feathers. The experience of participating in such a massive, moving group is special for each dancer. Around the edge, the traditional women dancers keep watch as they enclose the circle.

When Mexican Aztec dancers participate in the Grand Entry, their staged theatricality differs from how Native Americans express themselves. At the Honor the Earth Powwow in Northampton, Massachusetts, in 1997, Mexican Xavier Alacron stood out from the crowd. As he joined the circle, he moved forcefully around the other dancers. Instead of quietly presenting himself with the dignified self-containment of most powwow dancers, Alacron thrust himself into the space. His style was jolting, perhaps more professional but almost rude as the emcee commented, "Way to work it, Xavier" and "Shake it up, Xavier, shake it up, baby."

In another example of how dancers from outside the United States join the Grand Entry, at the United Tribes International Powwow in Bismarck in 2009, the Soweto Dancers from Africa took part in the Grand Entry as invited guests and moved freely around the arena with everyone else. However, most of the time they simply walked or marked their own dance movements; they did not dance full out as Mexican dancer Xavier Alacron did in Northampton.

Often during the Grand Entry the emcee encourages the dancers and informs the audience about who is participating, as he did at the Crow Fair Celebration at the Crow Agency in Montana in 1997: "Dancers have come from across Indian country, representing the Kiowa, the Northern Cheyenne, the Navaho, the Shoshone, the Sioux, the Blackfeet and the Crow. Many, many tribes are represented today." Later, when the young people appear, he added, "Look alive, dancers, look alive. Be proud that you're an Indian right here on this land that we call America. The freedom that we have that we can dance together, of all tribes, and of all nations. Dance your style. Dance your style. You're looking good."

In the Grand Entry, Native American identity is defined by age, gender, and especially tribal affiliation as individuals express themselves in dance. Harriett Skye (Lakota/Sioux) explains: "What Native dancers bring to the circle is the complex question of representation and self-definition. After years of being told who they are in their lives, religion, costumes, as well as dance, they are making a statement in the circle, and most are dancing with their ancestors. They are saying, 'This is who I am: Lakota, Kiowa, Comanche.' We all know who these dancers are. It is only the non-Indian who is unable to differentiate" (personal communication, 1999). For most Indians, coming into the circle during Grand Entry is not an act of performing for others but is instead a statement of their "Indianness."

In addition, Grand Entry is a social experience during which a lot of greeting goes on. For many individuals it is also a sacred act as they honor a greater power and spirit. Ultimately, the Grand Entry can be a presentational yet reverent intersection of formality and informality, punctuality and timelessness, polychronic and chronological time, and circles and lines.

On occasion, even at the smaller events, for example in Maine, the flashing cameras remind us of the display aspect of powwow in a way that resonates with the arts and craft festivals in the Southwest and Wild West shows of the past. People usually photograph and film whomever they want whenever they want. Cell phones are typically held in the air for yet another shot. Sometimes, but not always, these individuals, whom Indians consider to be disrespectful, are chastised. Other times there is a fee for using a camera. Of course, it's different if a family member wants to capture the dance of a grandchild or a nephew.

One drum group after another guides the Grand Entry. The emcee often exhorts the drums to "keep the beat." Bernard S. Mason wrote of the importance of the drum: "The drum is indispensable. It is to the dance as to the bow to the arrow. It is the spring to action" (1944, 8). At powwow, dancing and singing around the drum are closely related and operate in an ongoing dialogue.

Many others have already written extensively about this important relationship (Browner 2002; Burton 1993; Lassiter 1998), and I do not expand upon it here. However, it is crucial to note that music, movement, and regalia are always intricately connected.

As song and dance become one, the communal circular movement from east to west reaffirms the presence of Indian country beyond the arena circle. As the Grand Entry proceeds, everyone dances, even the men and women carrying the eagle staff and other flags.

## The Arena Program

After the Grand Entry, the arena program continues with a flag song, an invocation or prayer, often a victory song, and an intertribal. The order of these practices differs from powwow to powwow. At the Spring UNITY Pow-Wow in Manhattan in 1997, the flag song, a moment of silence to acknowledge the Great Spirit, and a greeting from the Youth Council preceded the Grand Entry. In contrast, at Schemitzun in 1995 and 1997 and at the United Tribes International Powwow in Bismarck in 2009, the flag song and invocation occurred after all the dancers were in the arena, facing the center. In general, at the Gateway to the Nations PowWow, the grass dancers begin, followed by the Grand Entry, the flag song, the invocation, and the victory song. The Park Slope Native American Dance Festival in 1998 began with the Grand Entry and a flag song after which the emcee invited people to dance for "the many victories yet to come" in a kind of round dance. The Sneak-Up Dance was next, followed by the Crow Hop. After a number of intertribal dances, Kenny "Martin" Jr. (Lakota) performed flute music.

The invocation was included at all events I attended, with the exception of some Thunderbird powwows. Usually spoken in a Native language, the invocation imbues the first rituals of a powwow with a strong sense of communal reverence for the sacred. The powwow prayer offered to the Great Spirit, the Creator, Wakan Tanka, or God is a crucial aspect of powwow. Spirituality is a cohesive force during powwow and in each dance that follows.

Typically, after the opening rituals, an intertribal is announced. The various dance categories follow, interspersed with such events as the Eagle Dance ceremony, honoring rituals, giveaways, and noncompetitive dances such as the Round Dance or the Potato Dance. The usual order of the dance categories is based on style and age—the youngest children, or tiny tots, dance first, followed by juniors (ages 6–12), teens (ages 13–17), goldens (ages 50 and over), and adults, who are sometimes subdivided into categories of junior (ages 18–30) and senior (ages 31–49 or older).

Dance styles usually, though not always, follow the same order as they appear in the Grand Entry: traditional, grass, jingle dress, and fancy. The men's fancy dance style, the flashiest, is last. The entertainment and specialty numbers—the Aztec dancers and other invited performers—are rarely brought in at this point in the program.

The length, quality, and makeup of the arena program are determined by the traditions of that particular powwow and by the quantity of dancers. At Schemitzun in 1995 and 1997, dancers performed into the night—as long as necessary until everyone had a chance to dance. In a polychronic sense of time, the satisfactory completion of an act is primary. Often, I have heard non-Indians comment on how long the program is and complain that the dances "go on and on." However, this relaxed, leisurely atmosphere is essential to powwow.

While the arena is alive with dancers, people are free to come and go, watch or not watch, wander about the performance area, look at and buy things from vending booths, have a meal, and socialize. Meanwhile, the emcee maintains the rhythm and order of the program. He is in charge. Largely because of the emcee—and his continual output of powwow information and stories, announcements, and jokes—things follow a schedule.

Periodically an emcee will prompt spectators to observe powwow policy. Visitors should not sit in the inside circle; that space is reserved for the dancers and the drums. Similarly, people who want to dance are expected to wear regalia or be respectfully attired. This means shoes for everyone, and it might mean shawls for the women. Alcohol and illegal drugs are not allowed. It is common knowledge that substance abuse continues to be a critical issue for Native populations. A zero-tolerance policy at powwows makes them places of safety, recovery, and healthy fellowship. This was the case at all the powwows I attended in my many years of fieldwork. Basic courtesy is expected as well. Finally, although the emcee invites people to move freely around the powwow area, the arena circle is reserved for the emcee(s), the arena director(s), those who judge the dances, the powwow dancers, and the drum groups. All these rules are plainly stated.

If the powwow involves competition, an emcee might speak directly to the dancers to remind them to register, to wear regalia that meets powwow standards, and to secure all the elements of their outfits securely. He also reminds them that points will be counted for participation in Grand Entry and intertribal dances. For example, at the United Tribes International Powwow in 2009, the emcee repeatedly told the grass dancers to make sure they were wearing the required bells on their ankles.

The ongoing, circular flow of activities reinforces the notion that what takes place at powwows has happened many, many times before, perhaps centuries ago. This is not to say that powwows as we know them existed in precontact times. But many of today's body actions and performance practices emerged from ancient times, including worship practices, storytelling, and socialization through dance.

## Dance Styles

> Dancing for me is a real community celebration that brings us together. We can have fun. And it is a real sense of connectedness to our culture. So those dances today, we're doing the same foot movements. The same body movements. Singing the same songs that our ancestors done and that is to me probably the most important thing about the dances.
>
> BARRY DANA (PENOBSCOT) IN THE VIDEO *OUR DANCES*

On the powwow circuit, I have seen dancers perform complex dance styles that embody characteristics shared throughout Indian country. Adrienne L. Kaeppler proposes that "dance is a cultural form that results from creative processes that manipulate (i.e., handle with care) human bodies in time and space in such a way that the formalization of movement is intensified in much the same manner as poetry intensifies the formalization of language. The cultural form produced, though transient, has a structured content that conveys meaning, is a visual manifestation of social relations, and may be the subject of an elaborate aesthetic system. Often, the process of performing is as important as the cultural form produced" (2001, 32). As a dancer performs, he or she produces a cultural form that is personal, social, and cultural. This leads to the meaning of the style, both in general and within the context of Native American powwow dancing.

In some instances, a style is a mode of moving based on aesthetic choice. For example, a ballet dancer incorporates an intricate combination of movements of the torso, limbs, hands, feet, and head that result in the Bournonville, Balanchine, or Vaganova style. These three styles could be considered substyles of the style of ballet. And each individual ballerina has her own nuanced version of these substyles. In the case of Native dance, each dancer develops a grass, traditional, jingle dress, or fancy dance style as well as his or her own way of moving within that style.

Dance scholar Lee Ellen Friedland states in her discussion of African American performance that style can be defined as "the means by which an individual progresses in the spiritual quest for aesthetic communication. The social prestige of being recognized as an artist in the culture, and in the community, can be achieved only through the cultivation of 'style'" (2001, 139). Though Native dancers may or may not consider themselves artists (in the way Friedland means), they challenge themselves to strengthen and enhance the execution of their styles at powwows and in other contexts such as in dance companies (e.g., the American Indian Dance Theater or the Native Pride Dancers) and on film. Movement style expresses a particular way of presenting oneself to a society. Many powwow dancers work very hard to refine their performances.

## The Intertribals

After the Grand Entry, the flag song, and the invocation, the emcee invites everyone to join the first intertribal (see figure 4). At powwows, the intertribal dances are most commonly called intertribals. In the intertribal, performers and spectators come together to dance at the emcee's invitation—Native dancers, invited guests, children, non-Indians, and wannabes.

This welcoming gesture on the part of the emcee to include non-Indians in an intertribal is especially common in the Northeast. It is not as prevalent elsewhere; I did not see it at the 1997 Crow Fair Celebration in Montana or at the 2009 United Tribes International Powwow in North Dakota. The differences between powwows in the Northeast and those in other parts of the country are a direct reflection of the early contact and postcontact period of the region, when European settlers, slaves, and Native Americans were compelled to interact in many ways and often in areas that were more congested than they were further to the west (Brooks 2008; Lepore 1998; Pritchard 2002). This integration of diverse peoples continues today in the Northeast, particularly in urban areas.

Intertribals occur at several points in the arena program, and depending on the specifics of each powwow a few dancers or hundreds might participate in them. At the Spring UNITY Pow-Wow in 1997, there were few dancers, so the emcee encouraged people from the audience to join in. At the three powwows I observed on reservations, Schemitzun '95, the Crow Fair Celebration in 1997, and the Shinnecock Labor Day Powwow in 1995, most people who participated in the intertribal dances were Indian.

Non-Indians and wannabes participate in the intertribal to varying degrees, depending on the powwow. In 1997, many non-Indians joined in at the Honor the Earth Powwow in Northampton and at the powwow in Sayerville. Curiously, all the dances were intertribal at a powwow in Wells, Maine, in 2009, and many wannabes participated. At the Gateway to the Nations PowWows, the Thunderbird Grand Midsummer Pow Wows, and the UNITY powwows I attended, non-Indians danced when they were invited to do so. In contrast, at the 1995 Shinnecock Labor Day Powwow and at Schemitzun in 1995 and 1997, they rarely took part, although the emcees often jokingly noted "a lot of wannabes out there."

The intertribal category includes a spectacular variety of dance styles and produces a flow of space, time, and energy that is full of dynamic diversity. Some dancers perform grass, traditional, jingle dress, or fancy dances "full out," while others just walk and talk with friends. As a result, a literal sea of bodies is created. When one watches an intertribal in a large arena, it seems at first as if all the participants are moving in similar ways, but with more careful observation the differences in styles become apparent. As Lillian Williams (Skidi Pawnee/Chicksaw/Cherokee) suggests in the video *Into the Circle*, participants are "all dancing to the same song but with a different melody." Most Indian dancers perform in regalia, but others join in street clothes, most likely individuals who are not at the powwow to compete or gain points for competition. Eager to dance, young people are usually the first to move into the circle.

The intertribal dances emphasize inclusivity and diversity. It is a gathering together of peoples. In an intertribal, exchanges clearly take place between people of different tribes, races, and generations. For example, a two-year-old may be performing the jingle dress dance for the first time alongside a woman in her eighties, or a young boy may be dancing with his father, both in full fancy dance regalia.

An intertribal, like the Grand Entry, often reveals the makeup of a particular host community. During the intertribal dances at Thunderbird powwows and at the UNITY powwow in New York City, Taíno Indians danced hunched over in a line that meandered through the crowd. The men were dressed in loincloths, almost naked, and the women wore long, loose, light-colored dresses. At Thunderbird, I also noticed "contraries," men who danced counterclockwise around the arena and wore regalia that tended to be a chaotic assortment of feathers, belts, and beads of many colors.

The intertribal invites questions about the meaning of the terms "tribal," "intertribal," and "pan-Indian" in relation to transcultural performance and powwows. William K. Powers writes that "tribalism, a tendency toward maintaining tribal distinction, becomes indicative of tradition, cultural identity, and continuity in culture, while intertribalism, the tendency toward exchanging cultural traits between tribes and between the Euroamerican society, becomes indicative of modernity, social identity, and cultural change" (1990, 11). Powers's use of the term "intertribal" can be used to refer to the kind of powwows examined in this book—especially those events in the New York City tri-state area as well as the dance category discussed above.

Nonetheless, I want to reiterate that the fact that many powwows are intertribal does not mean they are necessarily pan-Indian. "Pan-Indian" refers to social and political movements that have historically brought together different tribal nations and individuals from distinct tribal affiliations for a common purpose related to Indian rights. Intertribal powwows are pan-Indian in their cross-tribal sharing of traditional practices of dance, song, and so forth. Yet today, the tribal, the intertribal, and the non-Indian influences dominate. A powwow can be hosted and sponsored by a tribal nation and continue to be intertribal. At an intertribal powwow, while others from outside the tribe are welcome, the general sense of the event reflects the local tribal community.

Philip J. Deloria recognizes that "the understandable response of many historians and many Indian people has been to turn to the unique particulars of tribal and community histories" (2004, 11). However, he continues, "tribal histories also militate against efforts to generalize or synthesize, leaving us to wonder how to do justice to the variation among hundreds of tribal and community histories while at the same time reaching for general patterns concerning such things as colonialism and empire in North America" (2004, 11–12). There is always a tension between working to preserve the culture of a particular tribe and engaging with other tribal or ethnic groups in intercultural exchange.

During an intertribal, as Native and at times non-Native individuals dance together in the circle, there is a fluid exchange between them. Through transcultural exchange, they produce both multiplicity *and* unity through their moving bodies.

## Tiny Tots

The tiny tots are usually the first to perform after the opening ceremonies and intertribals. As youngsters venture forth into the wide-open space, they dance the initial moves of the fancy shawl, grass, jingle dress, or other dance styles. Often their relatives and friends accompany them: a mother carries a young toddler dressed in a jingle dress or a five-year-old performs the grass dance in the company of his older brother. Some children execute detailed moves in specific styles. At the United Tribes International Powwow in 2009, I was astounded by how many very young children performed their distinct styles remarkably well. However, children in this age group usually execute general, tentative bounces up and down, and their dance category is organized as an intertribal. Sometimes at the larger powwows there are separate dance categories for young children, as seen in the jingle dress dance in figure 13.

Native children dance as soon as they can walk, and often a grandfather, parent, or older friend teaches a youngster the steps. Dance becomes an integral aspect of a Native person's life from a very early age. For example, Paul A. Francis III (Penobscot), or "June Bug II," a young visual artist who worked at a vendor's table with his mother at Bar Harbor in 2009, told me that he started dancing at home at age three or four, moving in the kitchen around the washing machine (personal communication, July 16, 2009).

Dana Runs Above says that "some children were born 'powwow babies.' Other children are introduced to it in their later years. Our children are 'powwow babies'—that's all they've ever known. It's a part of their life" (qtd. in Roberts 1992, 58). As people travel the powwow circuit, children are encouraged to honor their elders and learn from them and to establish strong social and family relations within the Indian community. Perhaps because the United Tribes International Powwow is held on the campus of the United Tribes Technical College in Bismarck, Montana, an institution that promotes a philosophy of educating the whole family, there was an especially strong presence of children at the powwow in 2009. In New York City, the Redhawk Native American Arts Council, the American Indian Community House, and the organizers of the Thunderbird Grand Midsummer Pow Wow are also deeply invested in organizing powwow events for children. These organizations do a great deal of educational outreach in the area through classes, theatrical and other performances, videos, and so forth that encourage children and their families to participate in local powwows.

The following story from Harriett Skye (Lakota/Sioux) is a moving description of how a child can first experience powwow dancing:

> At the United Tribes Pow-wow in the 1970s, I was sitting with my husband watching an inter-tribal, when my eyes began to focus on a young boy about twelve years old. He didn't have a dance costume, just his jeans, T-shirt, and sneakers. What caught my eye was that he was literally spinning on one foot with his head arched sideways, his eyes were closed, his arms outstretched, completely oblivious to anyone else around him. He kept such exact time with the drum beat that at some point in that arena him and the drum became one. For a brief moment, I knew he was con-

> nected to everything around him, and when the last beat was sounded it was difficult to tell where he started, where the arena grounds ended and how high the sky was. He was all of it and more. His aunt was watching as well, and she was shocked. She remarked that he had never danced before and had no idea that he even wanted to, yet there he was, giving the performance of his life. It was a spectacular sight I will never forget because I knew that I had been touched in a very special way. (personal communication, March 19, 1998)

I saw a similar moment when I watched "June Bug II" jump into the arena. He would wait on the outside of the circle until he felt the beat, then he would join the circle. With high knee bends and sure footing, Paul's dancing expressed reverence, concentration, and energy. He called his style men's northern traditional, a style I will discuss below.

As the tiny tots dance, the emcee reminds attendees that Indian people make decisions in relation to the seventh generation, with the needs of children and *their* children and grandchildren and great-grandchildren in mind. Today's tiny tots will someday perform adult dance styles as ancient, social, and sacred memory transfers the power of dancing bodies across generations. The traditional dances are at the core of this process. Mature individuals and some younger adults, both men and women, perform these styles, which embody gender, spirituality, and storytelling.

## Men's Traditional Style

The men's traditional dances are derived from the times when warriors told their battle stories through dance (Stephenson 1993; White 1994). This performance practice is clearly evident during a men's traditional dance and in many dancers' oral narratives as they talk about what it means to be a traditional dancer (e.g., Browner 2002, 123–125; Roberts 1992, 1998; and evidence recorded in numerous videos and films). As R. C. Mowatt (Comanche) says, for traditional male dancers, "each movement has a significance of looking for a trail, looking for your enemy, swaying in and out" (qtd. in Contreras and Bernstein 1996, 30). Tara Browner situates today's dances in the context of powwow history: "Traditional dances have roots in old, tribal-specific warrior societies, old Omaha/Grass styles, and, to a certain extent, the Oklahoma Dream Dance of the 1890s that spread into the Great Lakes region. With so many variables, there is no one definite Traditional Dance. Each dancer presents a slightly different version, depending on tribal affiliation and personal preference" (2002,

49). Nonverbal narrative is the basis of men's traditional dance. Each dancer is engaged in the act of storytelling through dance (see figures 8 and 9).

The styles most frequently performed in the New York City area are the southern straight and the northern styles. At smaller powwows these are danced at the same time, though at larger events such as Schemitzun there are often separate competitions for each. I have also seen these dances performed in Maine, Montana, and North Dakota with slight variations. At the 1997 Crow Fair Celebration, men also danced the Crow traditional dance. They wore boned breastplates, strings of bells, tails of feathers or fur, and were relatively barechested. The body actions of this dance are similar to those of the traditional styles discussed here, but they do have some differences.

During the men's southern straight traditional dance, also known as the gentlemen's dance, dancers bend close to the ground and take two steps to the right then two steps to the left. Their posture seems to almost pull them to the ground. The straight dance, which is derived from early contact period dance societies, is dignified and graceful. Foresset Kassanavoid (Comanche) claims that the Poncas and Omahas first created it because they wanted a competitive dance—a feather or fancy dance; later, they passed it on to the Comanche and other southern Plains tribal groups (*Into the Circle*).

The dancers wear porcupine roach headdresses or beaver hats with one feather and often carry a feather fan, a hand mirror, a medicine wheel, a dream catcher, a war weapon, or a staff. Alert and aware of danger, the dancers quickly snap their heads from side to side. Each dancer's actions make an individual statement about himself as an Indian, a dancer, and a contemporary warrior. The regalia expresses that identity. Reminiscent of Plains Indian dress, it often includes a colorful cloth shirt with ribbonwork on the shirt and leggings, beaded bandoliers, bells worn at the knee, and moccasins. Some dancers wear a long train that is sometimes made of otter fur but is usually made of cloth to which feathers and smaller animal tails are attached.

In a competition, dancers are judged on how vividly a story comes alive. Southern straight dancers can improvise as long as their dance begins and ends with the drum. Body movements are affected by the particular song of the moment. An individual dancer will subtly shake his shoulders, bend down and up, and weave forward and around. Sometimes he might emulate "a bird coming off a perch, and going down, swooping down, picking up something" (Abe Conklin, Ponca/Osage, in *Into the Circle*).

The men who perform the southern straight traditional dance are stalwart and steady as they take two short steps, first with the right foot then the left, using a variety of toe-heel, flat-flat, flat-heel, and heel-toe movements. Knees bent, they seem to glide across the arena. The head initiates, tells the body which way to turn, as the hunter or warrior smells, hears, and sees where to go. The senses are especially active in this dance.

Dancers also tell stories in the men's northern traditional dance, which is said to have come from the Sioux Indians of South Dakota. The regalia features a distinctive roach headdress full of hundreds of magpie feathers, a bustle, and a coup stick. In this style, the basic move is two steps to the right and two to the left. The northern traditional style also uses a lot of sharp head movements while the body dips down and up and executes knee bends and weight shifts front and side to side. Many dancers paint their faces and bodies as a personal, spiritual, and political statement.

Diamond Brown (Eastern Band Cherokee), a traditional dancer, explains that when he paints his face, puts on his regalia, and dances, he engages in a contemporary form of warfare that involves spiritual practice: "I enjoy dancing. I am a Traditional dancer. I am a warrior for my people, in regalia and out of regalia. I fight for Indian issues. I believe in what is right for the Indian people. . . . Before I put my paint on, before I even knew how to paint, I had to pray to the Creator, and the Creator told me how he wanted me to paint. That's my identity between me and him" (qtd. in Contreras and Bernstein 1996, 69–70). When Brown paints his face black, white, and red, he links black with death, white with peace and security, and red with war. As he dances, he feels and thinks these meanings, and the act of performing traditional is integrated into how he relates to his Creator and to the spiritual world. Thus, he asserts what it means to resist, fight, and celebrate through dance.

Those who dance the Crow Hop, a dance that is related to the men's northern traditional style, perform multiple hops forward and backward, almost a skip, step side to side, and turn in place. Two other distinctions of the Crow Hop Dance are that the drum song is different and the dancers change feet on each beat.

In the Crow Hop Dance, as in other men's and women's traditional styles, dancers raise their fans or coup sticks on the honor beats of a song, beats that usually appear in the second part of a song: "And what they are doing is they're honoring their people, they're honoring the veterans, anybody who has ever been in war, and *Tunkashila*, the Great Spirit" (Norma Rendon qtd. in Browner 2002, 86). Honor beats vary somewhat from song to song, but they are usually four or five loud beats.

Reginald and Gladys Laubin describe an earlier dance called the Ruffle Dance that is quite similar to the contemporary Crow Hop Dance, the Sneak-Up Dance, and even the fancy dance style: "For the Ruffle Dance the drum throbs rapidly to start and the dancers 'ruffle their feathers,' shaking shoulders and bodies to make the feathers in their modern 'swing bustles' vibrate. Then the singers take up a fast 2/4 time, getting faster and faster, and suddenly stop, which requires great control on the part of the dancers who have been moving so rapidly. This sequence may be repeated several times before the contest is brought to a close" (1976, 459).

The Sneak-Up Dance is particularly dramatic. It begins with a rapidly beating drum and a drummed "ruffle." The dancers kneel on the floor to scout for an animal or enemy. Shielding their eyes, their heads move this way and that. At different moments, dancers abruptly rise to encounter the enemy with the usual two steps right, two steps left. Then a break segues into a casual walking around until the ruffle is heard again. This happens four times. Dancers constantly look over their arms while performing large, high, arc-like arm sweeps. They sometimes dance backward, which means they are retreating from the enemy. Each dancer follows the timing of his individual narrative. When several men are in the arena, this sequence happens in counterpoint.

During the men's traditional dances, starts and stops of the flow of movement relate to the real act of watching out for something or someone. Just as an animal freezes when it sees a hunter, a moving car, or another animal, traditional male dancers often stop dead in their tracks when in danger. Their attentive readiness is tempered by the steady, strong song of the drum. As they move on, their feet touch the ground in calm, firm steps and their heads jerk from side to side and bob up and down.

Damon Rough Face (Ponca) describes what others watch for when they observe male traditional dancers: "I like to see a Traditional dancer go low, a lot of body movement. You got different parts of your body, and they all need to be moving with the drum: the head and shoulders, legs, the bustle. But what I look for is the dancers' effortless expression because that's when they're dancing with their heart" (*Into the Circle*). Inner meaning is intrinsically linked to how movement and music interrelate and to the necessary coordination between different body parts. Ricky Stevenson, who is part Cherokee on his grandmother's side, told me that for him dancing to the drum is what makes powwow dancing so powerful. As one dances, the drum provides a direct "heart-line" from the spirit to the earth (personal communication, September 12, 2009).

The male traditional dance styles are less three-dimensional than the grass dance style and express a sturdy quality. As Kip White Cloud (Sioux) says, "Traditional is coming into manhood, very deliberate, confident and self-assured" (qtd. in Roberts 1992, 87).

## Women's Traditional Style

According to many sources, women didn't actively perform at powwows until after World War I. Then, after World War II, their participation increased because more women had served in that war. However, there are accounts of women's dance societies during the early contact period. Norma Rendon points out that women's traditional dance has a long history: "The women's Traditional has been around for a long time. Pow-wows have been around for a long time. We got pow-wows in our Origin Stories that go way back and just during the dance the woman would dress in her best attire. And because the woman has connection with the earth, because the earth is our mother and they're both female, then that is why the woman Traditional dancer should be as graceful and use more of a swaying motion than a hopping motion. That's where that connection is, and that's how the women's Traditional Dance came about" (qtd. in Browner 2002, 107). Thus, I question the notion that women did not dance in powwow-related performances until the twentieth century.

In contemporary intertribal powwows, women first danced in place on the edge of the dance area, as they continue to do. At Schemitzun in 1995 and 1997, the United Tribes International Powwow in 2009, and many other powwows I attended, traditional women dancers surrounded the others during the Grand Entry, making space for more people to enter and keeping time with the drum. As they gather on the periphery of the circle the traditional women dancers stand in place and move in a calm up-and-down motion. Radiating a powerful connection to the earth, they reinforce their role as givers and protectors of life by the gentle yet firm way their feet touch the ground. Women watch over the powwow arena and hence over the space/land of the community. By facing inward toward the sacred center of the circle, they also turn away from the outside—from the nation-state, mainstream U.S. society, capitalism, Anglo-American values, racism, and perhaps other factors that Indian women might want to exclude from their consciousness as they protect their community.

Dancers execute similar body movements in two styles of traditional women's dance, the southern cloth and the buckskin styles. The regalia and the use of energy in each dance style distinguish them from each other. Both cloth and buckskin dancers execute short, measured steps; maintain a vertical, dignified stance; and use their regalia as part of the action of the dance.

The regalia of women's southern cloth dancers consists of a one- or two-piece cloth dress decorated with appliqué, printed designs, fine embroidery, and, often, elk teeth, coins, and cowry and dentalium shells. The women might also carry a fringed shawl, a purse, or a hand fan. The dancers stand in place, moving their feet ever so slightly to turn in a move that is called a washboard. Stephenson suggests that this symbolizes how in the past women turned to look for their warriors as they came home and relates to the protective circle mentioned above (1993, 15).

Other cloth dancers bounce up and down while moving forward clockwise around the circle in such a way that the purse swings forward as the shawl fringe moves backward—and vice versa. Often the dress is so long that it's not possible to see what the feet are doing. In both the cloth and the buckskin style, the fringe itself seems to dance. It can represent "the continuous flow of a waterfall with its life-giving water and energy, and the perseverance of the Native mother" (White 1994, 15). Often beaded leggings and moccasins accentuate the delicacy of the steps.

Cloth dancers perform as one assemblage and use no superfluous movements. On the honor beats, all the women bend forward at the waist. As in the men's traditional style, dancers continually show respect for the drum with a variety of gestures indicating the dialogic interaction between movement and music. As a woman bows, her headgear, which might be a headdress with a single feather, a hairpiece, or a beaded crown, curves forward and downward with her. A poignant dignity is expressed in the relaxed yet calculated movements of both the cloth and buckskin dance styles. To watch traditional buckskin dancer Bobbie Orr (Salish) is "like seeing a field of wheat blowing in a gentle breeze. Her movements are slow, light, and precise, barely perceptible if not for the softly swaying fringe of her buckskin dress" (Contreras and Bernstein 1995, 5). Orr describes the buckskin style as "a very graceful, slow moving dance" (qtd. in Contreras and Bernstein 1996, 5).

The buckskin outfit is made of tanned deerskin with fringe on the bottom and along the edges of the garment, particularly on the large yoke, the shoulder cape, and the shawl. These dresses are sometimes so heavily beaded that they weigh sixty to eighty pounds. The placement, patterns, and color of the beadwork identify different tribal groups and individuals. Orr describes the personal investment her regalia required: "It took a while to get the money to make my dress. . . . You have thousands of dollars in these dresses, and I'm still working on mine. The more beadwork you add to it, it's a never-ending job" (qtd. in Contreras and Bernstein 1996, 5).

A dancer's regalia is an important element of any powwow dance style. It is her personal and aesthetic interpretation of the human and animal worlds and is different for each woman. The designs for both cloth and buckskin regalia are often handed down from grandmothers, mothers, and aunts. In the buckskin traditional style, as in the cloth style, women carry fans, shawls, and purses. Articles from earlier times such as beaded pouches, knife shields, and a "drag," a long strip with silver work that was originally used as a horse whip, sometimes hang from a silver belt decorated with conch shells.

A strong sense of the circular is expressed in these traditional dances. The women circle, slowly and sedately, in time with the drum. Norma Rendon describes the requirements of these styles: "But when you're dancing—and that's part why the Northern women are stationary when they dance—when you're watching and judging a women's Traditional dancer, their heels should always be together, and the closer they are together the better the dancer is. You watch for them to be on-beat. When that beat comes down, that dancer should be coming up. If that beat comes down and they're going down they're off-beat. The other thing is that they hold their head up and their fringe should be swinging the same way" (qtd. in Browner 2002, 109).

The movements of the buckskin dance style are slightly faster than those of the cloth dance style. Claudia Spicer (Otoe), a judge of buckskin dancers, describes the requirements of this style: "It [the fringe] has to go right in timing with the drum. . . . You don't have to dance hard or anything like that. Then . . . the costume—how nice it's made . . . and the way they're dressed. And, of course, they have to stop with the drum. When it stops your feet have to be on the ground" (*Into the Circle*). When the dancers don't stop with the drum, it's called overstepping. (This is true for all dance styles.)

Several elements of men's and women's traditional dance styles are different, leading to questions about gender roles. What do these distinctions indicate about what it means to be male or female in Indian country? Browner describes how this issue relates to upbringing: "As children grow to adulthood, the question of their dance category begins to tie more and more into concepts of gender identity and sexual orientation. At this point, choice of dance category becomes a statement to the powwow community of who a person is and how they wish to be perceived. Indian people tend to be more accepting of difference than the dominant society, primarily because they consider that it is not up to one human to criticize how the Creator has made another" (2002, 60). She continues: "I have never heard . . . of any dancer not being allowed to dance or being ejected from a pow-wow, harassed, or abused in any way for choosing to dance in a category not traditionally assigned to their sex or gender" (2002, 60). This level of acceptance of gender roles and sexual preferences illustrates the importance of inclusivity to Native peoples.

Men's and women's styles use the powwow arena space differently. Women dance together in a synchronized up-and-down motion as they move around and through the wide-open circular area. The men are less "orderly" and do not dance in unison. This could be because each man is telling his own story, while the women are not necessarily doing so. Still, each woman experiences and expresses her own personal meaning. Gender distinctions can also be observed in the bent-over posture of the men and the regal verticality of the women as they look forward into the distance with an inner focus. What is perhaps most important is how the traditional women dancers encircle the arena during the Grand Entry.

As transcultural beginnings, the Grand Entry, the intertribals, the tiny tots dance, and the traditional dances introduce the powwow. The energy in the arena and in the audience increases as the program continues. With each new dance category another way of embodying power is revealed.

# 6

# Performing Race

> The question of my "identity" often comes up. I think I must be a mixed blood. I claim to be male, although only one of my parents was male.
>
> JIMMIE DURHAM (CHEROKEE)

Native American intertribal powwows are open, public sites where Indian and non-Indian dancing bodies visibly perform race in complex ways. I use the term "perform race" to refer to all those who dance at powwows, although in this chapter the focus is on Native dancers. Maintaining the centrality of bodies in motion, here I examine how race and racism affect the quality and meaning of both Native dance performance and the production of power. In chapter 7, I continue with a discussion of how and why non-Indians dance as "wannabes" at powwows and what that might mean.

Intertribal powwows emerged in the historical and contemporary context of Indian hospitality. This is particularly true in the Northeast, where Indians had to deal with outsiders as early as the 1600s. As Lisa Brooks (Abenaki) explains: "Europeans were in the common pot, whether they knew it or not, and they had brought with them ideas, behaviors, and materials that could potentially disrupt or even destroy it. A central question that arose in Native communities throughout the northeast had to do with how to incorporate the 'beings' from Europe into Native space and how to maintain the network of relations in the wake of consequences—including disease and resource depletion—that Europeans brought to Algonquian shores" (2008, 7). The term "common pot" alludes to the Algonquian metaphor of the "dish with one spoon" and illustrates how Native concepts of a shared land and shared resources were so different from those of the newly arriving Europeans (Brooks 2008, 140).

Richard Drinnon offers another perspective on Indian hospitality during the first years of contact: "Throughout the Americas tribal people extended their hands in friendship because they affirmed the invaders as parts of the creation they worshipped all the days of their lives. . . . And at the spiritual center of their great affirmation was the dance, the moving means of interweaving life, culture, land" (1987, 109). For centuries, Native Americans have provided spaces for cultural interaction through dance and other means. This does not imply that non-Indians were or are welcome at all ceremonies. Many sacred events exclude outsiders, though non-Indians might be invited to observe a particular ritual at a respectful distance.

A key element of powwow as a performance genre is that Indians are the controlling majority, not Euro-Americans. During a powwow, the emcee gives a double message of welcome and friendly ridicule as he jokes about Indians and non-Indians alike. While continually reiterating that the powwow is open to everyone, he makes it clear that he and other Indians are in charge. As dance scholar Black Hawk Hancock points out in his discussion of the alternative social spaces African American communities create in Chicago, "These situations provide a counter-space to exercise cultural freedoms and expressions. In these spaces, a sense of community is constructed through an alternative set of values and social relationships than those of White society" (2005, 436). With the emcee "at the helm," powwows are alternative spaces in which Native Americans set the rules.

During a powwow, the emcee guides the arena program and, with the arena directors, dance judges, and others, maintains order in the entire performance area. He also reminds people about "those wonderful Indian things out there to look at and buy" and cordially invites powwow attendees to spend money at concession stands.

In a specific example of Indians in command, at the Honor the Earth Powwow in Northampton in 1997, the emcee invited anyone who had achieved sobriety to put his or her name on a list, noting the length of time he or she had gone without using alcohol or drugs. One by one Native and non-Native men and women came forward, forming a row in front of the emcee tent. An intertribal dance followed that included people from many racial groups, though Indians led the group around the arena. The emcee and other Indians were clearly in control of this moment as all participants celebrated sobriety and then performed race in his or her own way.

The astounding mix of people at intertribal powwows is a reflection of the diversity of the larger society. Individuals who attend powwows represent different ethnicities and varying degrees of ethnicity; some refer to themselves as mixed blood or hybrid. However, in a shift toward what Hancock calls "something deeper—culture and knowledge" (2005, 452), I choose to minimize the use of colors—white, black, red, yellow, and brown—to identify people. As

Hancock suggests, "The visual indicators of race evade the crucial question of racial formation and instead rely on the absolute and static notions of race as essential and marked by skin alone" (2005, 452). Even an expression such as "rainbow of colors" is simplistic and can detract from the complexities of racial discourse.

In addition, when people dance in the arena circle, it is not always easy to discern who is Indian and who is not. This is the case at events in the Northeast, especially those that take place in and around New York City. Originally a site of the Algonquian peoples, this region is now a gathering place for Indians from many diverse tribal groups, although the Shinnecock Nation is always present at powwows in this area. Similarly, the integration of Indians and non-Indians at powwows such as the annual Gateway to the Nations PowWow points to the ongoing, ever-changing process of transculturation in which "performances of race" are central to the meaning of powwow.

Years of intermarriage between racial groups have complicated categories of racial identity in the United States. Many people find it difficult if not impossible to identify themselves by race on government census forms, job applications, or other similar documents. Caucasian is not simply Caucasian and African American is not simply African American. A Native American person is not only Native American but is also descended from a specific tribal group or nation or from several groups or nations. Likewise, one can be Latino/a, Asian, and Caucasian or Chinese, Filipino, Caucasian, and Spanish, or some other complex mix of ancestors. Although census forms have now begun to provide a category called mixed race, the notion of single racial identity markers prevails as part of our national mindset, even though most of us are the product of generations of racial mixing.

Color and blood are still prominent in the thinking of many people in the United States, as is evidenced by the persistence of racial profiling in U.S. culture. Jill Lepore writes of how the link between color, blood, and race was already deeply ingrained in the European way of thinking when they arrived in North America: "Blood that flowed uncontrollably, for instance, signaled filth and chaos. Blood, the colonists believed, ought to be contained within the body, where it regulated all the vital forces. Blood might be 'let' to cure 'plethora,' but carefully, and, one hoped, by someone who could stop it" (1998, 100). Many Europeans of the sixteenth and seventeenth centuries believed that the blood that flowed when Indians engaged in violent acts was similar to the uncontrollable bleeding of menstruation. They saw both Indian blood and the blood of women as shameful (Lepore 1998, 100).

Racism is a prejudice against certain racial groups that sometimes becomes hatred. This bigotry is based on how one side or the other looks at and responds to a composite of genetically acquired physical features (skin color being the most obvious) and cultural factors such as language, religion, spiritual practices, and lifestyles. In relation to dance, some questions about race emerge: Is there an innate, "natural" way of moving and dancing that is dependent on one's race or racial mix? What is biological and what is cultural? How does the body interact with the social and how does social environment act upon the body? In order to explore these questions in relation to "performing race" at powwows, the concepts of essentialism and socially constructed racialized bodies must be examined.

As feminist scholar Diana Fuss suggests in *Essentially Speaking*: "On the one hand, to maintain a strict constructionist view which holds that there is no such thing as racial identity can block our understanding of the social production of 'race.' On the other hand, to advocate an even more rigid essentialist view which holds that 'race' is self-evidently hereditary or biologistic can also interfere with an analysis of the ideological and political formation of racial subjects" (1989, 92). In her study of race and "whiteness," Ruth Frankenburg argues that it is necessary to rehistoricize race and culture, "insisting on antiessentialist concepts of race, ethnicity, and culture, while at the same time emphasizing that these categories are made materially 'real' within matrices of power relations" (1994, 74). These issues are fully operative when Native peoples perform race at powwows.

What does it mean to be Indian in the twenty-first century? Is it an issue of blood? Is it an issue of culture? After many generations of mixed unions across races, tribes, and ethnicities, is there still something essentially Indian about Indian culture and traditional practices? These are not theoretical issues for Native Americans who attend and perform at powwows.

Native dancers are deeply invested in a history that has been passed down from generation to generation. Youngsters are steeped in powwow culture early in life and learn to dance as the result of years of practice. Indian dancers who come to powwows bring that history and that experience with them.

I have often observed differences of quality, style, and meaning between Indian and non-Indian dancers. These differences are not inherent or "in the blood." However, centuries of traditional cultural practices performed in the context of oppressive racism have affected Indian dance expression. Judith Butler observes that "bodies live and die; eat and sleep; feel pain, pleasure; endure illness and violence; and these 'facts,' one might skeptically proclaim, cannot be dismissed as mere construction. Surely there must be some kind of necessity that accompanies these primary and irrefutable experiences. And surely there is. But their irrefutability in no way implies what it might mean to affirm them" (1993, xi). The necessity that accompanies the lived experience of Indians in the United States often propels them to dance; for many, it is a need. And that need for dance is expressed in many individual practices within the styles of Native American powwow dance.

For example, traditional male dancing is precise, elegant, and often heavy in the way that men make contact with the earth. Male grass dancers move in rapid, urgent, full-bodied, and three-dimensional ways. In contrast, wannabes appear to dance on clouds far above the ground. They also have difficulty stepping in time with the drum. In a basic, physical way, wannabes move less energetically and "mark" or "trace" the steps of their chosen dance rather than fully engage their entire bodies. Frequently, they dance without defining any specific style. This could be an indication of the shy, uncertain respect of an outsider who is intruding on an unfamiliar culture, but it is also a demonstration of the absence of lifelong preparation and practice.

Renae Watchman (Diné/Tsalagi) writes of her lifelong training: "In North America, powwow traditions—such as obtaining and creating dance outfits, performing dance styles, and knowing origin stories and songs—are passed on orally and through experience. As a Fancy Shawl dancer since the Tiny Tots category, I learned powwow protocol from the teachings of elders, specifically family members" (2005, 248). This is not to say that a non-Native person who has been deeply immersed in Indian culture from a young age cannot also learn and execute certain dance styles in a visceral, meaningful way. However, during my fieldwork, I observed very few non-Indian people who had this ability. Indian dancers express the great complexity of Indianness; wannabes perform with body movements that seem tepid and vague in comparison. Sincere though they may be, wannabes are not Indians.

The overt and tangible bodily presence of Native American powwow dancers today contrasts with the invisibility that Indians have experienced for hundreds of years: "Native peoples in America remain invisible on their own land, precisely because it *is* our land. . . . The African, Asian and Latin American peoples are seen as having legitimate political struggles, as part of an important concept called 'human rights.' American Indians obviously cannot be called 'Americans.' We cannot, therefore, be considered politically. We must be spoken of mythically, as American Indians, or anthropologically, as 'Amerinds.' We are thereby effectively removed from the arena of political discourse in exactly the same way we are removed from artistic, literary, and cinematic discourse" (Durham 1992, 429). This notion of visibility lies at the core of powwow dancing. Powwow offers a complex discourse in one of the few places in which

Indians are plainly visible—by their own choice. Whether or not skin color, body types, and other physical attributes of "Indianness" are visible, moving, dancing bodies are viscerally present in the form of individuals and social beings with cultural histories and lived experience.

This voluntary manifestation of Indianness sharply differs from the racially biased images that appear in popular culture and in pre-1980s textbooks. Often these sources represent Indians using contradictory images of noble and savage, or good and bad, Indians. They are presented as drunks, warriors, or feathered icons. Robert F. Berkhofer (1978), Philip J. Deloria (2004), and others have written extensively about the history of these images. These contrived portrayals have very little to do with real Indians, their dance, and their lives.

Native Americans have taken control of how they are represented in U.S. culture in a variety of ways in recent years. Tribes have successfully sued the government over the mismanagement of tribal money and lands. Each year more tribes are added to the federal register of recognized nations. Gaming casinos on Indian reservations have brought prosperity to some parts of Indian country. Films produced by Native Americans have entered the mainstream in the last fifteen years, including *Smoke Signals* (1998), *Skins* (2002), *Skinwalkers* (2002), *The Song of Hiawatha* (2005), and *Dance Me Outside* (2008). Native American culture is represented in literature, poetry, and scholarship by Native Americans; in stores and galleries that sell Native art and crafts; and in museums such as the Smithsonian Museum of the American Indian in Washington, DC, and the Abbe Museum in Bar Harbor, Maine, both of which are operated primarily by indigenous peoples. However, this trend does not mean that conditions have significantly improved on reservations or for Indians who live off reservations. Many Native peoples are still treated as second-class citizens in a land that was originally theirs.

## Back and Front Regions

At powwows, race relations are manifest in the spatial organization of the performance area and behind the scenes. In elaborating on Erving Goffman's concept of front and back regions, Dean MacCannell proposes that "a back region, closed to audiences and outsiders, allows concealment of props and activities that might discredit the performance out front. In other words, sustaining a firm sense of social reality requires some *mystification*" (1976, 93). The multiple layering of front and back regions at intertribal powwows produces a mystification that is important for any analysis of these events.

At powwows, organizers of the host community control most of the front and back regions. Where the drums will be located is decided beforehand, as are the order of the arena program and conventions about protocol and respect. In the back regions, or inner workings of powwows, race and power shape the rules that regulate who can register as a dancer, a drum group, or a craft dealer. Flyers that advertise powwows frequently announce these restrictions with phrases such as “certified Indian,” “member of a certified tribe,” and “Natives only.” Dancers, artists, and craftspeople are required to identify themselves in this way, though there is some flexibility from powwow to powwow. Some Indians see these categories as the result of a long history of bureaucratization of the very meaning of Indian.

Attending powwows does not mean that one automatically experiences Indian country. Many social and political events and organizational decisions take place at powwow areas that are closed to the public. Powwows may serve as venues for political meetings, conferences, and sacred rituals, and those who attend powwows looking for the “authentic” or the exotic are prevented from intruding into those spaces.

For example, in 1976, the Mashpee Wampanoag Tribal Council went to court to fight for possession of about 16,000 acres of land in Indian Town, located in Cape Cod. In his testimony on behalf of the council, anthropologist Jack Campisi noted that “events such as the powwows or ‘homecoming’ are ways of identifying Mashpees as a distinct group. Although the powwow caters to outsiders and tourists, it also operates on other more exclusive levels. Gatherings of this sort have a social function, drawing together the dispersed community, and also a spiritual, educational function (their pageants and ceremonies are concerned with moral subjects and Indian history; they teach reverence for the earth). Parts of the unity conference are sacred and closed to outsiders” (qtd. in Clifford 1988, 319). The true reality of Indian country exists in the “back regions” of powwows.

The contrast between front and back regions and what is visible and what is not visible are often seen in crystallized moments of in-between space or transcultural exchange that express a kind of surreal illumination of postcoloniality itself. Examples include the tipi-lined entrance of the 1995 Gateway to the Nations PowWow right next to a busy two-lane highway in Brooklyn; the flashing cameras of tourists that assault people as they enter the arena in a Grand Entry with dignified reverence; an Indian fancy dancer in full regalia chatting informally with a few non-Indians in street clothes. These kinds of moments offer startling and sometimes absurd illustrations of how racial differences are performed at intertribal powwows.

## Racism: A Historical Paradigm with Contemporary Repercussions

The Europeans who first came to North America brought with them world views, ideological tenets, and economic goals that had a devastating effect on Native Americans. Bodies, and in particular dancing bodies, immediately captured the attention and curiosity of "civilized" Europeans, who observed Native American dancing through the lens of racial, ethnic, and sexual voyeurism. Thus, from the beginning of the contact period, racism against Indians has been expressed largely in reaction to their bodies. Even though violence between non-Indians and Indians existed from this time, Euro-Americans didn't use racism to justify their actions against Native peoples until the first third of the eighteenth century. However, the attraction and repulsion of dancing Indian bodies for non-Indians has been recorded from as early as the fifteenth century.

Christopher Columbus's reports of his first encounters with Indians emphasize the body. The descriptions recorded in his *Diario* focus on the "very handsome bodies and very fine faces" of the people he met. Like many white Europeans, he organized people in his mind by skin color: "They are of the color of the Canary islanders, neither black nor white" (qtd. in Drinnon 1987, 108). Drinnon records that Columbus's "very first thought" was to enslave the "gentle islanders" and that "from then on the entries to his *Diario* made plain that he had jumped at the chance to make himself and his men masters of those who were 'very poor in everything' and who went about 'naked as their mothers who bore them'" (qtd. in Drinnon 1987, 108). Many scholars affirm that the concept of race was not part of the world views of precontact indigenous peoples (Berkhofer 1978; Jaimes 1992, 1994; Takaki 1990, 1993; Allen [1986] 1992, 2004). Yet for Europeans, skin color and all that skin color implied determined how they viewed power relations between Native and non-Native people.

Indians have always conceived of themselves as groups of people distinguished by kinship, geographical location, and cultural affinities based on similarities in subsistence practices, performance rituals, and languages. Native American scholar M. Annette Jaimes explains how these elements have informed individual and group identity:

> Traditionally, individuals could become members of an indigenous society by kinship, intermarriage, adoption, or naturalization, which included "mixed-blood identities," no matter what their "racial" or cultural background. Later, Euro-Americans as "whites" could be adopted or nat-

> uralized by Indians through intermarriage and emphasis on exogamy. After conquest and forced assimilation, some translations of Indian statements indicate that groups continued to see themselves as distinct cultural entities, with a communal concept of nationhood as "a people." Yet this is not the same as perceiving and promoting themselves as a distinct "race." . . . While kinship, culture, and nationhood are the bedrock of Indian identity, race or ethnicity [are] not. (1994, 42)

Indians and non-Indians practice radically different ways of defining Native identity—and, for that matter, identity in general. Beginning in colonial times, Euro-Americans linked identity to racist beliefs that focused on experiences and expressions of culture that used the body.

Three key aspects of Euro-American interactions with Indians contributed to and implemented racist thinking: religious and scientific ideology, appropriation of land, and laws that sought to control and contain Indians. Scholar John Mohawk (1945–2006), once a spokesperson for the Six Nations Iroquois Confederacy, emphasizes that Christian theology was one of the first mechanisms by which Europeans imposed their ideologies on Native peoples (1992). Theology and science have both been used to justify harmful beliefs and practices. Two examples are the theory of manifest destiny and the use of science to "prove" that Caucasians were the superior race.

## Ideology

During the early contact period of the 1600s and into the period of intense colonization of Native peoples by Euro-Americans in the mid-eighteenth to early nineteenth centuries, Europeans often clothed ideology in religious, scientific, and political disguises in order to coerce Indians to give up their richest resources, their culture, and autonomous control over their own lives. Even though scientific racial ideology did not fully develop until the nineteenth century, from the start of contact Europeans considered themselves better than Indians. This belief was influenced by Europeans' misuse of Judeo-Christian theology.

The Christian religion was first imposed on Native peoples by Europeans whose goal was empire building. Spanish and French Catholic missionaries came to North America to "save" Indian peoples from eternal damnation caused by sin and a lack of faith. English Protestants shared the belief that the "heathenism" of Native Americans damned them. The arrogant belief that the Christian god was the only spiritual power led Christians to misunderstand and disrespect the worship practices they encountered in North America. This position clearly contrasts with the ideas of William Apess (1789–1839), a Pequot religious and intellectual leader and prolific writer who lived and worked in the Mashpee Wampanoag territory. In Apess's writings, "the realm of the earth is also 'God's' sphere, and the Christian God is merged with the 'God of Nature,' so that nature, nativity, and divinity are interconnected. In Apess's vision, the biblical God and 'the Indian's God' are one and the same, and the 'noble work' of this 'great Spirit' can be seen in, and is enacted by, the inhabitants of the earth" (Brooks 2008, 200). Apess practiced a theology of inclusion and unity across differences.

In contrast, the European Christians who came to North America believed that the body was the source of sin and had to be rigorously disciplined to prevent it from leading the individual into sinful behavior that could threaten the soul. The Christian conviction that the actions of the body could threaten the purity of soul caused many to distrust and fear people who had a freer attitude toward the body. Many of the Native peoples of the Americas that Europeans encountered in the contact period practiced an integration of body, mind, and soul as a vital aspect of healing and spiritual ceremonies. Dance was an integral part of these rituals. For Europeans who were striving to rigidly discipline their own bodies, this freedom of and respect for the body was deeply threatening. Almost immediately, European settlers focused on Native American dance as "heathen" and sinful and set about creating laws and policies designed to eradicate or at least control it. As noted earlier, Native peoples had to fight for their right to dance for decades.

The Enlightenment of eighteenth-century Europe brought secular accomplishments in science to the fore, and science began to replace religion as the dominant ideology. Theories of progress in human evolution, most notably Charles Darwin's *On the Origin of Species by Means of Natural Selection, or the Preservation of Favoured Races in the Struggle for Life* (1859), affected how people thought of Indians. Some influential thinkers used Darwin's theories to claim that non-white peoples belonged to a lower stage of human development. By the late nineteenth century, the field of anthropology had emerged as an ostensibly objective way of studying human culture (Berkhofer 1978, 38–61).

Robert F. Berkhofer defines racism as a "specific social doctrine" that evolved during this period and influenced European colonialism all over the world: "Racism rests upon two basic assumptions: (1) the moral qualities of a human group are positively correlated with their physical characteristics, and (2) all humankind is divided into superior and inferior stocks upon the basis of the first assumption. Racism, in other words, is an understanding of human diversity mainly or solely in terms of inherent racial differences (and the moral judgments thereon) and an explanation of that diversity entirely or mainly in terms of inherent racial inheritances" (1978, 55).

Twentieth- and twenty-first-century scholars have challenged the foundations of racism and their relationship to identity. We now know that "race is not something that one *is* as a static identity or predetermined category by physiology or biology, but rather a set of competences and embodied knowledges that one *enacts* in practices grounded in particular and historical contexts" (Hancock 2005, 427). Hancock's definition is an illustration of how Native communities have always understood identity. It is inclusive: it takes into account that all of us are the products of racial and ethnic intermarriage to some degree, a reality that racist ideology does not acknowledge.

## Appropriation of Land

In Indian country, the natural world and the land are of central importance. Each tribal nation honors its own sacred sites, and powwows are organized in the same location year after year as recognition of the deep ties people have to specific geographical areas. For Native Americans, land is a resource to honor, work with, and protect, not a commodity to be sold.

Europeans who came to the continent in the seventeenth century envisioned land as a "new" place that was a source of prosperity. At first, they entered into negotiations, agreements, and treaties with Native peoples to facilitate cohabitation. But as Euro-Americans expanded the areas they occupied and their commercial and industrial needs grew, the land that was covered in treaties became increasingly valuable, and the newer residents on the land began to formulate devious ways to get what they wanted.

Indians were deprived of their land in three distinct periods. In the first stage, treaties were made that limited Indians' access to land they had previously cared for. Although the federal government continued to make new treaties with Indian groups about a range of issues into the late nineteenth century, this first stage lasted until approximately the 1830s. In the second stage, the U.S. military forcibly removed Indians from their land (Awakuni-Swetland 2008; Churchill 1992; Jaimes 1992; Takaki 1990, 1993). The policy of Indian removal forced eastern groups to move to western reservations. The reservation period began in the 1830s and lasted until the 1930s. During this stage, the federal government tried to impose a European notion of land ownership on Indian people by giving them allotments of land on reservations. Finally, in the third stage, Indians began leaving reservations and moving into urban centers as individuals who lived separate from their families and their communities.

In the Northeast, no official policy was needed to separate Indians from the land. The diseases Europeans brought, to which Native groups had no immunity, decimated indigenous populations within several generations, and those who remained blended into the general population to such an extent that they became barely visible. Also in this region, wars between Indian nations and European colonists further disrupted Indian cultural traditions. For example, in the late eighteenth century, King Philip's War, which was waged by Algonquian peoples against Europeans who had encroached on their land, cost thousands of lives for a population that was already decimated by disease (Lepore 1998).

The struggle over land became particularly intense in the nineteenth century, when U.S. citizens began moving into the territory of the Plains Indians. To a great extent this period in U.S. history is identified with the presidency of Andrew Jackson. Historian and ethnic studies scholar Ronald T. Takaki writes convincingly of how Jackson personified the cultural need to control the body and to control Indians that was so prevalent in the mainstream of the nineteenth-century United States. Jackson had been wounded in a duel and almost died from an infection. One observer wrote of how Jackson stayed alive by sheer force of will, seemingly by "some miraculous agency." Takaki notes that for Jackson, using violence to bring Indians under control was a way to integrate a struggle to control his own body and the need to control Indians: "Military campaigns in the Creek War enabled him to subordinate his physical self and to destroy Indians. Indians, for Jackson, personified the body. He believed that they were impulsive and lacked 'discipline'" (1990, 95). For Jackson, controlling his body and controlling Indians were both part of a necessary process.

As president of the United States, Jackson signed the Indian Removal Act in 1830. Some Indian nations acceded to the inevitable and voluntarily signed their land away in exchange for western lands. This is the choice the Choctaw nation in Mississippi made in 1830. Other nations chose to fight the new law in court; the Cherokee nation took their argument for the right to stay on their land all the way to the U.S. Supreme Court. The Court ruled against them, and the result was a journey from Georgia to what is now Oklahoma that cost thousands of lives:

> The march took place in the dead of winter. . . . The exiles were defenseless against disease. . . . "Long time we travel on way to new land," one of the exiles recalled bitterly. "People feel bad when they leave Old Nation. Women cry and make sad wails. Children cry and many men cry, and all look sad when friends die, but they say nothing and just put their heads down and keep going towards West." (Takaki 1993, 97)

The physical, psychological, spiritual, and social impact of these experiences continues to resonate in Indian country across generations in dance: "Because dance is an embodied practice, the body is central to cultural meaning, not only because it serves as the medium of enactment, but because the body is the locus and embodiment of those very practices. . . . The body effectively serves as a 'memory pad' by which [the] most serious and essential knowledges we have are rooted" (Hancock 2005, 440). The bodies of today's Indians carry the memories of what happened to their ancestors: the annihilation of hundreds of thousands by disease, the removal of entire nations from their land, the dispersal of tribal nations. These individual, community, and tribal experiences were etched into the collective soul of Indian country. These experiences have been integrated into how Indians perform contemporary powwow dance styles.

The reservation system violated the right of Indian nations to maintain their own sovereignty in a bilateral relationship between Native peoples and the U.S. government (Jaimes 1992; Churchill 1992). The reservation, a form of supposedly scientific management, was actually "a reformatory, a place where the government could prepare Indians for citizenship and inculcate them in republican and Protestant habits of self-control and domination over the 'strong animal appetites'" (Takaki 1990, 187).

Today some tribal nations have reclaimed their land rights. In the New York City area the Shinnecock Indian Nation, one of the largest of thirteen tribes on Long Island, now lives on one of the oldest reservations in the United States after being moved from place to place for generations (Pritchard 2002, 326–329).

## Laws

In 1887, the U.S. government passed the Dawes Act, which empowered the federal government to divide reservation land into small parcels, or allotments, that were assigned to individual Indians. Jaimes explains the provisions of the law:

> The function of this piece of legislation was to expedite the process of Indian "civilization" by unilaterally dissolving their collectively (i.e., nationally) held reservation land holdings. Reservation lands were reallocated in accordance with the "superior" (i.e., Euroamerican) concept of property: *individually* deeded land parcels, usually of 160 acres each. Each Indian, identified as being those documentably of *one-half or more Indian blood*, was entitled to receive title in fee of such a parcel; all others were simply disenfranchised altogether. Reserved Indian land which remained unallotted after all "blooded" Indians had received their individual parcels was to be declared "surplus" and opened up for non-Indian use and occupancy. (Jaimes 1992, 126)

From 1887 to 1934, the Indian land base was reduced from about 138 million acres (by one conservative estimate) to about 48 million acres. The blood quantum concept, the notion that the only true Indians were those who had a certain percentage of Indian blood, is intrinsically linked to the body and had severe consequences for Indian societies, economies, culture, and political bodies.

Genocide, exile, forcible confinement on reservations, and the imposition of European languages, religious beliefs, and so forth are only the most obvious forms of oppression Indian peoples have endured. During the late nineteenth and early twentieth centuries, when many Indian ceremonies and dances were banned, Native Americans were encouraged to perform "as Indians" at events that were organized by non-Indians. Performance studies scholar José E. Muñoz analyzes these as performances of "disidentification," "a cultural imperative within the majoritarian public sphere that denies subalterns access to larger channels of representations while calling the minoritarian subject to the stage, performing her or his alterity as a consumable local spectacle" (1998, 217).

A ludicrous example is when Indians were asked to perform at "celebrations" of land allotment: "On these occasions, the Indians were ordered by the government to attend a large assembly on the reservation. Dressed in traditional costume and carrying a bow and arrow, each Indian was individually summoned from a teepee and told to shoot an arrow. He then retreated to the teepee and reemerged wearing 'civilized' clothing symbolizing a crossing from the primitive to the modern world" (Takaki 1993, 235).

In 1924, the U.S. government passed the Indian Citizenship Act. Until this law, Indians had an uncertain relationship to U.S. citizenship. Some Indian women had acquired citizenship by marrying Euro-American men. Some Indian men had become citizens by other means, such as military service, receiving allotments, or through special treaties. But no federal law existed that offered citizenship to all Indians. The new law was not passed in response to requests from Indians; rather, it is generally seen as an attempt by Congress to bring Indians further into the mainstream of U.S. society. The law created enormous confusion for Indians. "Full-blooded" Indians became dual citizens of their tribal nations and the United States. But "hybrid" Indians, or those who were less than "half-bloods," became U.S. citizens without the right to be Indian. Harriett Skye (Lakota/Sioux) explains:

> What the Indian Citizenship Act in fact did was to give citizenship to Native people who were the original inhabitants. What that Act depended on were the enrollment records that were initiated by the federal government (BIA). Indians were required to come forward with their families

> and at this time each Indian was given a number as well. They were enrolled as allotted or unallotted, depending on whether or not they had land. I am an unallotted Indian at Standing Rock. . . . The confusion arises because some Indian people denied they were Indian, which is understandable. If they didn't they might have been shot on sight. Others left never to return and assimilated. The confusion wasn't in "dual citizenship or half-bloods," it came from people like Alice Fletcher [a white anthropologist], who . . . was sent out to Indian Country to determine who was Indian and who wasn't. (personal communication, 1999)

Ten years later, the Indian Reorganization Act was passed in order to "finally and completely usurp the traditional mechanisms of American Indian governance (e.g., the traditional chiefs, councils of elders, etc.) replacing them with a system of federally approved and regulated 'tribal councils'" (Jaimes 1992, 128).

During this period, 55 percent of Indians earned less than $200 a year. Only 2 percent of all Indians earned more than $500 a year. A 1933 study revealed that almost all Indians who lived on reservations who had participated in allotment were landless. By that year, Indians had lost almost 60 percent of the land base that existed at the time the Dawes Act was passed in 1887 (Takaki 1993, 238). By the time the allotment program was discontinued and tribal self-government was restored in 1934 by the Indian Reorganization Act, the situation for Indians of all nations was dire.

Although Indian dance was now permitted, the long period of removal, reservations, and allotment had irreversibly changed Native lives and cultural expressions. Significantly, as power relations began to shift, powwows as we know them today emerged as spaces controlled by Indians. Within those spaces, the concept of people of mixed blood continued to evolve.

Today the notion of mixed blood is critical to understanding powwow. At events in the New York City area (Gateway, Thunderbird, Schemitzun, Shinnecock, and Northampton), most powwow participants are of mixed race. This is characteristic of the region and is a significant difference from powwows further west.

For instance, I met Ricky Stevenson at the United Tribes International Powwow in Bismarck in 2009, who told me that he is part Cherokee but is considered to be white. When he started to go to powwows in his area of the country (Minnesota), he never "pushed" his "part Indian blood." Stevenson explained that many of the tribes out west are "quite closed" and would have rejected him based on his physical appearance. Eventually, as a dedicated and accomplished dancer, he was accepted and welcomed along the powwow circuit (personal communication, September 12, 2009). Had Stevenson been going to powwows on the East Coast, he might have been accepted more quickly because his appearance as a tall, blond Caucasian would have been less conspicuous. It is important to note that he first went to powwows with his (Cherokee) grandmother, who provided a "blood" link to other Indians as well as a social and cultural tie. Also, Stevenson appeared to be personally invested in and respectful of powwow in a serious way.

Indians generally identify other Indians using broad parameters. It is racist non-Indians who look down on mixed bloods. As Jaimes explains: "'Mixed blood' Indians, like other 'hybrids,' are denigrated as 'mud people' by the Ku Klux Klan and other white supremacists. We are a subject of scorn and ridicule for being weak and confused inferior types, due to the abomination of the mixing of the races" (1994, 41). The attitude toward mixed-blood Indians at powwows depends on both local mores and on a person's standing within any given tribal community. Although mixed-blood individuals are sometimes differentiated from "full-blooded" Indians, they are definitely considered more Indian than wannabes.

Under the first Bush administration the Indian Arts and Crafts Act (Public Law 101-644), which went into effect on November 30, 1990, relates to the issue of mixed bloods at powwows. This truth-in-advertising law defines an Indian artist or craftsperson as a member of any federally or state recognized tribe or as an individual certified as an Indian artisan by an Indian tribe. Although this law deals primarily with Indian artisans and the selling of artwork, it has also affected powwow dancers who compete at the larger events. At many powwows I attended, flyers would advertise the dance competitions as for "Native only" and "certified Indian." Though the law might curb non-Indians opportunists, I agree with Jaimes's assessment:

> Grotesquely described as "an Act to promote the development of Indian arts and crafts," the statute legally restricts definition of American Indian artists to those possessing a federally issued "Certification of Degree of Indian Blood"—derogatorily referred to as "pedigree slips" by opponents—or those certified as such by "federally recognized tribes" or the "Alaska Native Corporation." Excluded are not only those who fall below blood-quantum requirements, but anyone who has, for politico-philosophical reasons, refused to cooperate. . . . Further, the entire populations of federally unrecognized nations such as the populous Lumbees of North Carolina, Abenakis of Vermont, and more than 200 others, are simply written out of existence even in terms of their internal membership identification as Indians. (1992, 131)

Jaimes quotes historian Patricia Nelson Limerick's statement in *The Legacy of Conquest: The Unbroken Past of the American West*: "Set the blood quantum at one-quarter, hold to it as a rigid definition of Indians, let intermarriage proceed as it had for centuries, and eventually Indians will be defined out of existence. When that happens, the federal government will be freed of its 'Indian problem'" (1992, 132). To decide who you are and where you come from becomes not the decision of your immediate community but that of standard percentages of blood set by the federal government.

Many Indian artists, activists, political leaders, and tribal nations have rebelled against these identity markers. The right to belong to a particular group should be decided by that group, not by outsiders. Nonetheless, this issue has created division, power struggles, and confusion in Indian country. Many believe that federal recognition based on the blood quantum is a necessary deterrent to those who appropriate Indian identity (Sanchez 1995, 116–119, 136–143). One thing is certain: the blood quantum is intrinsically linked to the domination of federal and state government institutions over Native individuals and Indian tribal nations.

## Performing Race

> When an Indian dances, he dances with freedom, and every movement is vivid and natural. This is, perhaps, the most significant difference between the dance of the Red and White man. . . . An Indian has said, "The White man dances with his legs; the Indian with his muscles." His dance is certainly rather a body vibration than a limb motion.
>
> JULIA M. BUTTREE, *THE RHYTHM OF THE REDMAN*

As Native dancers ground themselves in the earth and stamp, step, and turn, their dance reveals a strong, clear affirmation of what it means to be Indian in the twenty-first century. Although tribal individuals and nations each have their own accounts of colonization, in Indian country there are many shared experiences. Some of these include endurance and warrior-like persistence alongside humiliation, illness, pain, and manipulation of many kinds.

As historical memory spills into contemporary life and Indians respond to the effects of many kinds of racism, their flesh, bones, and blood embody power relations in visceral articulation. Many of the specific styles that Native dancers express have emerged from their very real contemporary lives. In the contemporary grass dance, the traditional styles, the intertribal, and the tiny tot category, Indian dancers execute a particular "performance of race" of complex and forceful beauty.

As Indians enter the powwow circle and invite or allow other indigenous peoples or wannabes to join them, they express diverse psychic, cultural, and body experiences. Indians have become increasingly aware of their unique power. As Deloria makes clear: "Indian people have, for more than one hundred years, lacked military power. Being militarily defeated, they found that social, political, and economic power were often hard to come by as well. Native people have been keenly aware, however, that in their relations to white Americans they do in fact possess some mysterious well of cultural power" (1998, 178). Powwows represent a way to break out of the cycle of exploitation through performance.

Today, Indians continue to seek, assert, and accomplish a proactive control over their identity as tribal nations and as individuals. Contemporary powwows are a part of that process. In rejecting the blood quantum policy as a defining factor in deciding access to health care, education, and other entitlements, some tribal nations, like that of the Oglala Lakota on the Pine Ridge Reservation in South Dakota, have developed other means of tribal affiliation based on such factors as residency on the reservation, affinity and cultural knowledge, intermarriage, and naturalization (Jaimes 1992).

Predictably, in response to these initiatives, the federal government has fought back by repeatedly refusing to support services for Indians who are not registered as members of a federally recognized tribal nation. Organizations such as the Indian Resource Center, National Indian Youth Council, and the International Indian Treaty Council have become forums for debate and activism about such issues. Jaimes observes: "We are currently at a crossroads. If American Indians are able to continue the positive trend in which we reassert our sovereign prerogative to control the criteria of our own membership, we may reasonably assume that we will be able to move onward, into a true process of decolonization and reestablishment of ourselves as functioning national entities" (1992, 137).

As Indian dancers perform in the stark reality of powwows as postcolonial performances, the power and beauty of their dance makes it clear that generations of Native peoples have lived and danced under the shadow of racism. These dancers mobilize and access a transcultural process that is open and in which they are in control. At intertribal powwows, when powwow dancers enter the communal arena circles of Indian country, they affirm Indian identity and resist colonization and assimilation. In this way, bodies in motion offer a performative challenge to centuries of genocidal policies.

# 7

# Contemporary Wannabes

When non-Indians dance at intertribal powwows, what does their participation signify in the context of interracial and transcultural exchange? How do these people perform race? Why are some non-Indians so intensely invested in what could ultimately be called a game of dress-up? In this chapter, I explore how some of these individuals play Indian through dance at powwows primarily in the United States, though it is also a common practice in Canada, Europe, and elsewhere in interesting ways. By focusing on the details of body movement, one can begin to understand why wannabes, hobbyists, New Age practitioners, and tourists are motivated to join the powwow circle not as themselves but as Indians for many reasons in the twenty-first century. Their complex and varied motivations include entertainment, the search for an American identity, a desire to participate in a communal and alternative reality that is different than their own, and the desire for a new or renewed spiritual experience.

## History

In the United States, the phenomenon of non-Indians playing Indian goes back to the eighteenth century, when we have our first written reports of Europeans dancing with or "like Indians." The earliest accounts deal with French and British officials in the mid-eighteenth century who participated in Indian dance to help "create alliances with and between Indian tribes" (Young 1981, 119). Though the motivations of these officials was distinct from that of other non-Indians who would later "perform Indian," nonetheless, they recognized the importance of dance for Indians and participated in that activity to facilitate Native and non-Native relations. James Mooney's 1896 narrative of an incident that took place in 1750 serves as an example: "When a governor of Canada and a general of his army stepped into the circle of braves to dance and sing the war song with their red allies, thirty-three wild tribes declared on the wampum belt 'the French are our brothers and the King is our Father'" (qtd. in Young 1981, 120–121).

Non-Indian play has taken on many different forms since then. However, what is of interest here is how dance was a specific and integral aspect of these forms. For example, in the early nineteenth century, the Tammany societies of New York City performed May Day rites that were largely derived from European carnival practices. As David Ridgely reported in 1841 in the *Annals of Annapolis*, at these festival-like gatherings, after dancing around the maypole in an "Indian war dance," the participants would form "a large company usually assembled during the course of the evening, and when engaged in the midst of a dance, the company were interrupted by the sudden intrusion of a number of the members of 'St. Tamina's Society,' habited like Indians, who rushing violently into the room singing the war songs, and giving the whoop, commenced dancing in the style of that people" (qtd. in Deloria 1998, 17).

Another group that traces its history to the first half of the nineteenth century is the Improved Order of Red Men, which was formed during the 1812 War and was first called the Society of Red Men. The origins of this group lie in pre-revolutionary era secret societies of colonists who objected to the British Crown. The organization persisted after the Revolution as a patriotic fraternity. This group provides some of the first instances of non-Indians actually dancing and practicing "pow-wows, victory dances, braves and princesses" (Green 1988, 36). The secret "costumed rituals" of the group were performed by members who wore regalia patterned after a Euro-American version of Native American regalia. It is likely that dance played a role in these ceremonies. In the 1950s, the Improved Order of Red Men had hundreds of chapters or what they called tribes throughout the United States, and it still exists today.

According to chroniclers Bunny McBride and Harald Prins, the Improved Order of the Red Men was "the oldest of various patriotic societies in the country" and was also "the most widespread, especially in the eastern states." The chapter on Mount Desert Island in Maine (now the site of the Annual Native American Festival) was one of 116 chapters in the state. It took its name from "one of the five so-called 'civilized' tribes—the Cherokee" (2009, 63–64). The authors explore the disjuncture between "playing Indian" and being Indian: "One cannot help wondering what the Penobscot and Passamaquoddy Indians, almost all of whom were Roman Catholics in addition to belonging to authentic tribes, actually thought when they found out that their . . . white Protestant 'brothers' had become 'Cherokee'" (McBride and Prins 2009, 64). The Mount Desert Island chapter was located in an area of the Northeast where Indians and non-Indians interacted cordially, especially during the summer months, and it is safe to assume that no disrespect was intended.

The Euro-Americans of the Tammany societies and the Improved Order of Red Men were the precursors of today's wannabes. By the late nineteenth century, camps and programs developed for boys and girls such as the Woodcraft Indians, the Boy Scouts, and the Camp Fire Girls had incorporated dance as a way to explore and often exploit the meaning of Indianness. Indian dance was considered part of training for these young people; they also learned about how Indians dealt with survival in the wilderness, the relations of Indians with animals and birds, and so forth. Scout manuals often gave explicit instructions on how to perform an "Indian" dance. Ernest T. Seton's *Boy Scouts of America: A Handbook of Woodcraft Scouting, and Life-Craft* provides an example in this didactic description of a "crouch dance": "Each brave takes his club, and now begins the crouch dance. Going three times around, and each time crouching lower while the squaws stand or sit in a circle, arms down tight to side, but bodies swaying in time to the music" ([1910] 2010, 81). Thus in the very "American" activity of scouting, Indian dance played a central role in the formation of thousands of youngsters over decades of U.S. history. My father, an avid Boy Scout in the 1930s, won numerous Indian badges. Many of us with male relatives have heard stories about "Indian" experiences in the Boy Scouts. "Dancing like an Indian" has become ingrained in the scouting experience for generations of boys and girls in the Boy Scouts and the Camp Fire Girls in the United States, Great Britain, Mexico, and elsewhere.

Many contemporary hobbyist first encountered and developed an interest in Native American rituals and practices by participating in these groups. An honor society of scouts, The Order of the Arrow, which "gathered around camp bonfires in ritual Indian costume to tap out and induct new members" also emerged in the early twentieth century; by the late 1920s and late 1930s, it had chapters throughout the country (Deloria 1998, 126).

American Indian hobbyist groups began to organize during the late nineteenth and early twentieth centuries, the period when the U.S. government banned Indian dance and the paradoxical phenomenon of non-Indians playing Indian emerged in full force. This practice was particularly prevalent in the East; figure 11 depicts a group of Caucasian college students dressed up as Indians at Oberlin College in 1915. In another example, John D. Rockefeller's youngest son, David, was photographed as a young boy wearing a "fancy dance" outfit as he participated in a fancy dress competition at the Bar Harbor horse show in 1925 (McBride and Prins 2009, 61). But it was not until after World War II that hobbyists began to make their presence felt at intertribal powwows along with New Agers and other wannabes.

Philip J. Deloria (1998), Rayna Green (1988), and others have examined the history of how and why these groups have played Indian through the centuries. In archival sources, the actual body movement of "White Indian" dance surfaces in momentary glimpses as part of dressing up and costuming, festivals, and ceremonial rites. By the late nineteenth and early twentieth centuries, non-Indians were emulating two versions of "Indian dance": the woodland version based on an interpretation of Algonquian cultural traditions of the eastern tribes and the stereotypical version of Plains Indian dance promoted by organizers of the Wild West shows. A Plains Indian representation that was transmitted to the U.S. public through the Wild West shows and later Western films became the predominant model of "Indian" (Green 1988, 39).

Some of the most notable body movements were most likely replicated from the Plains Indian dancers of the Wild West shows and were recorded in descriptions of the childhood game of cowboys and Indians:

> In the Cowboys and Indians game . . . the "Indians" "walk Indian file," they howl and yell, putting their flattened palm repeatedly against their pursed mouths in an imitation of the shrill, ritual "lu-lu" of Plains women or the battle cry of men. They greet each other with the upraised right forearm, saying "how" in an abasement of the Sioux greeting "hau." They stand or sit with arms folded over each other in front of the chest, repeating the word "ugh!" as a form of communicative discourse. They "creep up" on the cowboys, who, of course, do not engage in such secretive behavior, this embodiment left over from the shock endured by British troops when Indians would stealthily attack from the shadows rather than lining up and marching straight towards the enemy in a line of men, as characterized 17th and 18th century European warfare. In the game, Indians are allowed to "run wild," whooping, hollering, behaving in a completely unorthodox manner, while cowboys must behave scrupulously, not playing dirty, staying taciturn and calm. Their noise comes from their guns alone. (Green 1988, 39)

In Green's description, people perform their own race, their own ethnicity, even as they aspire to perform Indian identity. Underneath the Indian outfits, they continued to be Euro-American. The stereotypical gestures, sounds (lu-lu, hau, and ugh!), and full body movements reveal an ignorance of real Indians and how they move and dance. As some have said, the moving body never lies. This becomes especially evident when contemporary non-Indians dance "Indian" in the public spaces of intertribal powwows.

## Contemporary Wannabes

Today many non-Indians are motivated "to dance like an Indian." Frequently, people of Euro-American ancestry claim to have a great-great-grandmother who was a "Cherokee princess." Others simply lie about a fantasy Indian heritage. Many of these wannabes dance at powwows.

Barre Toelken describes a dance at the Arlee Pow-Wow in Montana jokingly called the Wanabi initiation dance:

> The announcer—often Bearhead Swaney or Colonel Doug Allard—asks all Indian people to leave the center of the arena so that non-Indian visitors can be honored by induction into the Wanabi society. Hippies in beads, German and Japanese tourists festooned with cameras, elderly California matrons heavy with Navajo jewelry, grandpas on vacation in Hawaiian shirts and sandals are all dragged into the arena and given basic instructions on how to stamp their feet in time to the drums, and then, as they dance in a mixture of honor and embarrassment, they are told they are now the possessors of the Wanabi Dance, the special ritual dance for those who "wanna be" Indians. (1991, 149)

Wannabes rarely perform in the grass, traditional, jingle dress, or fancy dance categories, but they tend to join the Grand Entry and dance in intertribal dances. I have seen many non-Indian women and men, young and old, dressed in regalia, sitting around the arena. As they wait to dance, they often seem subdued as if they are aware that they are in the wrong place. How do these people present themselves at intertribal powwows? What is the significance of their presence?

Wannabes were very present at many of the powwows I attended during my fieldwork, including the Thunderbird Grand Midsummer Pow Wow in Queens, New York; the Return to Beaver Creek Native American Powwow in Belvidere, New Jersey; the Honor the Earth Powwow in Northampton, Massachusetts; the Gateway to the Nations PowWow in Brooklyn, New York; and the Native American Pow Wow in Wells, Maine. Particularly at Beaver Creek, I noticed many non-Indians running the concession stands and dancing. During an intertribal, I watched a Native woman dancing with tall serenity, eyes looking forward, feet calmly and securely on the ground. Nearby, a young woman with long blonde hair wearing a flowing, silky shawl, street clothes, and dark glasses moved as if in a trance. Rapt in her own enjoyment, her dance was easily distinguishable from the dance of Native women around her. Oblivious to the drum or the other dancers in the arena circle, she bobbed about and moved her torso in and out, exuding an ongoing involvement with self.

At the same powwow, several teenage boys sat around the arena in what appeared to be store-bought outfits. As they bashfully began to dance, their rigid and hesitant movements contrasted sharply with a young champion fancy dancer about their age who was concentrating on how his physical moves, which were often intricate and arduous, united with the drum and his own inner meanings. One can differentiate wannabes by the absence of stylistic detail in their regalia and by how they move their bodies when they try to dance the grass, traditional, or fancy styles.

At the Native American Pow Wow in mid-coast Maine, I saw a Grand Entry, intertribals (there were no exhibits or competition dances in specific styles), and a smudging ritual that I had never seen anywhere else. Norma Rendon, a member of the Oglala Lakota Nation, told Tara Browner about the meaning of feathers and smudging in the context of powwow traditions: "Those feathers are treated with respect. My son was taught that you should always smudge—and my girls—should always smudge your feathers and plumes before you dance. Take the time to pray for that eagle that those feathers came from. When you're done dancing, you should smudge them again and put them [feathers] away in a proper place where they will be taken care of" (qtd. in Browner 2002, 106).

Before each dancer came into the arena to dance at the Maine powwow, he or she stood before one of the leaders of the group, who burned sage and then fanned the smoke up and down the front and back of the dancer's body. The organizers of the powwow and the men who did the smudging were veterans dressed in military clothes. Though this isolated example coheres with Rendon's explanation, in the context of this Maine powwow, the ritual seemed artificial. Something did not ring true. Perhaps this was because later on, the smudging that had been obligatory at the beginning of the day was no longer required and people went freely in and out of the circle without it, even new arrivals who had not been smudged earlier on.

The dancers' outfits at the Native American Pow Wow in Wells were elaborate and highly individualized. With the exception of the attire of a few young grass dancers and something similar to fancy shawl regalia that one middle-aged woman wore, most outfits did not approximate those worn by Native peoples who dance in the grass, traditional, jingle dress, or fancy styles.

Although there is no doubt that the wannabe dancers at this powwow were enthralled as they moved around the arena, with a few exceptions all the dancers moved in a similar way. They stepped forward two steps at a time, both women and men moved with slightly bent-over torsos, and some skimmed the ground hopping and skipping sometimes on half-toe. The overall quality of their movement was light and feather-like as they extended their arms away from the body out into space. One of the singers who sat most of the morning at the drum came out later without regalia to dance several times. In marked difference to the majority of the other male dancers, his movement was clearly grounded in a men's traditional dance style. This tall male singer and dancer seemed to be listening intently to the drum and danced with ease and an intense inner focus. However, at the Native American Pow Wow, most of the participants appeared to play at being the "right kind of Indian." This was evident in the quality of their dancing and in how they tried to adhere to strict rules about how the flags should be held during the Grand Entry; it was as if they were following an instructional pamphlet on powwows.

In contrast, at this same event, an Indian woman in her late seventies was moved to dance during the lunch break while a guitarist played. She began to circle the arena slowly, stepping forward two steps at a time. It was wonderful to observe this elderly person dance with a fullness of being that integrated body, movement, and inner meaning, so engrossed in the pleasure of the dance that she seemed unaware of the audience. Little by little others, mostly young girls, joined her. Philosopher Pierre Bourdieu describes this kind of movement in a way that resonates with the integration of history and body movement in Native American dance in the United States: "The body believes in what it plays at; it weeps if it mimes grief. It does not represent what it performs, it does not memorize the past, it enacts the past bringing it back to life. What is 'learning by the body' is not something that one has, like knowledge that can be brandished, but something that one is" (1990, 73). The older Indian woman, the singer who danced in street clothes, and the non-Indians who participated in the Grand Entry and the intertribal dances at the powwow in Wells all performed race, identity, and meaning, each in his or her own way.

As wannabes attend and participate in powwows, questions of meaning, authenticity, appropriation, and race come up again and again. Hobbyists and New Age practitioners are the two major groups of wannabes that dance in the powwow circle today. Tourists are a more general category of individuals that represents non-Indians who come to powwow out of curiosity or a sincere interest in Native American cultures. One can observe them joining intertribal dances and enjoying the many performances and activities at powwows. Often they come to powwows only once. But hobbyists and New Age practitioners attend repeatedly over a period of years, and many are deeply invested in everything "Indian."

## Hobbyists

Hobbyists participate at two types of powwows: those they organize themselves and those organized by Native peoples. Hobbyists attend the latter in a variety of capacities. In this book, I write about the hobbyists who attend intertribal powwows organized by Indians. Often hobbyist powwow circuits run parallel to or close to Indian-organized events. During the 1960s and perhaps earlier, Indians and non-Indians participated in powwows run by both Indians and non-Indians: "Some Indian people alternated between the two powwow circuits, visiting hobbyist gatherings to sell crafts and sing songs for cash and their own events to see friends and relatives in the larger Indian community. Many serious hobbyists engaged in a similar kind of cultural crisscrossing. They sang and danced in full regalia not only at white powwows, where they were surrounded by fellow hobbyists, but also at Indian events, where they joined Indian people in the dance circle" (Deloria 1998, 129).

Philip J. Deloria offers analysis that organizes American Indian hobbyists into two groups: object hobbyists and people hobbyists. Object hobbyists "favored the replication of old Indian artifacts and costumes," while people hobbyists "enjoyed the intercultural contact and boundary crossing they found at contemporary powwows" (1998, 135). The differences between these groups points to the many ways that non-Indians have chosen to relate to Indians.

Object hobbyists are more interested in the "authentic" replication of material for their regalia and a "perfect" performance of powwow dances, the Grand Entry, and, as noted above in the example from the powwow in Wells, Maine, the most "correct" smudging ceremony. Their primary reasons for consulting Native peoples are to learn from them about Native traditions and to receive validation for what they are doing.

As Deloria reminds us, the search for the authentic that is prevalent among American hobbyist groups has a long tradition that reaches back to many of the fraternal societies of the eighteenth and nineteenth century. The journal the *American Indian Hobbyist*, which was published from 1954 to 1960, "served as a clearinghouse for information, traders, and dealers" (Deloria 1998, 137). Though this journal later focused its attention on people hobbyists, many other books and especially Web sites continue to cater to hobbyists' interest in replicating the "authentic" Indian tipi, fancy dance outfit, and much more. People hobbyists emphasize the importance of interacting with real Native peoples; this term more closely approximates the kind of hobbyists that one observes in the powwow arena today. These two definitions sometimes become blurred, as in the example of the practices at the Native American Pow Wow in Wells.

Jack Campisi observed that the hobbyists of the 1970s were deeply invested in learning about "authentic costumes" and dances. They participated in specific dance competitions for hobbyists at intertribal powwows and were willing to do mundane jobs at powwow events such as parking cars, organizing publicity, and "policing the area" (1975, 42). Campisi also found that at the powwows he studied, where participants included Iroquois, Indians from other tribal groups, and hobbyists, "white hobbyists were primarily engaged in performing the dances" and perfecting their regalia (1975, 39). By today's standards these were not strictly white hobbyists' powwows; they were intertribal events.

Campisi describes a number of different powwows in the New York area in the 1970s whose practices resonate with the practices I observed at many of the events I attended three decades later. But it is possible to make several distinctions between the powwows Campisi attended in the 1970s and those I attended in the twenty-first century. These differences reiterate how fluid and ever-changing powwow is as a performance genre. In the 1970s, "each dancer would give the name of the dance he was to perform and a group of singers would provide the accompaniment. . . . Common titles were the Calumet or Peace Pipe Dance, Blanket Dance (Mohawk), Harvest Dance (women only), War Dance, Arrow Dance, Saw Grass Dance, Hunting the Deer Dance, etc. There was little relationship between what the singers chanted and the performer did" (1975, 34). In comparison, at today's powwows dancers don't announce their dances and one of the key aspects of powwow dance is the profound integration of dance, music, and regalia.

When one looks into the arena circle during a powwow, it is often difficult to differentiate American Indian hobbyists from the many mixed-blood participants who are simply enjoying the powwow or wannabes who call themselves New Age spiritualists. This is perhaps more true in 2013 than it might have been thirty or forty years ago. At the powwow in Wells, Maine, several young grass dancers were Caucasian in outward appearance. During the powwow they practiced their grass dance style along the sidelines, and in the arena they worked hard and compared notes. At this powwow, these teenagers were part of only a handful of dancers who danced in a specific style. Their dancing approximated the grass dance style, but their movements were not as full-bodied or as vigorous as the hundreds of Native grass dancers I have observed.

## EARLY DANCE SCHOLARS AS HOBBYISTS

During the 1930s and 1940s, Bernard S. Mason, Ernest T. Seton, and Julia M. Buttree studied Native American dance and directed the reconstruction of rituals complete with dance, costumes, stage sets, and music. These enactments, staged productions that took place either outside in a large, circular, arena-like space or in a theater, were based on a wide variety of Indian dances and ceremonies that the scholars and dance practitioners had seen or read about. Their version of "powwow dances" was included in these productions, which were created to teach young people, primarily boys, about Indian culture through dance and to "preserve" Indian dance by writing about it and teaching it to others.

Mason considered powwow dance to be a "dance of celebration, a festive dance of solid fun participated in for the pure joy of dancing." He describes the dancing as having "two characteristics: first, the movements are bold, strong, vigorous; and second, each dancer is a law into himself, dancing as he chooses and following no hampering ritual, and with no story to tell. To dance in powwow fashion is to dance vigorously, lustily, usually with the characteristic toe-heel and flat-foot movements" (1944, 61). Mason generalized powwow dancing as a free, individual kind of dance—almost frenetic and not particularly spiritual—with a single style. These comments reveal the limitations of his understanding of powwow dance.

Nonetheless, Mason, Seton, and Buttree insisted that Indian dance was beautiful and developed ways to describe and analyze the actual body movements in writing. As dance scholars they are little known. Although dance scholars in Europe, for example Rudolf Laban, were beginning to write about dance by focusing on the movement in the early twentieth century, this approach was less common in the United States. Mason, Seton, and Buttree wrote about Native dance in a way that prioritized body actions and movement quality and expression. In addition, they took responsibility for their version of appropriation and made clear distinctions between Indian dance and wannabe dancing.

In *Dances and Stories of the American Indian*, Mason revealed his identity as a non-Indian practitioner of powwow dancing; he dedicated the book to "the Camp Fairwood Dancers with happy memories of those inspired Grand Council nights when together we donned our moccasins and plumes." From this racial positioning, Mason asked key questions about the differences between Indian and non-Indian dancers:

> To what extent are these modern feet of non-Indian dancers capable of filling these ancient moccasins? . . . Much has been said on the point that there is an indefinable something about the dancing Indian that no other seems able quite to duplicate, an intangible element in style that is distinctively, inimitably Indian. . . . This margin of the supposedly unattainable is narrow and fleeting, and may doubtless be more a matter of individual differences than of racial ones. . . . Many a sincere and thorough interpreter of the Indian way has entered the Redman's dance arena and blended with the dancing Indians so harmoniously that

even the practiced eye could not label one as Indian and another as not. (1944, 7)

Mason clearly believed that some followers of "the Indian Way" could "dance like an Indian."

However, he complicates the issue in his discussion of the meaning of Native dance: "It becomes clear that behind the visible dancing movements is a depth of meaning, a seriousness of purpose, a sense of responsibility, often a reverence that comes only from deep concern for the purpose for which the ceremony is danced. Those of us who are foreign to Indian culture and possess no such understanding find it difficult to cope with those intangibles of feeling and mood in our dancing, but the bodily movements are capable of analysis and reproduction. And in the study of movements something of the feeling should evolve" (1944, 41). Mason suggests that if one actively studies the "bodily movements," some "authenticity" can be executed, a cross-cultural understanding of sorts achieved through studying, doing, and dancing.

## Early American Modern Dancer Choreographers as Hobbyists

While Mason and his colleagues were writing about Indian dance and "powwow dances" during the 1930s and 1940s, several pioneers of American modern dance were also taking an interest in Indian culture. In *The People Have Never Stopped Dancing* (2007), Jacqueline Shea Murphy examines principal modern dance figures Ted Shawn, Lester Horton, Martha Graham, and Erik Hawkins and two Native choreographers: Mexican-born José Limón and Tom Two Arrows (Thomas Dorsey), of Lenni Lenape descent. These choreographers were inspired by Native American dance. To my knowledge, none of them participated in or studied powwow dance. However, they did observe, learn, and use Indian dances that relate to powwow dance practices. Their use of Native dance for their own creative work also pertains to a key question in this book: How do Indians and non-Indians "perform race" differently?

Were Shawn, Horton, and Graham wannabes? It is clear that they were not hobbyists in the sense discussed here. However, all of them in different ways were attracted to Native American culture and were affected by it. Most important, like hobbyists, they recognized the unique beauty of Native culture and tried to relate to it as honestly as possible. The choreographic work of each one of these dance artists is testimony to Murphy's argument that the influence of Indian dance on American dance is often unrecognized.

For example, Shawn did extensive research and fieldwork for his "Hopi Indian Eagle Dance" (1923). Unlike Mason, Shawn believed that Native American dance could not be learned by non-Indian dancers. He wrote in his 1926 book *The American Ballet*: "I have seen Hopi men do the Eagle Dance. There is no living white man today (and that included all of the greatest of the Russian Ballet, as well as American dancers, including myself) who, after spending a year studying this dance, would be able to do it" (qtd. in Murphy 2007, 120). Shawn, an accomplished modern dancer, thus acknowledged that the Eagle Dance is difficult to do. Later, he went on to create many more dances based on Native themes.

Horton, who based many of his dances on cultural practices from around the world, produced large Native American pageants and "cultivated an 'Indian' identity for himself as a dancer," incorporated Indians into his dances, and studied dance directly with Native peoples (Murphy 2007, 130–131). Graham's relationship to Indian culture is most evident in some of her earlier pieces, inspired in large part by her travels to the Southwest in the 1930s–1950s. Her 1931 dance "Primitive Mysteries" is representative of this period. In contrast to the work of Shawn and Horton, Graham's choreography sought to "evoke Indianness" rather than to "represent Indians" (Murphy 2007, 154). The work of these seminal artists of twentieth-century American modern dance provides another version of what it means to play Indian through dance.

This brings us back to the ongoing question about performances of race by both Indians and non-Indians. At what point are these acts based in biology and blood and at what point are they socially constructed? Black Hawk Hancock proposes one answer that suggests that this is the wrong question: "Viewing the practice of identity through cultural forms, not as natural or essential practice, opens up the possibility for a new understanding of race. Because of the visceral grounded nature of culture in the body, dance is a seminal place to investigate the connections between the body, culture, and racial identity" (2005, 442).

I have found the writings of Chris Roberts useful in my study of powwows, especially powwow dance styles. He has danced at powwows, although I am not certain he would call himself a hobbyist:

> When I was sixteen, my family moved to Montana, the heart of northern Indian country. I was active in the Boy Scouts and I started an Order of the Arrow Indian Dance Team. With the intent of being authentic our troupe attended local powwows to study the costumes and dances. It was the mid-sixties and no literature was available to provide the informa-

> tion we needed. Everything I found dated Indian culture to the turn of the century or before. Photographs of powwow dancers seemed limited to tourist postcards. In order to research "outfit" construction I made detailed observations and took simple 110-format pictures for many years.
>
> In 1968 I built a "fancy dance" outfit complete with beadwork and bustles and participated in my first powwow as a dancer at the Flathead Reservation's Fourth of July Celebration in Arlee, Montana. Although dancers were curious about my interest, I was made to feel welcome and developed powwow fever. Since then I have danced Grass, Fancy and Traditional on the northern circuit. (1992, 6)

Roberts's books are sold along powwow circuits, where they are popular and respected. His work is an example of transcultural exchange in powwow communities. I have never seen him dance, though I expect that he must be a strong performer given his long-term involvement with powwow along the northern circuit and his deep knowledge of powwow. Roberts consistently defers to Native voices and expertise when he writes about powwow culture. His work illustrates an important point about change over time in the process of transculturation. I believe that in this ongoing process, there is an undeniable shift in power toward Indian authority and agency.

### New Age Practitioners

New Age practitioners are wannabes of a particular kind. In the arena circle, they often sway in a trance around the space, surrounded by a community of moving, dancing bodies. They believe that here they will find comfort, solace, and spiritual renewal. It is easy to distinguish their light-footed, formless movement. Some of these people call themselves Native American spiritualists.

Deloria offers a definition of the term New Age that highlights its differences from Native American spirituality: "Like *counterculture* itself, *New Age* spans an ambiguous time period and serves as a general rubric for a wide range of practices. . . . Heavily based in self-help and personal development therapies, its proponents await a large-scale change in human consciousness and a utopian era of peace and harmony. . . . New Age thinking tends to focus on ultimate individual liberation and engagement with a higher power, having little interest in the social world that lies between self and spirit" (1998, 170). This "little interest in the social world" becomes apparent in the self-involvement many of these individuals demonstrate when dancing at powwows.

For example, one young woman at the Native American Pow Wow in Maine joined the circle with disheveled dark hair hanging freely. Her feet were bare and she was dressed in a buckskin outfit. At times, she would stand face upward with closed eyes and shake her entire body. Her enraptured movements were loose and repetitive and followed no particular powwow dance style. Like so many wannabes, she appeared to be totally absorbed in her own experience, almost as if she was alone in the arena.

Chris Butterfly, a gaunt, rather shy man in his thirties, was one of most active participants at this powwow (see figure 12). He carried a flag during the Grand Entry and participated in all of the intertribal dances. In the afternoon he led a special children's activity during which they played a game that involved chasing stuffed animals thrown into the arena. Chris explained that though he is "not Native," he feels that he and many of his fellow "Native American Spiritualists" are more knowledgeable about Native practices than some Indians: "Many times," he told me, "Indians who live on the rez know only that and not about their own history and heritage" (personal communication, July 18, 2009).

As Chris circled around the arena and moved about the powwow grounds, he was completely engaged in a silent and devotional surrender to the day. As all the dances at this powwow were intertribals, he danced continually for over six hours. However, like the other non-Indian dancers at this event, his movements did not fit any traditional dance style.

Much of the New Age phenomenon is derived from the counterculture trends of the 1960s and 1970s, when a naïve understanding of Native culture was used on many levels as an example of a better way of life. This was typified by slogans such as "back to the earth," "in tune with nature," and "away with consumerism." Though these slogans did not necessarily allude to Indians or Indian culture, they resonated with how Native Americans relate to the natural world.

Native American scholar Lisa Aldred feels that the trend emerged during the 1980s and that the term New Age "probably was coined to reflect adherents' vision that the world would enter a literal 'New Age' of harmony, health, and spirituality through personal transformation" (2005, 270n2). The key concept here is *personal transformation* in a movement that is very much about individual self-discovery and "improvement" without any serious regard for the reality of Native American traditions or the repercussions of blatant appropriation of elements of Native American culture.

Aldred analyzes the body movements of New Agers at powwows:

> New Agers can be spotted by their dance styles at powwows, which usually take one of two patterns. Some dance free form, in the fashion of fans

> at a Grateful Dead concert. They pay little attention to other dancers on the floor or to what particular style of dancing is taking place at the time. Rather, they appear to be in their own worlds, emoting and improvising steps as they dance to the beat of their own imagined drum. Those who fall into the second pattern try too hard to replicate Indian peoples' dances. In their quest for "authenticity," they exaggerate the movements involved and their expressions are so deadly serious that they are quite humorous. (2005, 261)

This description closely approximates what I have seen at various powwows.

Aldred's point that New Agers dance in two distinctive modes—improvisational and in mimicry—is important. Neither mode has much to do with the forceful beauty of powwow dance styles. Moreover, these dancers often demonstrate a lack of knowledge of and respect for the most basic of powwow rules and even for actual Indians. They insist on "dressing in their own stereotyped, and often inappropriate, versions of powwow dress and [on] interrupting and insulting Indian peoples with bizarre or mimicking dance styles" (Aldred 2005, 269).

For instance, Ritchie Plass (Menominee) was surprised at the differences between New Age culture and Indian culture when he attended a New Age powwow in Austin Village, Ohio. Plass later wrote about his experience on powwow.com, a legitimate Web site for powwow dancers. Aldred summarized his reaction: "He was shocked at the powwow's disorganization and failure to follow any recognized protocol for Grand Entry. One of the three drums there consisted of eight white women, one of whom shook a rattle while drumming with one hand, a practice he had never seen before. They called themselves 'Mother Earth Beat'" (Aldred 2005, 264).

The number of New Age powwows is increasing, and non-Indians now run hundreds of Internet Web sites about powwow. The authenticity of the information on these sites can easily confuse someone unfamiliar with the complexity of powwow culture. Both Indian- and non-Indian-run Web sites cater to what might be a sincere interest in Native American cultures and often use them to make money online by selling Native American (or fake replicas of Native American) powwow regalia, arts and crafts, jewelry, musical instruments, tipis, and many other articles that appeal to those attracted to Native cultures (Aldred 2005, 268–269).

Deloria analyzes the possible motivations of those who "play Indian" in both the counterculture movement of the 1960s and 70s and the New Age movement of today: "Those original rebels . . . had used Indianness to shift the location of their identities from Britain to American. Since the early twentieth century, people had put on Indian clothes to search for authenticity in a modern America more alienating than welcoming. Now, counterculture rebels became Indian to move their identities away from Americanness altogether, to leap outside national boundaries, gesture at repudiating the nation, and offer what seemed a clear-eyed critique" (1998, 161). Unfortunately, the activities of the "counterculture rebels"—like the early "white Indians" and the first hobbyists—frequently had little to do with real Indian lives or the political struggles of the time. The stark differences between playing Indian and the reality of being Indian continues.

During the counterculture years, many Indian activists were working to protect tribal lands and water rights and to contest tribal treaties. The Seneca battle over the building of the Kinzua Dam on the Allegany River, the occupation of Alcatraz Island by seventy-eight Indians in 1969, the 1973 occupation by members of AIM (American Indian Movement) of the Pine Ridge Reservation near the South Dakota town of Wounded Knee, and the filing of a lawsuit by the Passamaquoddy tribe and Penobscot Nation to claim 12.5 million acres that had been taken away from them are just a few of the legal and political struggles Indians were engaged in during these years. Yet most non-Indians in the counterculture were not well informed about these movements and did not offer support.

New Agers today often know little about the protocol of powwows. Deloria reports that "New Age participation in Plains Sun Dances, for example, has been so overwhelming and so lacking in etiquette that many dances have been closed to non-Indians" (1998, 240n45). Although intertribal powwows are open for the most part to non-Indians, this hospitality is done in such a way that Indians are in charge. Powwows are open to outsiders under certain conditions. This indicates a change in power relations between Indians and non-Indians.

## Wannabes on the World Stage

A few years ago, in Budapest, Hungary, I visited a "Native Teaház" (teahouse) at which Hungarian waiters were dressed as Indians. When I asked the proprietor if any "real" Indians were involved in the operation of the teahouse, she answered, "No! But we have a deep connection with everything 'Indian.'" One has only to search the Internet to find thousands of links to Web sites that are run by people who have an unabashed, fervent, and sometimes shameless interest in "Indian ways."

In 2013, thousands of non-Indians engaged in powwows around the world. Hobbyists have been active in Europe for many years, particularly in the United

Kingdom, Germany, Holland, Belgium, Sweden, Italy, Poland, the Czech Republic, and Russia. Though this book does not examine these groups in depth, suffice it to say that the interest of Europeans in playing Indian and in Indian dance has a fascinating and long history that began as early as the 1600s and most likely differs from the history of wannabes in the United States. Today Germany is a particularly important center of Indian playacting.

In an intriguing article in *The New Yorker*, Rivka Galchen discusses an annual summer event in the town of Segeberg in northern Germany at which 3,000 people participate in Indian-like spectacles that feature "live horses, live chickens, gunfights, flaming-spear fights, and tumbling from roofs." She adds that "there are thousands of children in the audience, many in face paint and feathers—most come as Indians, though a small number dress up as cowboys—and many with parents and grandparents who attended as children" (2012, 40). In Germany and elsewhere in Europe, this strong interest in everything Indian is so prevalent that one can divide non-Indian powwows into two separate categories. Traditional hobbyists focus on "pre-reservation" Indians and try to stay "true" to "real" traditions, while the more contemporary contest powwows attempt to replicate the larger competition events in North America such as Schemitzun in Connecticut, the Crow Fair Celebration in Montana, and the United Tribes International Powwow in North Dakota. The contest powwows in Germany (and in other countries on the continent) rely to a great extent on Native Americans living in Europe who mentor non-Indians, share knowledge with them, and expose them to powwow (Watchman 2005).

In her informative essay on German powwows, Renae Watchman (Diné/Tsalagi) poses an important question: "Good intentions aside, the issue of appropriation becomes complicated and—perhaps for some—unsettling when we consider . . . the active involvement of a number of Native mentors, acquaintances, and paid participants in transferring powwow overseas. When German powwow people are instructed in person by Natives, sometimes at the urging of a Native mentor or friend who may encourage even further commitment to this 'alternative lifestyle,' then we must ask: is those Germans' participation in powwow an act of appropriation per se?" (2005, 252).

Many Europeans do not receive coaching from Native Americans but instead learn from books or film clips on the Internet. It is impossible to learn to dance by reading a book or watching a video, DVD, or television program. Nonetheless, people insist on trying to learn powwow dances in this way—another indication of the superficiality of their venture. This mode of learning and the subsequent representations that emerge from it—the dubious body movements and random regalia seen at venues such as intertribal powwows, hobbyist and New Ager events in the United States, and at powwows and festivals in Europe—raise a question: Why *are* these people so invested in Indian culture and dance?

## Bodies, Masking, and Appropriation

Sometimes wannabes—for example, Chris Butterfly—are not just pretenders but express a sincere desire to learn about Native world views, Native spirituality, and a sense of community that is absent from their lives. Perhaps powwow dancing gives these "students of Indian culture" self-esteem and a purpose that they might not experience elsewhere. Green suggests that they are trying to resolve a sense of guilt and validate for themselves what it means to be an American: "This most American of performances suggests that playing Indian is one of the most subtly entrenched, most profound and significant of American performances" in which "Anglo-American players are connecting to the America that existed before European invasion; they are connecting to the very beginnings of the mythological structure called America. . . . And they are connecting to both the real and to the primally mythic shaping of the country, perhaps through the reenactment of conflict between Indians and their ancestors, perhaps through the affirmation of victory over Indians by their ancestors, real or spiritual" (Green 1988, 48).

Playing Indian in the context of an intertribal powwow is also profoundly "American" in the sense that it is a multi-racial, multi-ethnic reflection of a society full of complex ambiguities. At the powwow in Wells, Maine, I asked Harry Tinker/Laughing Wolf, a man whose outward appearance was Caucasian, if he ever felt that wannabes were out of place at powwows. "Oh, no!" he exclaimed. "Everyone gets along just fine" (personal communication, July 18, 2009). Tinker/Laughing Wolf is an older man who had come to the powwow with a large extended family and danced with the same undefined body movement as Chris Butterfly and other dancers at this powwow. He told me that he was half Passamaquoddy and was from Old Town, where the Penobscot Reservation is located on Indian Island. The Native American Pow Wow in Wells was evidently a place where he felt comfortable as a person of mixed-blood descent and a member of this powwow community.

As hobbyists, New age practitioners, other wannabes, and even tourists join the powwow arena, their bodies in motion reveal a great deal about who they are. Deloria proposes that those who "play Indian" validate an imagined Indian identity through performance: "The donning of Indian clothes move[s] ideas from brains to bodies, from the realm of abstraction to the physical world of concrete experience. There, identity [is] not so much imagined as it [is] performed, materialized through one's body and through the witness and recognition of others" (1998, 184). By actually "becoming Indians"—putting on Indian clothes and engaging in the physical enactment of "Indian" movements through dance—these non-Indians take part in a kind of masking.

In many cultures, masking and dance go hand in hand. The act of moving within a mask is transformative, whether the mask is constructed or painted on; whether it is a facial mask, a partial body mask, or a full body mask; whether it is elaborate or as simple as a veil. When a person puts on a mask, it covers the face or body but also reveals and elicits—from deep within that person—other layers of the self.

As non-Indians hide behind their "Indian disguises," they move into another reality that is not their own. Their moving bodies create an illusory tie with Indians. They lack the understanding of the profound symbolism of the intensely elaborate regalia that Indian dancers create for themselves. They lack the knowledge of how regalia is an integral part of the various Indian dance styles. Instead of disguising the dancer, Indian regalia illuminates both a dance style and the identity of a particular dancer and his or her tribal nation and community. The difference here is between using masks and other regalia to cover, to disguise, to become something one is not and using it to complete the spiritual and communal process of powwow dancing. In other words, Indians, including those who perform for touristic, commercial, and financial reasons, know why they are doing it, while the motivations of wannabes are less clear.

How do Indians respond to wannabe dancers at powwows? Of course, the responses vary. But in some places they are perceived as a threat to Native American culture. Powwow scholar Victoria E. Sanchez writes that in central Ohio "wannabes are regarded as extremely dangerous when they attempt political or cultural representations of Native Americans. Their sense of understanding in these areas usually does not reflect tradition-oriented Native American values" (1995, 138). Sanchez adds that often the public cannot distinguish between Native and non-Native, thus making it even more imperative that Indians are "in charge of their own representation" (1995, 138). She also warns against instances in which wannabes assume they can speak in public for Indians in situations related to legislative decisions (1995, 116). Green proposes that when non-Indians play Indian, "Indians . . . are loved to death . . . while despised when they want to act out their real traditional roles on the American landscape. For

Indians to be Indians, or rather to be Indian in their some 200 distinct tribal roles, to be Indian in the historical future, non-Indians must give up the role" (1988, 50).

Many people in Indian country are deeply concerned about the appropriation of their culture. For decades there has been a movement to reveal the truth about play-acting Indians and the dangers they pose to Native American cultural traditions, individuals, and tribal groups. Hopi/Miwok author Wendy Rose (1992) calls these people "whiteshamans" or the "Great Pretenders." Native American Greg Sarris cautions: "The New Age Movement with its appropriation of American Indian religion is a good example of how citizens of a dominant society take what they find—what they came into Indian territory wanting to know—for their own purposes. Here the interests, or need to know, may not directly affect the political well-being of a particular Indian community, but the interests nonetheless ultimately result in re-creations of Indian life and ideology that may, through the creation of stereotypes and so forth, be damaging in the long run" (1993, 71n10).

As these scholars point out, many writers, pseudo-shamans, and supposed experts on Indian culture—for example, Adolph Hungry Wolf, Jamake Highwater, Joseph Epes Brown, Sun Bear, Rocking Thunder, Lynn Andrews—lecture in Indian dress and profess to contain Indian wisdom of one sort or another. The criticism is directed primarily at non-Indian authors and lecturers but can also be applied to powwow wannabes who dance as if they were Indians. This is especially the case when wannabes distance themselves from the very people whose culture they emulate as they profess to have a "superior," more authentic knowledge of traditional powwow practices. Rose proposes a conclusion that is generous but serves as a warning of the delicate yet important line between inclusion and exclusion: "We accept as given that whites have as much prerogative to write and speak about us and our cultures as we have to write and speak about them and theirs. The question is how this is done and, to some extent, why it is done" (1992, 416).

The presence of wannabes at Native American intertribal powwows has far-reaching ramifications. Their actions at these events are the result of a complicated production of desire, imitation, yearning, and at times ignorance. Each individual's motivation to dance is revealed by his or her body in motion. How that body moves is key to understanding the meaning of the wannabe dance.

# 8

# Power in Motion

## A Conclusion

*Mawkeka* (They come together dancing)

PASSAMAQUODDY-MALISEET WORD

In this book I have suggested numerous ways that moving bodies perform and generate power. At powwows throughout North America, power is manifest in the longevity and constancy of Iruska and the repetitive actions and practices performed across centuries of Native American dance. It is also manifested in the ways that bodies in motion engage in space and in time and in the complex fluidity of transcultural exchange as powwow attendees cross borders of race, ethnicity, gender, age, and class. At powwows, power is a force that is deeply embedded in Indian experiences of racism and survival. Dance is an essential part of this process.

W. Richard West Jr. (Southern Cheyenne), the first director of the National Museum of the American Indian, elaborates: "Dance reflects the vast capacity of native peoples to endure culturally and to continue as a vital contemporary cultural phenomenon, notwithstanding historical oppression and a way of being that stands in stark contrast, if not rebuttal, to much that drives the current technological age. The dance of native peoples is thus both a vital means of surviving culturally and a powerful expression of that survival" (1992, ix). Dance has been and is a fundamental aspect of resistance to colonization and is a force for revitalization in Indian country. Along with the drum, dance is a constant of powwow practice that produces a distinctly Native energy. This chapter further explores the power inherent in powwows and how it is expressed in specific dance styles.

Artistic practices are tools for social change as Native Americans and other colonized peoples across the globe rebel against centuries of violence and injustice. Ernest Fischer writes in *The Necessity of Art*: "We may conclude from a constantly growing wealth of evidence that art in its origins was *magic*, a magic aid towards mastering a real but unexplored world. . . . This magic role of art has progressively given way to the role of illuminating social relationships, of enlightening men to recognize and change social reality. . . . Art is necessary in order that man should be able to recognize and change the world. But art is also necessary by virtue of the magic inherent in it ([1959] 1963, 13–14). Indians manifest this magic power to change the world through the aesthetic skill, beauty, and sacred traditions of powwow dancing, singing around the drum, and creating and wearing regalia. Specific dance styles emerge from bodies in motion to reveal this power in motion.

Three styles serve as vivid examples of how dance creates power: the women's jingle dress style, the women's fancy shawl style, and the men's fancy style. In this concluding chapter I examine how these dances embody and express power.

## Women's Jingle Dress Style

> According to one account, the jingle dress style evolved from Mill Lacs, Minnesota: in a holy man's dream, four women wearing jingle dresses appeared before him. They showed him how to make the dresses, what types of songs went with them, and how the dance was performed. In his dream, the dances made a pretty sound to him.
>
> Upon wakening, he and his wife made four of the dresses, called the four women who in his dream wore them, dressed them in the dresses, brought them forth at a dance, and told the people about the dream and that this is the way the women were to dress and dance.
>
> From there, the jingle dress spread throughout the Chippewa/Ojibway territories.
>
> In the late 1920s, the White Earth people gave the jingle dress to the Sioux/Lakota, and it spread westward into the Dakotas and Montana.
>
> LISA STEPHENSON, *POWWOW*

A similar version tells about an Ojibwe holy man whose daughter is very ill. In a dream, he is told that if his daughter dances every day for a year while wearing a dress with seashells hanging from it, she will heal (Jones and Jones 1996, 279). The notion of dreaming a dance highlights how individual and communal inner visions shape the meaning of specific dances and imbue them with power. Paula Gunn Allen writes about how dreams are connected to power in Native American cultures: "It is likely that the power embodied in the Irriaku (Corn Mother) is the power of dream, for dream connections play an important part in ritual life of the Pueblos as of other tribes of the Americas" ([1986] 1992, 22).

In her book on Pocahontas Allen adds:

> The state of awareness when one is in or communicating with this realm was long identified as Dream-Vision, or *powa*, in the Algonquian world. It is allied to the Native Australian concept of Dream Time, a way of organizing reality, including via sensory data, that brings phenomena into awareness that are absent from perceptual fields in another brain state. [It is] variously known as "alternative consciousness," "shamanic consciousness," "walking in balance," "walking in beauty," "walking in a sacred matter," a state or condition of *inanyi*, *orenda*, *waken*, *hozho*, the "paranormal," the "transcendent"—there are as many ways of speaking about it as there are traditions in the world. (2004, 21)

The links between dream and magic, dance, and power are very important in Indian cultures. As Tara Browner—who is a jingle dress dancer herself—writes, in the jingle dance style power is embodied as a spiritual and healing force "which originates as an energy generated from the sound of the cones [on the dress] that sing out to the spirits when dancers lift their feet in time with the drum. The very act of dancing in this dress constitutes a prayer for healing, and often spectators, musicians, and other dancers will make gifts of tobacco to a dancer and request that she pray for an ill family member while she dances" (2002, 53).

The various origin stories of the jingle dress style demonstrate how dance styles evolve through exchanges of tribal knowledge across geographical regions and across generations. Browner discusses one narrative that relates to a woman named Maggie White, who was part of the Ojibwe community in Whitefish Bay in southwestern Ontario. In this account, "the Jingle dress and dance were given to the Anishnaabeg sometime soon after the end of World War I through the medium of White's father's vision, which he sought after she was ill." Subsequently, White and three other girls created the "nucleus of the Jingle Dress Dance Society" (2002, 53–54). Browner also tells two other jingle dress stories: one from Norma Rendon of the Lakota tradition and another that was told to her by Randy Talmadge (Ho-Chunk) (2002, 55–58).

As with the grass and traditional styles, there is no "correct" historical origin story for the jingle dress style. The jingle dress dance seems to have been around since the 1920s, with a pause during the 1960s, and is now performed at most intertribal powwows (see figure 13). The fact that the jingle dress society that originated with Maggie White has "lost control" over the dance has caused some concern in traditional Ojibwe communities: "On one hand, many consider the dance to be a gift from the Ojibwe to the larger Native North American community. On the other hand, however, the regalia of many women is far beyond that deemed proper, and skin-tight dresses, metallic glitter fabrics, and lace sleeves are coming into vogue. . . . Many competitive pow-wow dancers also wear eagle feathers, a practice frowned upon by the dance society" (Browner 2002, 58). As a partial solution to the conflict, "the society may be considering allowing branches to form in other communities and even allowing Indians who are not Anishnaabeg to join" (Browner 2002, 58). This solution would enable the original Women's Jingle Dress Society to maintain and preserve its traditions and styles while providing venues for women who perhaps have other tribal affiliations to dance in ways that modify the jingle dress style and adorn themselves in ways that depart from the Anishnaabeg tradition. Native peoples have always exchanged and gifted their dances across tribes. They also have a long experience of coping with changes that come from outside their traditions in ways that enable them to preserve core elements of culture that are important to them.

In the arena circles in the northeast region of the United States, the jingle dress is a younger women's style. It is not an easy style to execute; it requires dancers to coordinate their body movement and the jingles with the drum. The synchronization of body movement, music, and the movement of certain elements of the jingle dress regalia is especially important in this dance.

Jingle dress dancers usually wear a minimum of 200 jingles. Through the years jingles have been made from bones, animal teeth, shells, and hammered copper, but today they are often hand-made from chewing tobacco lids. (Dancers can also buy jingles.). They are sewn in rows or in zigzag chevron designs across a colorful fitted cloth dress. As dancers move, their jingles bounce up and down and side to side. At night, floodlights gleam on the shiny metal surfaces. On a sunny afternoon, the brightness illuminates each jingle while the dancers bob this way and that. This movement is carefully controlled, as J. R. Matthews explains: "A good dancer moves so that the jingles rise and fall together in unison, in rhythm with the drum" (*Native American Men's and Women's Dance Styles*).

Dancers also wear wide beaded belts or concho belts, braids and hair ties, neck scarves, beaded leggings, and moccasins that may have beads and sequins. They might carry a scarf, a fan, or a purse and are bareheaded or wear a simple single feather or plume. In the jingle dress style, as in other styles, dancers embody a sense of Iruska as they move in sync with kinetic, auditory, and visual stimuli.

Two basic songs accompany jingle dress dancers. During the slide, or shuffle, song, jingle dress dancers perform in place with the feet together. Their bodies are regal and straight, and their knees bend as they spring energetically up and down. Often they execute tiny turns right and left. Dancers may also twist and shuffle to the side while the entire body is propelled upward. Yet the feet don't leave the ground. Making short, slight hunches with the shoulders and outwardly held elbows, dancers lift their fans high and away from their chests during the honor beats.

In the straight song, also known as the jingle dress song, dancers move more fully in space while gazing inward and downward toward the floor. They hold their fans close to their bodies in a vertical position and lift them only at particular moments. Even though their stance is tight and narrow, this dance is free and lively. As Diane Rogers (Oneida Chippewa) explains: "The Jingle Dance, it's a bouncing dance. Your feet are constantly moving" (qtd. in Contreras and Bernstein 1996, 119). The footwork combines short steps performed on the toes as the legs cross and open, steps that move forward and backward, and hops with both feet together that move sideways, forward, and especially backward. As in the grass dance style, the dancer uses space behind the body as she turns in place to the right and to the left. I have also observed tiny twists of the feet as spirals of movement ripple up the body.

In the arduous physicality of synchronizing all aspects of the jingle dress dance, each dancer performs her personal version of the required actions while simultaneously maintaining a quiet and attentive expression of inner spirituality. Jingle dress dancers are innately aware of one another as they circle clockwise around the communal space. This dance and the men's and women's fancy dances are the most flashy powwow styles, and their intensity is one illustration of how modern-day Indians assert and affirm power.

## Power

Oral and written sources in many tribal traditions emphasize the notion of power, a visceral and spiritual energy. This sacred power is connected to magic and dreams. Native terms such as Iruska fire power, *wakan*, Wakan Tanka, or Wakon'da, and *powa* all refer to this power. The Comanche term *puha* is related to a spiritual power that resides in speech and can be related to the emcee's role at powwow (Gelo 2005).

In northeastern tribal traditions, power is present in all forms of life—in human beings, in animals, and in plants. The Algonquian tribes refer to this power as *manitou*, and the Iroquians call it *orenda* (Calloway [1991] 1999, 36–40). The power of the natural world is present everywhere at powwows. It is present in the regalia dancers wear; in the dance movements that embody the movements of animals, birds, and insects; in the outdoor settings of most events; in how all participants have access to an experience of all the senses; and in the coordination of those senses in dance through body movement, music, and regalia. This intricate relationship with the natural world reflects a deep connection to the sanctity of all life and a profound sense of spirituality.

When dancers enter the arena circle at contemporary powwows, they experience a feeling of closeness to one another and to a greater spirit. This is best expressed by a narrator in the film *I'd Rather be Powwowing*: "As you're dancing, you feel yourself stand taller and show everything you've got because the creator has given you everything you have. And as you look around you, you could see other dancers and they're all feeling that same feeling . . . people dancing, dancing the way they dance, the sound of the bells in time with the drum . . . the beat of the drum, the voices of the singers, and it's a feeling of worship. The creator is telling you that this is the right way to do." Often, to dance with others is to share a profoundly religious experience.

Mircea Eliade eloquently writes about the meaning of the sacred: "The *sacred* is equivalent to a *power* and, in the last analysis, to *reality*. The sacred is saturated with *being*. Sacred power means reality and at the same time enduringness and efficacy. . . . Thus it is easy to understand that religious man deeply desires *to be*, to participate in *reality*, to be saturated with power" (1961, 12–13). It is this very visceral sense of being that runs through powwows as a constant presence. The act of dancing for the creator is an empowering experience. Furthermore, because powwow dances are executed with other dancers in relation to the drum and as worship to a greater spirit, a sense of a sacred sharing enlivens and deepens the meaning of the communal circle.

Power is also a matter of endurance and survival. It can refer to a growing capacity to express one's own point of view—in this case, Native ways of operating in the world. As a unique performance genre, powwow can join other artistic projects and political movements that guide us out of the quicksand of status quo that exists today in the United States and many areas of the so-called developed world. There are many other ways to gauge the success of a society or a nation than industrial development. Euro-Americans have a great deal to learn from indigenous world views.

Part of the Native world view is how Native American societies perceive and value competitive games and dance contests. When dancers compete in the arena circle, they perform another layer of reality and power.

## Competitions

At many contemporary intertribal powwows, competitions or contests are held in all categories. These contests are organized by dance styles and age groups. At the larger powwows, more categories are added. For example, at Schemitzun in 1997, there were competitions in men's and women's team dances as well as in the categories of the Eastern Blanket Dance, the Smoke Dance, and the Chicken Dance.

Intertribal powwows also often feature in hand game competitions, drum contests, and even basketball games and other sports. In 2009 at the 40th Annual Sipayik Indian Day Celebration on the Passamaquoddy tribe's Pleasant Point Reservation near Perry, Maine, an entire day was set aside for children's games and sports competitions such as canoe races, weight-lifting contests, and golf tournaments.

During a dance competition, each style and corresponding song has particular requirements. Browner describes these standards: "There are internal (and external during competition) sets of standards that define good regalia design, footwork, and musical performance, and they vary regionally to a certain extent" (2002, 9–10). She states that powwow dancers follow all of these requirements but also know how to dance best through an "internal aesthetic sense." Powwow dancers are dancers in the fullest meaning of the word—they are trained, they are skilled, and they are intimately aware of how their bodies move and express themselves.

Judges look for the quality of the regalia and the dancing and at how well each dancer stops with the drum. They also notice how the nuanced particulars of each style are executed. Each dancer wears a number for the duration of the event so that everyone who is registered can be identified (see figure 10). Points are earned for competing in individual dances. In order to encourage participation in all aspects of the program, points are also awarded for dancing in the Grand Entry and intertribal dances. After a competition, the winner shakes hands with other competitors.

Bernard S. Mason observed contests between dancers in the 1940s. These were called challenge powwows or spot powwows:

> If an Indian powwow is studied carefully with a view to determining what is going on, it will be found that two or three of the dancers are dancing brilliantly and with all spectacle, while the remainder are dancing very quietly, perhaps doing little more than marking time or jarring their heels to the drumming. Presently two or three of the latter leap forward in dashing style while the first ones join the ranks of those moving quietly. Later still others replace these. This serves two useful purposes—it gives each a chance to feature his dancing at its most colorful best, and it gives everyone a rest, protecting against the exertion of constant full-bodies dancing. (1944, 63)

Though today's competitions are organized differently, they feature a similar balance of courtesy, rivalry, and respect.

Dance competition is a debated topic in Indian country, and not all tribal groups or individuals approve of them or include them at their celebrations. For example, contest dancing was not a strong component at the Shinnecock Labor Day Powwow in Southampton in 1995, which featured several traditional dances from the Shinnecock Indian Nation and a modern dance piece. The latter type of dancing, which was performed on the "drum" proscenium stage, was more theatrical and less inclusive. In contrast, at Schemitzun in 1995 and 1997 and at the Crow Fair Celebration in 1997, dance contests were lengthy and ran late into the night. Steve Lang, a photographer who has worked with the Redhawk Native American Arts Council, told me that how and why contests are managed affects the tone of each gathering (personal communication, January 1998).

In his essay on powwows in North Carolina, music historian Chris Goertzen lays out some of the conflicting issues: "Many types of American festivals employ the contest format to impose order on and add suspense to long series of short songs or dances. The disadvantage of this for powwows is that they become less spiritual, according to numerous organizers. There tends to be less room for 'specials,' such as giveaways and social dances. But contest powwows attract skilled dancers and thus larger crowds, making it easier to achieve a high energy level and for dancers to lose themselves in the attractive communion of flow" (2005, 295). This flow, or the presence of power, is a positive support for both the dancers and the spectators.

In her early research on powwows, renowned dance ethnologist Gertrude Prokosch Kurath wrote in 1957 about festivals in the Great Lakes region: "Does this complex have any meaning besides the spectacle? Anyone accustomed to the leisure and dignity of native rituals may indeed be appalled at the crowds, the blaring public address system, the booths selling trinkets, may remember the integration of the old ritual dances with social structure and all phases of life, and may judge these powwows to be a bit of fluff on par with ballroom dances and show business. But anyone who watches long enough will discover underlying and specific values" (183). Kurath's study, which was done long before powwow scholarship existed, points to an intrinsic, core meaning of powwow events, even in the face of commercial influences and more recent developments such as dance competitions.

Many powwow dancers are professionals; they earn their livelihood from dancing. Some of these dancers do not attend powwows when cash prizes are not offered. Native American scholars Patricia C. Albers and Beatrice Medicine

(Standing Rock Sioux) offer information about professional dancers at competition powwows:

> We can now speak of "professional powwow families," who spend much of their time on the circuit and are able to earn a decent living through their winnings in contest singing and dancing. . . . Professionalization is also apparent in other areas. Today well-known and respected announcers, judges, and arena directors are invited and paid to work at events far from their home communities; some are able to make a respectable living not only during the summer powwow season but also at the larger urban and college events generally held at other times during the year. . . . Today's "star" dancers are now recognized over wide regions, some even nationally. The presence of these well-known and much admired artists adds to the prestige of an intertribal powwow, and some powwow goers organize their summer itineraries to take in the powwows that their favorite dancers typically attend. (2005, 38–39)

Numerous nationally known emcees work at intertribal powwows in the New York City tri-state area. Star dancers and singers come from all over North America to compete at Schemitzun. The truth is that dancers do sometimes attend a particular event mainly for the cash prizes, which range from under $100 to thousands of dollars. For example, a local newspaper reported that a total of $80,000 was awarded at the 2009 United Tribes International Powwow in Bismarck.

In the Northeast, many festivals do not include competitive dancing. For instance, the 1998 Spring UNITY Pow-Wow in Manhattan had few dancers and offered no competition money. Contest dancing would have been out of place at a family-run powwow I attended in 2006 in Caribou, Maine, and at the Annual Native American Festival in Bar Harbor. These examples echo a trend in the West of reverting back to smaller powwows "to avoid the insidious distinctions, 'bad feelings,' and 'bad medicines' that have been reported to surround the heated competition at some of the bigger ones" (Albers and Medicine 2005, 40). Albers and Medicine report that "some of the smaller celebrations are now gaining reputations for putting on good 'traditional' events and are attracting more participants who wish to experience the sociality and intimacy of an 'old-style doings' rather than the glitter, bustle, and anonymity of the big powwow" (2005, 40). Many of the powwows I attended during my fieldwork fit this category of event, including the 1995 Shinnecock Labor Day Powwow, the powwow the New Jersey American Indian Center organized in Sayerville, New Jersey, in

1997, the Thunderbird Grand Midsummer Pow Wows, and the 1997 Honor the Earth Powwow in Northampton, Massachusetts. Even though both Shinnecock and Thunderbird are rather large, they have few contests and maintain a feeling of an extended tribal and family get-together.

Last, cash prizes are not the only reason competitions are held at powwows. Competitions are a kind of contemporary warfare between competing individuals from distinct tribes and communities. In addition, dancers challenge the hegemony of the nation-state with these expressions of artistry and prowess; they are announcements that Indian country is alive and well, strong and growing. This is also true of the dancing that takes place at powwows that do not have contests, where dancers perform in subtle yet powerful ways, for instance in the calm centeredness of the traditional styles or the spiritual healing of the jingle dress. Both the women's and men's fancy dance styles execute power in another way that makes a statement about what it means to dance in Indian country.

## Women's Fancy Shawl Style

As colorful fringed shawls open and twirling female bodies spin and hop, fancy shawl dancers create images of butterflies flitting over windswept wheat fields. Many elements of this style link it to the jingle dress style, including repeated crossings of the dancers' legs, vertical up-and-down bounces, turns in place, and hops in all directions. Yet in the fancy shawl style, which is sometimes referred to as the northern fancy shawl style, the space around the dancer extends outward. As thighs lift, hops become skips. Behind the body, kicks are high. The intricate footwork of this style is even more complex than that of the jingle dress style: dancers' feet tap right and left and their bodies shift weight on each beat of the drum.

The fancy dancer's splendid, colorful shawl is carried over her back. She grasps the corners of the cloth in order to lengthen it with her arms (see figure 14). As the dancer moves, her arms and the shawl become one as she tips and carves the space with her upper body. The shawl is usually a solid color that is decorated with appliqué, painted designs, beadwork, or ribbons in multiple shades of red, turquoise, blue, and yellow. The designs can be geometric or they may represent an animal or a bird. Some younger girls wear the shawl over street clothes while others perform in complete regalia. The key is how the shawl is used in harmony with body actions and the drum.

The fancy shawl dancer might adorn her dress with sequins, wear moccasins, and put one or two feathers on her head. In movement, the fringed edging along her shawl repeats the same energetic lightness and fluidity in space as in other dance styles that use fringe—the women's traditional buckskin style and men's grass dance style. In the fancy shawl dance, as the arms reach beyond and above the dancer's lower body, her torso curves. Sometimes she bends her elbows to enclose herself with the shawl, like a cocoon, while her feet continue to move.

The work of the feet and legs requires enormous expertise. The dancer balances on the balls of her feet while performing steady, quick weight shifts and turns. In the traditional way of doing this dance, at least one foot should touch the ground, but today some dancers bend that requirement and seem to soar across the arena.

The difficulty of this dance lies in how the dancer coordinates hops and skips that cover a great deal of space while simultaneously opening and closing her shawl with sweeping curves in space. This is especially difficult because the fringe of the shawl must not touch the ground. J. R. Matthews describes how the dance is judged: "Judges watch for graceful steps, fluid and continuous movement, originality, and endurance. Most of the dance is done on the balls of the feet, which gives the dancers the look of butterflies floating above the ground" (*Native American Men's and Women's Dance Styles*).

Some say the fancy shawl style first appeared in North Dakota during the 1950s, while others claim that it emerged at the turn of the twentieth century or during the 1930s. Browner suggests that it "either developed shortly before World War II or during the war. Numerous (non-Lakota) oral sources place the dance's birthplace on one of the Lakota reservations in South Dakota" (2002, 58). She adds that the women's fancy shawl or "butterfly" dance most likely emerged from the men's fancy style: "According to pow-wow tradition, in the early 1940s a number of teenage girls grew frustrated that only men were permitted to perform the Fancy Dance. In a challenge to convention, they dressed in men's outfits and danced at a South Dakota pow-wow. That and other similar actions led women to develop a Fancy Dance for females" (2002, 59). This history explains why so many of the body actions of the men's and women's fancy styles coincide. However, the fancy shawl dance is a distinctly female dance expression because of the use of the shawl and the extreme lightness of the nimble footwork it requires.

Julia C. White recounts two origin stories about the women's fancy dance: "One is that a butterfly lost her mate in battle and, grief-stricken, she withdrew into her cocoon (her shawl). She vowed to travel the world stepping on each stone until she found beauty in one and could start her life over. The other story is that women gradually gave up the buffalo robes and heavy blankets they wore as the lighter weight shawls came into their hands from European traders. The dance was developed as a way to show off their beautiful, new clothing" (1994, 11). The fancy shawl dancer does look as if she were stepping quickly from stone to stone, afraid to get her feet wet while at the same time accentuating her beautiful clothing.

Fancy shawl dancer April Renae Wachman (Navajo Western Band Cherokee) says that the dance is a celebration of life over death: "There's a story behind the Fancy Shawl Dance. It originated in the '30s and was looked down upon at first, but now it's making a comeback. The story I know well. A woman had lost her husband and had gone into mourning and enclosed herself in a cocoon. Her grandfather came and told her that she was done mourning and that she could go dance again, and that this dance would be for her. So she emerged from the cocoon as the butterfly emerges from its cocoon" (qtd. in Contreras and Bernstein 1996, 50). Multiple origin stories only add to the rich variety and complexity of powwow dancing.

During a contest, a fancy shawl dancer is often expected to perform other styles even though she is dressed in shawl regalia. For example, a song might include a beat from the Crow Hop Dance in the middle. When this happens, dancers transition from their intricate footwork to the even, steady, and rather heavy step right, step left of the Crow Hop Dance. The drum might also lead dancers to change their tempo from fast to slow and then back to fast. This requires coordination, physical dexterity, and stamina.

As with other female styles, the fancy shawl dancer seems almost weightless, and although each dancer performs her own choreography, she is aware of others in the arena. The attention of a fancy shawl dancer is concentrated downward and outward beyond her footwork. The shawl itself becomes a performer as it sways above fast-moving feet. This quick footwork is also an important aspect of the men's fancy dance.

## Men's Fancy Style

> A swirl of feathers and color, powerful music, and spirited moves. It's the fastest and flashiest, the hundred-yard-dash of the Native American dance world. It is a young man's dance that older men still remember.
>
> NARRATOR, *FANCY DANCE*

Sometimes called a crazy dance, the men's fancy style is the hallmark of contemporary powwows (see figure 15). The style is very complex. It includes many types of steps, including hops of all kinds on one leg or two; jumps; turns; crossings and openings of the legs while moving sidewise, forward, and backward (similar to the women's jingle dress and fancy shawl styles); rapid changes of weight and direction; high thigh lifts; splits and cartwheels; and even a type of low-level hop in which both legs jut out, one after the other, from a crouching position. In addition, although the fancy dancer's posture is upright but slightly bent over, because of the full-bodied movements he executes throughout, he vigorously explores the three dimensions while his feet are doing intricate stallion-like steps. Drum songs can be any tempo and might include a medium, straight song; a Ruffle Dance song; a Crow Hop song; or a song created especially for a particular dance.

A consensus exists along powwow circuits that the first fancy dancers were Gus McDonald, Dennis Rough Face, and Henry Snake, all members of the Ponca tribal nation (*Fancy Dance*). During the 1920s, these men became bored with the more sedate traditional dances and wanted to perform a livelier dance in which each dancer could create his own individual steps. It is said that these men were often ridiculed and referred to as clowns, perhaps because their movements were so different from the traditional styles (*The World of American Indian Dance*).

Competitiveness was part of the men's fancy dance style from the beginning. The first world championship contest was held as part of a homecoming celebration in 1926 at the Haskell Institute, an Indian school in Lawrence, Kansas. Because McDonald won that contest, his tribe was designated to host the annual world championship at their Ponca powwow (*Fancy Dance*). Through the years the dance has changed constantly. From the 1940s through the 1970s, women also dressed in fancy dance regalia and competed. Now most women have changed to the fancy shawl style or other styles.

The bustles worn by contemporary fancy dancers can be traced to the "crow belts" that the Omaha and Ponca wore in the Omaha war dance, a dance that also influenced the grass dance style. Early feather dancers moved much like the traditional dancers of today with a lot of upper body and head movement. In the late 1940s and 1950s, the emphasis switched to footwork (Roberts 1992; Laubin and Laubin 1976). The prolific use of feathers began in the early 1900s, when non-Indian organizers of large arts and crafts festivals asked Indian performers to "dress up" more (Stephenson 1993, 13). Curiously, some of the earlier fancy dancers—who can be seen performing in film clips of the Wild West shows—reveal the quick leg crossings and jumpy up-and-down actions characteristic of the Charleston, a dance that was popular in the 1920s. During this time, dancers wore many small bustles that twirled as they danced.

The agile, fast movements of the fancy dance must be coordinated with the regalia and the drum, as is the case in all the other powwow dance styles. The dancer dashes around and across the arena, wearing a colorful outfit that includes twin feathered bustles with long ribbon fringe. He holds a long whip stick in each hand, and the open expansion of the enormous bustles flows with feathers and ribbon fringe as the dancer sweeps and curves through space.

Browner points out the differences between the regalia dancers wear in the northern and southern men's fancy dance styles: "Northern dancers by tradition attach their feathers into what are referred to as 'spinners,' allowing each feather to move independently. Southern dancers use a device called a 'rocker,' which is shaped like a horizontal capital *H*. A feather is attached to each end of the top crossbar; the bottom ends of the main bar (which is somewhat shorter than the top bar) attach with rubber bands to make a free-floating 'hitch.' The result is that the two feathers move together as a single unit, but the rocker moves independently from the dancer's head" (2002, 59). In addition, in the northern version, "one *Catabwa* (small bustle) is usually worn on each upper arm" (Browner 2002, 58).

A fancy dancer commonly wears hard-soled moccasins that need to be replaced several times during a summer season. His outfit might also include anklets, or "goats," made of angora goat fur around the lower leg, sheep bells below the knee, beaded aprons in front and back, side tabs, and a belt. He also wears a cape decorated with appliqué, a harness around his neck, and sometimes a beaded medallion necklace. Cuffs with ribbon fringe, a roach headdress similar to the headdresses worn in other styles, and a beaded headband complement the outfit. Colors are coordinated so that the regalia functions as a unit. The dancer's clothing and accessories are made by hand by relatives and friends and are personal for each dancer.

As the fancy dancer moves through the arena circle, his arms constantly curve and sweep the space with up-and-down gestures. As the arms open and close, the ribbons on the whips blend with the ribbons on the bustles. All of this is done with incredible urgency. Level changes are especially startling: the performer bends his knees, jumps up to the sky or the ceiling and down to the ground, then quickly he is up again, all in an instant. Moreover, movements are repeated on the right and then on the left. Many say that champion dancers try to balance their footwork and do everything in fours. All of these movements require the fancy dancer to be in top physical condition. Alvin Windy Boy (Cree), a champion dancer, says, "Fancy dance is just like any other sport. . . . If you're not in good shape you are not a competitor" (qtd. in Roberts 1992, 72).

During a Ruffle Dance song, the fancy dancer often stays in place, low down, and literally "ruffles" his shoulders, bustles, and headgear to attract attention. This move is reminiscent of the movements in the Sneak-Up Dance, in which the traditional dancer, low, close to the ground, shakes his body in preparation for the hunt or a war party. Yet in the fancy dance the movement has a different purpose. It is more indirect, almost coquettish, and is overtly theatrical.

When a fancy dancer competes, he must work to maintain his balance on one foot, coordinate his head movements with the music, sustain a lightness of expression, and stop with the drum. The dancer combines body actions, music, regalia, spirituality, and "the desire to be the best and to express the excitement and dramatic power of the dance" (*Fancy Dance*).

As Calvin Burns (Cherokee/Shinnecock) explains in the film *Traveling the Distance*, each dancer has his own reasons for dancing. Burns, who also calls himself Wild Eagle, tells how he lost interest in dancing when his father died: "Back in 1988, my father had passed away and for a short time I stopped dancing. I lost interest, I lost my heart, you know . . . 'cause I used to dance on stage for my father and it was at those moments I really felt that my father was really proud of me . . . winning competitions, coming in first place, coming home with trophies. Big glow on my face to see a glow on my father's face. And when he died it was my best friend [who] died. I lost interest." After a while Burns realized how much the fancy dance was a part of his own identity and he began dancing once again in memory of his father, Gray Fox: "Recently, about . . . the past five years, I just started back dancing. . . . This is who I am. A dancer. A fancy dancer at that. And this is where I felt my father was most proud of me. And even now, I still feel that he is most proud of me. Right now, he's with me when I dance and I dance for my father. I dance for him, for my pop, for Gray Fox."

Dance is an integral part of who Native American powwow dancers are. This identification of self, which is based on a deep connection between body and spirit, leads to a sense of agency that is clearly expressed in specific dances. Agency can be defined as the power to assert oneself against all odds. This power has the capacity to transform lives—the dancer's own life, the life of the dancer's community, and the lives of others beyond the dancer's community.

## Comparing the Dances

Native American powwow dance styles share many characteristics. For example, as seen above, in the grass, women's traditional, and shawl styles, fringe is incorporated to depict the motion of plains grasses, enhancing the beauty of the dancer's performance. In these three styles, it's as if the fringe itself is dancing along with the dancer. Similarly, the women's jingle dress and fancy shawl styles and the men's fancy style all use quick steps and foot crossings.

Yet differences exist. The quiet, forward-looking vista and verticality of the women's traditional style contrasts with the more bent-over posture of the men's dances. In addition, traditional men tend to dance in space as individuals while each tells his story, while women are consciously aware of one another as they move clockwise around the circle. Gender distinctions are also revealed during the Grand Entry, when the traditional women dancers, after entering with the others, surround the arena in an inward looking circle. This invites questions about how gender roles play out in Native culture.

In all dances, the use of the space behind the body indicates an acute awareness of the past and how it relates to the present and to the future. This aspect of powwow dance styles illustrates the belief that time and space are both circular. In addition, all dancers pay close attention to how they are relating to the floor (the ground, the earth) as they strive to maintain a dialogic flow between body movement, the drum, and their regalia. This is accomplished with careful attention to how, where, and why they place their feet. A large part of a powwow dancer's skill is the ability to coordinate fringe and jingles with the drum, and a sense of groundedness supports this process. This strong link with the earth is one of the most obvious differences between how Indians and non-Indians dance at powwow.

These three elements—use of back space; coordination of body movement, music, and movement of regalia; and contact with the ground—also mark key differences between Native American dance and other dance styles, both western and nonwestern. In addition, when dancers gather in an intertribal or a particular dance category, they might narrate a story, as in the men's straight or northern traditional style, or create a kinetic image or metaphor, as in the movements grass or fancy shawl dancers make that imitate "swaying wheat fields on the plains." Storytelling and image-making are two strong elements of powwow dance.

All of these characteristics illustrate the complex ways the fire power of Iruska threads its way through all powwow dance styles. Because these skills are learned from an early age and are an intricate part of their culture, dancers become enormously proficient performers who execute both athleticism and fine, aesthetic nuances. I cannot emphasize enough how physically and artistically difficult it is to perform these dances, which have evolved from centuries of performance practice.

Two added aspects of powwow dance are worth mentioning. First, though this book has focused on the most commonly seen dances at intertribal events in the northeastern United States, I have also frequently observed other styles such as the Rabbit Dance, the Stomp Dance, and the Hoop Dance. In addition, many traditional dances surface at some powwows in the Northeast. For example, at the Shinnecock Labor Day Powwow of 1995, the Shinnecock Youth Dancers presented the Traditional Corn Planting Dance, the Hunter's Dance, the Calumet Dance, the Partridge Dance, the Robin Dance, the Duck Dance, the Fish Dance, the Horse Dance, the young men's Challenge Dance, and the Blanket Dance. The Eastern Calumet Dance is performed at Schemitzun, among other events. The Stomp Dance and the Snake Dance are occasionally used as exhibition dances in venues in New England.

In Maine, the Round Dance, a type of intertribal dance that integrates Indians and non-Indians, is a popular aspect of festivals. The Round Dance and the Wedding Dance are typical of Wabanaki tribes (Speck [1940] 1998, 273–283). However, when anthropologist Frank G. Speck was doing his fieldwork in Maine in the 1930s, these dances were done with rattles rather than drums. This was because many Christians believed that beating the drum was pagan, and Christianity was very strong in the region at that time. The result was "the substitution of the 'holy song,' the Indianized church liturgies, for the original prayer-appeals in song and dance which we may imagine to have existed before conversion several centuries ago. . . . The holy songs, I believe, have usurped the function of an original spiritual repertory, leaving the social dances to survive" (Speck [1940] 1998, 270). The impact of colonization followed Native American dance well into the twentieth century. But the dance endured.

Today, as exemplified in local powwows throughout Maine and in projects such as the 1997 video *Our Dances*, which features the Penobscot Student Dance Troupe, many traditional dances are being revived. These include not only the Round Dance but others such as the Snake Dance, the Green Corn Mother Dance, the Pine Cone Dance, the Duduwas Dance, and the Warrior (Mtoape Kuwin) Dance. Some of these dances demonstrate the use of space behind the body, moving backward, and footwork that is similar to that of the jingle dress and fancy styles. In 2009, I saw Paul A. Francis III (Penobscot) dance a traditional men's style at Bar Harbor more than a decade after he participated as a student in *Our Dances*.

In addition, new styles are constantly emerging. These are usually local and tribal developments. One can glimpse some of these on YouTube; they can also be seen in each new powwow season. Powwow dance is an ongoing, ever-transforming process that is full of surprises and of the creativity that is specific to each dancer and to the collective of Native powwow dancers.

## Conclusion: Power and Transculturation

> Here in Minneapolis, a growing number of Native American women wear red shawls to powwows to honor survivors of sexual violence. The shawls, a traditional symbol of nurturing, flow toward the earth. The women seem cloaked in blood. People hush. Everyone rises, not only in respect, for we are jolted into personal memories and griefs. Men and children hold hands, acknowledging the outward spiral of violations women suffer.
>
> LOUISE ERDRICH, "RAPE ON THE RESERVATION"

At the beginning of this project, my sense was that intertribal powwows were a kind of revivalist movement in which Native American traditional practices were expressed and renewed. But powwows do much more than renew. In this book each chapter has dealt with a discrete aspect of how the force of Iruska and dance is present in the history of powwow, space and time, transcultural exchange, and performances of race. The arena circle becomes the symbolic and actual forum for the intermixing and sharing of body actions and performance practices as dancers perform in the grass, traditional, jingle dress, and fancy styles. As the circle multiplies into thousands of circles across the land, a sense of collective, *moving* power is generated.

Because genocide and racism in the United States are body-based and visceral, power relations between Indians and non-Indians have always been of a physical order and are exercised upon the body in overt and convert ways. The power that is produced by Indians as resistance and revitalization is also physical and must ultimately be understood in the context of an ever-deepening process of spirituality and transculturation.

The many modalities of transculturation are a fluid and constant "reinvention of tradition." As Silvia Spitta proposes, "even though the term 'transculturation' can be useful in describing the dynamics of cultural contact very generally, it has to be continually redefined for specific contexts" (1997, 163). Thus, it offers a trope for addressing "the dynamics of the colony from the space and the perspectives of the colonized" (Spitta 1997, 166–168). Within the context of intertribal powwows, mutual exchange between Indians and non-Indians has always been part of how power is negotiated between Indian country and the United States.

Central to the transculturation process at intertribal powwows is the presence of spectators and non-Indians. As we have seen here, spectators participate for reasons that are sometimes controversial. Contemporary powwows are sites of negotiation in postcolonial times, and Indians and non-Indians at these events are in constant interaction in an Indian-controlled space. In this context, the impact of cultural appropriation by non-Native people is a serious issue that both Indians and scholars will continue to debate.

I have also pointed to the ability of Indians to assimilate and transform, both consciously and unconsciously, the culture that the colonizer enforces. Although powwow dance styles are based in traditional practices, they fully utilize a modern-day concept of athleticism in dance performance. Another example is how Indian organizers have taken control of powwows and allowed non-Indians into their world—on their terms. As Coco Fusco points out, "Taking elements of an established or imposed culture and throwing them back with a different set of meanings is not only key to guerrilla warfare: the tactics of reversal, recycling, and subversive montage are aesthetics that form the basis of many twentieth-century avant-gardes" (1995, 34). Thus, as Native Americans and powwow dancers maintain their traditions, creatively adapt to the imposition of outside influences, and transform their ways of survival and resistance, they exercise a form of "guerilla warfare."

Dancing bodies are vital to this process. At powwows, actions and practices have been repeated thousands of times in a process of transcultural exchange and appropriation that supports a gathering of power that is revealed in the bodies of powwow dancers. Power and transculturation happen at powwows in the context of a complex combination of many elements that includes sensory experience, expression, and memory; spirituality; interactions between participants; travel, geography, and diaspora; the family as the framework in which class, age, and gender are fluid identity markers; humor; and tourism, commercialism, and the dance competitions that attract both Indians and non-Indians.

•

I have argued here that powwows are a positive force within Indian country. For a moment, I want to problematize the issue. I foresee, as have many others, a potential danger in the commercialism of dance competitions, the inclusion of entertainment elements that do not necessarily share in the spiritual or communal aspect of powwowing, and the visitors who "play Indian."

From the early contact dance societies to the first hints of specific powwow dances years later, the grass, traditional, jingle dress, and fancy styles have gone through many transformations. Competition has had an impact on that process. Because of national contests, the dances have become more generic, less local and traditional in relation to certain tribal practices. In *The World of American Indian Dance*, a film produced by the Oneida Indian Nation, the narrator states that maintaining traditions in Native American dance while at the same time accommodating the values of generosity and sharing in the powwow circle is a challenge for Indian people.

It is clear that the intrinsic spiritual quality of powwows has survived. As Sherman Alexie (Spokane/Coeur), one of our most outstanding contemporary writers has written in his poem "Powwow":

> today, nothing has died, nothing
> changed beyond recognition
> dancers still move in circles
> old women are wrapped in shawls
> children can be bilingual: yes and no. (qtd. in McMillin 2006, 240)

Perhaps the shift toward the commercial is attributable to the changing times. This, however, does not make such developments right or positive. As Barre Toelken suggests, "One of the most difficult aspects of Indian life concerns competition, for in nearly every tribe it carries a negative connotation and may be seen as related to moral decay, selfishness, and even witchcraft" (1991, 150–151). Renowned Native American author, theologian, and activist Vine Deloria Jr. (Standing Rock Sioux) also warns about changes that seem to move away from spirituality: "In some instances ceremonies are considered part of the tribal social identity rather than religious events. This attitude undercuts the original function of the ceremony and prevents people from reintegrating community life on a religious base" (1994, 248). The possibility that the commodification of Indianness may replace spiritual, religious, and communal principles must be addressed.

One is reminded that intertribal powwows, and the astounding beauty of powwow dancing, often function as a tourist cover-up or as an illusionary front region that ignores the inequalities between Indian country and the United States. The just, combative, and difficult struggles for land, education, health, and the right for Indian individuals and communities to define their own identities are primary and critical. Hence, one must not gloss over very real, unresolved needs and conflicts. Nonetheless, powwow people and their dance—these bodies in motion—can inspire us with wonder, hope, and the energy to continue the struggle for survival and much, much more.

# Bibliography

## Powwows Attended during Fieldwork, 1995–2009

### Connecticut


Schemitzun, hosted by the Mashantucket (Western) Pequot Tribal Nation, Mashantucket Reservation near Ledyard, Connecticut

Schemitzun, hosted by the Mashantucket (Western) Pequot Tribal Nation, Hartford, Connecticut


### Maine


Annual Native American Festival, sponsored by the Abbe Museum, College of the Atlantic, and the Maine Indian Basketmakers Alliance, Bar Harbor, Maine

44th Annual Sipayik Indian Day Celebration, Passamaquody Pleasant Point Indian Reservation, Perry, Maine

Mawiomi of Tribes, Aroostook Band of Micmacs, Caribou, Maine

Native American Pow Wow, sponsored by the New Hampshire Intertribal Council, Wells Harbor Community Park, Wells, Maine


### Massachusetts


6th Annual Honor the Earth Powwow, sponsored in part by the Western Massachusetts Intertribal Spiritual Council, Northampton, Massachusetts


### Montana


76th Annual Crow Fair Celebration, hosted by the Apsáalooke Nation, Crow Agency, Montana


### New Jersey


Powwow, organized by the New Jersey American Indian Center Organization, Sayerville, New Jersey

Return to Beaver Creek Native American Powwow, Matarazzo Farms, Belvidere, New Jersey


### New York


Annual Spring UNITY Pow-Wow, organized by the American Indian Community House Youth Council, American Indian Community House, Manhattan, New York

49th Annual Shinnecock Labor Day Powwow, hosted by the Shinnecock Indian Nation, Southampton, New York

Gateway to the Nations PowWow, presented by the Redhawk Native American Arts Council, Brooklyn, New York

Park Slope Native American Dance Festival and Winter Social, sponsored by the Redhawk Native American Arts Council, Brooklyn, New York

Thunderbird Grand Midsummer Pow Wow, Queens County Farm Museum, Queens, New York

### North Dakota

40th Annual United Tribes International Powwow, Bismarck, North Dakota

### Washington, DC

1st Pow Wow on the National Mall, organized by the Smithsonian National Museum of the American Indian, Washington, DC

## Films

*American Indian Dance Theater: Finding the Circle*. (1989) 1996. Directed by Merrill Brockway. WNET/Thirteen in association with Tatge/Lasseur Prod. Phoenix, AZ: Canyon Records & Indian Arts.

*American Indian Dance Theater: Dances for the New Generations*. (1993) 1996. Directed by Phil Lucas and Hanay Geiogamah. Produced by Barbara Schwei and Hanay Geiogamah in association with Phil Lucas Prod. Phoenix, AZ: Canyon Records & Indian Arts.

*Fancy Dance*. 1997. Native American Dance Series Vol. 1. Directed by Scott Swearingen. Tulsa, OK: Full Circle Videos.

*I'd Rather be Powwowing*. 1983. Directed by Larry Littlebird. PBS and Buffalo Bill Historical Center.

*Into the Circle: An Introduction to Native American Powwows and Celebrations*. 1992. Directed by Scott Swearingen. Tulsa, OK: Full Circle Communications.

*Jingle Dress*. 2002. Native American Dance Series. Directed by Scott Swearingen. Tulsa, OK: Full Circle Videos.

*Naamikaaged: Dancer for the People*. 1996. Directed by Thomas Vennum Jr. Washington, DC: Smithsonian Folkways.

*Native American Men's and Women's Dance Styles*. Vol. 1. 1994. Directed by Scott Swearingen. Tulsa, OK: Full Circle Videos.

*The 1996 Crow Fair and Powwow*. 1996. Directed by Alfred B. Linney. Hardin, MT: Cold Camp Productions.

*Our Dances*. 1997. Directed by Tiana Vermette. Featuring the Penobscot Student Dance Troupe under the direction of Barry Dana. Indian Island, ME: Penobscot Nation.

*Powwow Highway*. 1988. Directed by Jonathan Wacks. Troy, MI: Anchor Bay Entertainment, Inc.

*The Right to Be*. 1995. Directed by Harriett Skye. New York: Filmakers Library.

*The World of American Indian Dance*. 2003. Directed by Randy Martin. Presented by the Oneida Indian Nation. Oneida, NY: Four Directions Entertainment.

*Thunderheart*. 1992. Directed by Michael Apted. Burbank, CA: Columbia TriStar Home Video.

*Traveling the Distance: The Shinnecock 50th Anniversary Pow Wow and Its People*. 1997. Directed by Ziggy Attias and Ofer Cohen. East Northport, NY: Ziggy Films.

*Schemitzun '94*. 1995. Executive producer Wayne Reels. Ledyard, CT: Mashantucket Pequot Tribal Nation.

## Publications

Adams, James Ring. 2012. "'A Great Charge': How Native Dance Changed American Ballet." *National Museum of the American Indian* (Winter): 14–15, 18–20.

Albers, Patricia C., and Beatrice Medicine. 2005. "Some Reflections on Nearly Forty Years on the Northern Plains Powwow Circuit." In *Powwow*, edited by Clyde Ellis, Luke Eric Lassiter, and Gary H. Dunham, 26–45. Lincoln: University of Nebraska Press.

Aldred, Lisa. 2005. "Dancing with Indians and Wolves: New Agers Tripping through Powwows." In *Powwow*, edited by Clyde Ellis, Luke Eric Lassiter, and Gary H. Dunham, 258–274. Lincoln: University of Nebraska Press.

Alexie, Sherman. 1992. *The Business of Fancydancing*. Brooklyn: Hanging Loose Press.

———. 1995. *Reservation Blues*. New York: Atlantic Monthly Press.

———.1996. *Indian Killer*. New York: Atlantic Monthly Press.

Allen, Paula Gunn. (1986) 1992. *The Sacred Hoop: Recovering the Feminine in American Indian Traditions*. Boston: Beacon Press.

———. 2004. *Pocahontas: Medicine Woman, Spy, Entrepreneur, Diplomat*. New York: HarperCollins.

Ancona, George. 1993. *Powwow*. San Diego: Harcourt Brace.

Anderson, Benedict. 1983. *Imagined Communities: Reflections on the Origin and Spread of Nationalism*. London: Verso.

Appadurai, Arjun. 1996. *Modernity at Large: Cultural Dimensions of Globalization*. Minneapolis: University of Minnesota Press.

Ashworth, Kenneth Albert. 1986. "The Contemporary Oklahoma Pow-Wow." PhD diss., University of Oklahoma.

Austin, J. L. 1975. *How to Do Things with Words*. 2nd edition. Edited by J. O. Urmson and Marina Sbisà. Cambridge: Harvard University Press.

Awakuni-Swetland, Mark. 2008. *Dance Lodges of the Omaha People: Building from Memory*. Lincoln: University of Nebraska Press.

Axtmann, Ann M. 1993. "Rudolf Laban: Movement Language and the Choreographic Process." Master's Thesis, New York University.

———. 1999. "Dance: Celebration and Resistance. The Native American Indian Intertribal Powwow Performance." PhD diss., New York University.

———. 2000. "Space, Time, and Popular Culture: Native American Indian Intertribal Powwows." *Mid-Atlantic Almanack* 9: 107–128.

———. 2001. "Performative Power in Native America: Powwow Dancing." *Dance Research Journal* 33(1): 7–22.

Barba, Eugenio, and Nicola Savarese. 1991. *A Dictionary of Theatre Anthropology: The Secret Art of the Performer*. London: Routledge.

Barriero, José, ed. 1994. *Native American Expressive Culture*. Ithaca, NY: Akwe:kon Press.

Bartenieff, Irmgard, with Dori Lewis. 1980. *Body Movement: Coping with the Environment*. New York: Gordon and Breach Science Publishers.

Benthall, J., and Ted Polhemus, eds. 1975. *The Body as a Medium of Expression*. New York: E. P. Dutton.

Berkhofer, Robert J., Jr. 1978. *The White Man's Indian: Images of the American Indian from Columbus to the Present*. New York: Alfred A. Knopf.

Birdwhistell, Ray L. 1975. *Kinesics and Context: Essays on Body Motion Communication*. Philadelphia: University of Pennsylvania Press.

Black Elk and John G. Neihardt (1932) 1988. *Black Elk Speaks: Being the Life Story of a Holy Man of the Oglala Sioux*. Lincoln: University of Nebraska Press.

Blackstone, Sarah J. 1986. *Buckskins, Bullets, and Business: A History of Buffalo Bill's Wild West*. New York: Greenwood Press.

Bourdieu, Pierre. 1990. *The Logic of Practice*. Translated by Richard Nice. Stanford, CA: Stanford University Press.

Bradley, Karen K. 2009. *Rudolf Laban*. London: Routledge.

Braine, Susan. 1995. *Drumbeat . . . Heartbeat: A Celebration of Powwow*. Minneapolis: Lerner Publishing.

Brandt, Keith. 1985. *Indian Festivals*. Illustrated by George Guzzi. Mahwah: Troll Associates.

Brascoupé, Simon. 1994. "Strategic Adaptations: Native Aesthetics through Time and Space." In *Native American Expressive Culture*, edited by José Barriero, 93–96. Ithaca, NY: Akwe: kon Press.

Brooks, Lisa. 2008. *The Common Pot: The Recovery of Native Space in the Northeast*. Minneapolis: University of Minnesota Press.

Brown, Vanessa, and Barre Toelken. 1987. "American Indian Powwow." In *Folklife Annual*, edited by Alan Jabbour and James Hardin, 46–69. Washington, DC: Superintendent of Documents, Government Printing Office.

Browner, Tara. 2002. *Heartbeat of the People: Music and Dance of the Northern Pow-Wow*. Urbana: University of Illinois Press.

Browning, Barbara. 1995. *Samba: Resistance in Motion*. Bloomington: Indiana University Press.

Buckland, Theresa J., ed. 1999. *Dance in the Field: Theory, Methods, and Issues in Dance Ethnography*. New York: St. Martin's Press.

Buff, Rachel-Jennifer. 1996. "Calling Home: Migration, Race, and Popular Memory in Caribbean Brooklyn and Native-American Minneapolis, 1945–1992." PhD diss., University of Minnesota.

Burton, Bryan. 1993. *Moving within the Circle: Contemporary Native American Music and Dance*. Danbury, CT: World Music Press.

Butler, Judith. 1993. *Bodies That Matter: On the Discursive Limits of "Sex."* New York: Routledge.

Buttree, Julia M., with Ernest Thompson Seton. 1930. *The Rhythm of the Redman: In Song, Dance and Decoration*. New York: A. S. Barnes.

Call, Dwight William. 1991. "The Sacred Tree Flowers: The Continuation of Culture within the Niches on Cheyenne River Reservation (Lakota Sioux, South Dakota)." PhD diss., Drew University.

Callahan, Alice Anne. 1990. *The Osage Ceremonial Dance: I'n-Lon-Schka*. Norman: University of Oklahoma Press.

Calloway, Colin G. (1991) 1999. *Indians of the Northeast*. New York: Checkmark Books.

Calloway, Colin G., and Neal Salisbury, eds. 2003. *Reinterpreting New England Indians and the Colonial Experience*. Boston: Colonial Society of Massachusetts.

Campisi, Jack. 1975. "Powwow: A Study of Ethnic Boundary Maintenance." *Man in the Northeast* 9:34–46.

Carlson, Marvin. 1996. *Performance: A Critical Introduction*. New York: Routledge.

Catlin, George. [1836] 2002. "The Manner, Customs, and Condition of the North American Indians." In *I See America Dancing: Selected Readings, 1685–2000*, edited by Maureen Needham, 21–25. Urbana: University of Illinois Press.

Champagne, Duane, ed. 1994. *Native America. Portrait of the Peoples*. Foreword by Dennis Banks. Detroit: Visible Ink Press.

Churchill, Ward. 1992. "The Earth Is Our Mother: Struggles for American Indian Land and Liberation in the Contemporary United States." In *The State of Native America: Genocide, Colonization, and Resistance*, edited by Annette M. Jaimes, 139–188. Boston: South End Press.

Churchill, Ward, and Winona LaDuke. 1992. "Native North America: The Political Economy of Radioactive Colonialism." In *The State of Native America: Genocide, Colonization, and Resistance*, edited by Annette M. Jaimes, 241–266. Boston: South End Press.

Clifford, James. 1988. "Identity in Mashpee." In *The Predicament of Culture: Twentieth-Century Ethnography, Literature, and Art*, edited by James Clifford, 277–346. Cambridge, MA: Harvard University Press.

Cohen, Matt. 2010. *The Networked Wilderness: Communicating in Early New England*. Minneapolis: University of Minnesota Press.

Collier, John. (1949) 1995. *Patterns and Ceremonials of the Indians of the Southwest*. Illustrated by Ira Moskowitz. New York: Dover Publications.

Comstock, Tamara, ed. 1972. *New Dimensions in Dance Research: Anthropology and Dance—The American Indian*. New York: Committee on Research on Dance.

Conklin, Abe. 1994. "Origin of the Powwow: The Ponca He-Thus-Ka Society Dance." In *Native American Expressive Culture*, edited by José Barriero, 17–21. Ithaca, NY: Akwe:kon Press.

Connerton, Paul. 1989. *How Societies Remember*. Cambridge: Cambridge University Press.

Contreras, Don (photography), and Diane Morris Bernstein (texts). 1996. *We Dance Because We Can: People of the Powwow*. Marietta, Georgia: Longstreet Press.

Corrigan, Samuel W. 1970. "The Plains Indian Powwow: Cultural Integration in Manitoba Saskatchewan." *Anthropologica* 12(2): 253–277.

Cronk, Michael Samuel, with Beverley Cavanagh and Franziska von Rosen. 1987. "Celebration: Native Events in Eastern Canada." In *Folklife Annual*, edited by Alan Jabbour and James Hardin, 70–85. Washington, DC: Superintendent of Documents, Government Printing Office.

Crum, Robert. 1994. *Eagle Drum: On the Powwow Trail with a Young Grass Dancer*. New York: Four Winds Press.

de Certeau, Michel. (1984) 1988. *The Practice of Everyday Life*. Translated by Steven Rendall. Berkeley: University of California Press.

Deloria, Philip J. 1998. *Playing Indian*. New Haven, CT: Yale University Press.

———. 2004. *Indians in Unexpected Places*. Lawrence: University of Kansas Press.

Deloria, Vine, Jr. (1970) 1988. *Custer Died for Your Sins: An Indian Manifesto*. Norman: University of Oklahoma Press.

———. 1994. *God Is Red: A Native View of Religion*. Golden, CO: Fulcrum Publishers.

Drinnon, Richard. 1987. "The Metaphysics of Dancing Tribes." In *The American Indian and the Problem of History*, edited by Calvin Martin, 106–113. New York: Oxford University Press.

Durham, Jimmie. 1992. "Cowboys and . . . Notes on Art, Literature, and American Indians in the Modern American Mind." In *The State of Native America: Genocide, Colonization, and Resistance*, edited by Annette M. Jaimes, 423–438. Boston: South End Press.

Dyck, Noel. 1979. "Powwow and the Expression of Community in Western Canada." *Ethnos* 44(1–2): 78–98.

———. 1983. "Political Powwow: The Rise and Fall of an Urban Native Festival." In *The Celebration of Society: Perspectives on Contemporary Cultural Performance*, edited by Frank E. Manning, 165–184. Bowling Green, OH: Bowling Green University Popular Press.

Edmunds, R. David. 1995. "New Visions, Old Stories: The Emergence of a New Indian History." *OAH Magazine of History* 9(4): 3–9.

Eliade, Mircea. 1961. *The Sacred and the Profane: The Nature of Religion*. New York: Harper and Row.

Ellis, Clyde. 2003. *A Dancing People: Powwow Culture on the Southern Plains*. Lawrence: University Press of Kansas.

Ellis, Clyde, Luke Lassiter, and Gary H. Dunham, eds. 2005. *Powwow*. Lincoln: University of Nebraska Press.

Erdrich, Louise. 1994. *The Bingo Palace*. New York: HarperCollins.

———. 2012. *The Round House*. New York: HarperCollins.

———. 2013. "Rape on the Reservation." *New York Times*, February 26.

Farnell, Brenda. 1999a. "Moving Bodies, Acting Selves." *Annual Review of Anthropology* 28: 341–373.

———. 1999b. "It Goes without Saying—but Not Always." In *Dance in the Field: Theory, Methods, and Issues in Dance Ethnography*, edited by Theresa J. Buckland, 145–160. New York: St. Martin's Press.

———, ed. 2001. *Human Action Sign in Cultural Context: The Visible and the Invisible in Movement and Dance*. Lanham, MD: Scarecrow Press.

Feest, Christian F., ed. 1989. *Indians and Europe. An Interdisciplinary Collection of Essays*. Herodot Edition. Aachen, Germany: Rader-Verlag.

Fenton, W. N. (1941) 2005. *Masked Medicine Societies of the Iroquois*. Ontario: Iroqrafts.

———. (1953) 1991. *The Iroquois Eagle Dance: An Offshoot of the Calumet Dance*. Syracuse: Syracuse University Press.

Fischer, Ernst. 1963. *The Necessity of Art: A Marxist Approach*. Anna Bostock, trans. New York: Penguin Books.

Fletcher, Alice C. (1915) 1994. *Indian Games & Dances with Native Songs: Arranged from American Indian Ceremonials and Sports*. Intro. Helen Myers. Boston: First Bison Book.

Foucault, Michel. (1977) 1995. *Discipline and Punish: The Birth of the Prison*. Translated by Alan Sheridan. New York: Vintage Press.

———. (1978) 1990. *The History of Sexuality*. Vol. 1, *An Introduction*. Translated by Robert Hurley. New York: Vintage Books.

———. 1980. *Power/Knowledge: Selected Interviews & Other Writings 1972–1977*. Edited by Colin Gordon. Translated by Colin Gordon, Leo Marshall, John Mepham, and Kate Soper. New York: Pantheon Books.

———. 1989. *Foucault Live: Collected Interviews, 1961–1984*. Edited by Sylvere Lotringer. Translated by Lysa Hochroth and John Johnston. New York: Semiotext(e).

Frankenberg, Ruth. 1994. "Whiteness and Americanness: Examining Constructions of Race, Culture, and Nation in White Women's Narratives." In *Race*, edited by Steven Gregory and Roger Sanjek, 62–77. New Brunswick, NJ: Rutgers University Press.

Frazier, Ian. 2000. *On the Rez*. New York: Farrar, Straus and Giroux.

Friedland, Lee Ellen. 2001. "Social Commentary in African-American Movement Performance." In *Human Action Sign in Cultural Context: The Visible and Invisible in Movement and Dance*, edited by Brenda Farnell, 136–157. Metuchen, NJ: Scarecrow Press.

Fusco, Coco. 1995. *English Is Broken Here: Notes on Cultural Fusion in the Americas*. New York: New Press.

Fuss, Diana. 1989. *Essentially Speaking: Feminism, Nature & Difference*. London: Routledge.

Galchen, Rivka. 2012. "Wild West Germany: Why Do Cowboys and Indians So Captivate the Country?" *New Yorker* 88(8): 40–45.

Gardner, Howard. 1993. *Frames of Mind: The Theory of Multiple Intelligences*. New York: Basic Books.

Geertz, Clifford. 1973. "Thick Description: Toward an Interpretive Theory of Culture." In Geertz, *The Interpretation of Cultures*, 3–30. New York: Basic Books.

Gelo, Daniel Joseph. 1986. "Comanche Belief and Ritual." PhD diss., Rutgers State University.

———. 2005. "Powwow Patter: Indian Emcee Discourse on Power and Identity." In *Powwow*, edited by Clyde Ellis, Luke Eric Lassiter, and Gary H. Dunham, 130–151. Lincoln: University of Nebraska Press.

Gilbert, Tamara B. 1991. "Urban Powwows: Form and Meaning." *UCLA Journal of Dance Ethnology* 15: 78–90.

Gilley, Brian Joseph. 2005. "Two-Spirit Powwows and the Search for Social Acceptance in Indian Country." In *Powwow*, edited by Clyde Ellis, Luke Eric Lassiter, and Gary H. Dunham, 224–240. Lincoln: University of Nebraska Press.

Giurchescu, Anca. 1999. "Past and Present in Field Research: A Critical History of Personal Experience." In *Dance in the Field: Theory, Methods, and Issues in Dance Ethnography*, edited by Theresa J. Buckland, 41–54. New York: St. Martin's Press.

Goertzen, Chris. 2005. "Purposes of North Carolina Powwows." In *Powwow*, edited by Clyde Ellis, Luke Lassiter, and Gary H. Dunham, 258–302. Lincoln: University of Nebraska Press.

Goffman, Erving. 1959. *The Presentation of Self in Everyday Life*. New York: Anchor Books.

Goldman, Ellen. 2004. *As Others See Us: Body Movement and the Art of Successful Communication*. New York: Routledge.

Green, Rayna. 1988. "The Tribe Called Wannabee: Playing Indian in America and Europe." *Folklore* 99(1): 30–55.

Greenhalgh, Paul. 1988. *Ephemeral Vistas: The Expositions Universelles, Great Exhibitions, and World's Fairs, 1851–1939*. Glasglow, UK: Bell and Bain.

Gregory, Steven and Roger Sanjek, eds. 1994. *Race*. New Brunswick: Rutgers University Press.

Haberland, Wolfgang. 1987. "Nine Bella Coolas in Germany." In *Indians and Europe: An Interdisciplinary Collection of Essays*, edited by Christian Feest, 337–373. Aachen, Germany: Rader Verlag.

Hall, Edward T. (1959) 1973. *The Silent Language*. New York: Anchor Books.

———. (1966) 1990. *The Hidden Dimension*. New York: Anchor Books.

———. (1976) 1989. *Beyond Culture*. New York: Anchor Books.

———. 1983. *The Dance of Life: The Other Dimension of Time*. New York: Anchor Books.

Hancock, Black Hawk. 2005. "Steppin' out of Whiteness." *Ethnography* 6(4): 427–461.

Herndon, Ruth Wallis, and Ella Wilcox Sekatau. 2003. "Colonizing the Children: Indian Youngsters in Servitude in Early Rhode Island." In *Reinterpreting New England Indians and the Colonial Experience*, edited by Colin G. Calloway and Neal Salisbury, 137–173. Boston: Colonial Society of Massachusetts.

Heth, Charlotte, ed. 1992. *Native American Dance: Ceremonies and Social Traditions*. Washington, DC: National Museum of the American Indian Smithsonian Institution with Starwood Publishing.

Hinsley, Charles M. 1992. "The World as Marketplace: Commodification of the Exotic as the World's Columbian Exposition, Chicago, 1893." In *Exhibiting Cultures: The Poetics and Politics of Museum Display*, edited by Ivan Karp and Steven D. Levine, 344–350. Washington, DC: Smithsonian Institution Press.

Hohman, John George. 1989. *Powwows or Long Lost Friend—The Long-Suppressed, Reviled & Referred Pennsylvania-German Folk-Healing Classic*. Cody, WY: Buffalo Bill Historical Center.

Horst, Louis, and Carroll Russell. 1961. *Modern Dance Forms in Relation to Other Arts*. New York: Dance Horizons.

Howard, James H. 1955. "The Pan-Indian Culture of Oklahoma." *Scientific Monthly* 81(5): 215–220.

———. 1976. "The Plains Gourd Dance as a Revitalization Movement." *American Ethnologist* 3(2): 243–259.

Huenemann, Lynn F. 1992. "Northern Plains Dance." In *Native American Dance: Ceremonies and Social Traditions*, edited by Charlotte Heth, 125–134. Washington, DC: National Museum of the American Indian, Smithsonian Institution with Starwood Publishing.

Humphrey, Doris. (1959) 1987. *The Art of Making Dances*. Princeton, NJ: Princeton Book Company.

Jaimes, M. Annette, ed. 1992. *The State of Native America: Genocide, Colonization, and Resistance*. Boston: South End Press.

———. 1992. "Federal Indian Identification Policy: A Usurpation of Indigenous Sovereignty in North America." In *The State of Native America: Genocide, Colonization, and Resistance*, edited by Annette M. Jaimes, 123–138. Boston: South End Press.

———. 1994. "American Racism: The Impact on American Indian Identity and Survival." In *Race*, edited by Steven Gregory and Roger Sanjek, 41–61. New Brunswick, NJ: Rutgers University Press.

Jones, Blackwolf, and Gina Jones. 1996. *Earth Dance Drum: A Celebration of Life*. Salt Lake City: Commune-a-Key Publishers.

Kaeppler, Adrienne L. 1999. "The Mystique of Fieldwork." In *Dance in the Field: Theory,*

*Method, and Issues in Dance Ethnography*, edited by Theresa J. Buckland, 13–25. New York: St. Martin's Press.

———. 2001. "Visible and Invisible in Hawaiian Dance." In *Human Action Sign in Cultural Context: The Visible and Invisible in Movement and Dance*, edited by Brenda Farnell, 31–43. Metuchen, NJ: Scarecrow Press.

Kavanagh, Thomas W. 1992. "Southern Plains Dance: Tradition and Dynamics." In *Native American Dance: Ceremonies and Social Traditions*, edited by Charlotte Heth, 105–123. Washington, DC: National Museum of the American Indian, Smithsonian Institution with Starwood Publishing.

Kehoe, Alice Beck. 2006. *The Ghost Dance: Ethnohistory and Revitalization*. 2nd ed. Long Grove, IL: Waveland Press.

King, Sandra. 1993. *Shannon: An Ojibway Dancer*. Photographs by Catherine Whipple. Minneapolis.: Lerner Publishing.

Kirshenblatt-Gimblett, Barbara. 1992. "Objects of Ethnography." In *Exhibiting Cultures: The Poetics and Politics of Museum Display*, edited by Ivan Karp and Steven D. Levine, 386–443. Washington, DC: Smithsonian Institution Press.

Koch, Ronald R. 1977. *Dress Clothing of the Plains Indians*. Norman: University of Oklahoma Press.

Kracht, Benjamin R. 1994. "Kiowa Powwows: Continuity in Ritual Practice." *American Indian Quarterly* 18(3): 321–348.

Krouse, Susan Applegate. 1991. "A Window into the Indian Culture: The Powwow as Performance." PhD diss., University of Wisconsin.

Kurath, Gertrude Prokosch. 1957. "Pan-Indianism in Great Lakes Tribal Festivals." *Journal of American Folklore* 70(276): 179–183.

———. (1964) 2000. *Iroquois Music and Dance: Ceremonial Arts of Two Seneca Longhouses*. Mineola, NY: Dover Publications.

Laban, Rudolf. (1939) 1974. *The Language of Movement: A Guidebook to Choreutics*. Annotated and edited by Lisa Ullmann. Boston: Plays.

———. (1950) 1971. *The Mastery of Movement*. Revised by Lisa Ullmann. Boston: Plays.

Lassiter, Luke E. 1996. "Towards Understanding the Power of Kiowa Song: A Collaborative Exercise in Meaning." PhD diss., University of North Carolina.

———. 1998. *The Power of Kiowa Song: A Collaborative Ethnography*. Tucson: University of Arizona Press.

Laubin, Reginald, and Gladys Laubin. 1976. *Indian Dances of North America: Their Importance to Indian Life*. Norman: University of Oklahoma Press.

Lefebvre, Henri. (1974) 1991. *The Production of Space*. Translated by David Nicholson-Smith. Oxford: Blackwell Publishers.

Leonard, Elizabeth Jane, and Julia Cody Goodman. 1955. *Buffalo Bill: King of the Old West*. Edited by James Williams Hoffman. New York: Library Publishers.

Lepore, Jill. 1998. *The Name of War: King Philip's War and the Origins of American Identity*. New York: Alfred A. Knopf.

Lesser, Alexander. 1933. *Pawnee Ghost Dance Hand Game: Ghost Dance Revival and Ethnic Identity*. New York: Columbia University Press.

Letay, Miklos. 1987. "'Redskins at the Zoo': Sioux Indians in Budapest, 1886." In *Indians and Europe: An Interdisciplinary Collection of Essays*, edited by Christian Feest, 375–381. Aachen, Germany: Rader Verlag.

Lipsitz, George. 1990. *Time Passages: Collective Memory and American Popular Culture*. Minneapolis: University of Minnesota Press.

Lowie, Robert H. (1913) 1916a. "Eastern Dakota Dances." In *Societies of the Plains Indians*, edited by Clark Wissler, 101–142. New York: The Trustees of the American Museum of Natural History.

———. (1913) 1916b. "Societies of the Hidasta and Mandan Indians." In *Societies of the Plains Indians*, edited by Clark Wissler, 219–358. New York: The Trustees of the American Museum of Natural History.

———. (1913) 1916c. "Military Societies of the Crow Indians." In *Societies of the Plains Indians*, edited by Clark Wissler, 143–217. New York: The Trustees of the American Museum of Natural History.

MacCannell, Dean. 1976. *The Tourist: A New Theory of the Leisure Class*. New York: Schocken Books.

Malinowski, Bronislaw. (1947) 1995. Introduction. In Fernando Ortiz, *Cuban Counterpoint: Tobacco and Sugar*, lvii–lxiv. Translated by Harriet de Onís. Durham, NC: Duke University Press.

Mann, Charles C. 2002. "1491." *Atlantic* 289(3): 41–53.

———. 2006. *1491: New Revelations of the Americas before Columbus*. New York: Vintage Books.

Marra, Ben. 1996. *Powwow: Images along the Red Road*. New York: Harry N. Abrams.

Martin, Randy. 1998. *Critical Moves: Dance Studies in Theory and Politics*. Durham, NC: Duke University Press.

Mason, Bernard Sterling. 1944. *Dances and Stories of the American Indian*. Photographs by Paul Boris and others. Drawings by Frederic H. Koch. New York: A. S. Barnes.

McBride, Bunny, and Harald E. L. Prins. 2009. *Indians in Eden: Wabanakis & Rusticators on Maine's Mount Desert Island, 1840–1920*. East Peoria, IL: Versa Press.

McMillin, Laurie Hovell. 2006. *Buried Indians: Digging Up the Past in a Midwestern Town*. Madison: University of Wisconsin.

McNamara, Brooks. 1976. *Step Right Up*. Garden City, NJ: Doubleday.

Mitchell-Green, Bonnie Lynn. 1995. "American Indian Powwows in Utah, 1983–1994: A Case Study in Oppositional Culture." PhD diss., University of Texas.

Mohawk, John. 1992. "Epilogue: Looking for Columbus: Thoughts on the Past, Present, and Future of Humanity." In *The State of Native America: Genocide, Colonization, and Resistance*, edited by Annette M. Jaimes, 439–444. Boston: South End Press.

Momaday, Scott N. 1987. "Personal Reflections." In *The American Indian and the Problem of History*, edited by Calvin Martin, 156–161. New York: Oxford University Press.

Mooney, James. (1896) 1965. *The Ghost-Dance Religion and the Sioux Outbreak of 1890*. Chicago: University of Chicago Press.

Moore, John H. 1993. "How Give-a-Ways and Pow-Wows Redistribute the Means of Subsistence." In *The Political Economy of North American Indians*, edited by James H. Moore, 241–269. Norman: University of Oklahoma Press.

Muñoz, José Esteban. 1998. "Pedro's Zamora's Real World of Counterpublicity: Performing an Ethics of the Self." In *Living Color: Race and Television in the United States*, edited by Sasha Torres, 195–218. Durham, NC: Duke University Press.

———. 1999. *Disidentifications: Queers of Color and the Performance of Politics*. Minneapolis: University of Minnesota Press.

Murie, James R. (1914) 1916. "Pawnee Indian Societies." In *Societies of the Plains Indians*, edited by Clark Wissler, 543–644. New York: The Trustees of the American Museum of Natural History.

Murphy, Jacqueline Shea. 2007. *The People Have Never Stopped Dancing: Native American Modern Dance Histories*. Minneapolis: University of Minnesota Press.

Napier, Rita G. 1987. "'Across the Big River: American Indians' Perceptions of Europe and Europeans, 1887–1906." In *Indians and Europe: An Interdisciplinary Collection of Essays*, edited by Christian Feest, 383–401. Aachen, Germany: Rader Verlag.

Neel, David. 1996. "Schemitzun: The World Championship of Powwow." *Native Peoples* 9: 58–62.

Ness, Sally. 1992. *Movement, Body, and Culture: Kinesthetic and Visual Symbolism in a Philippine Community*. Philadelphia: University of Pennsylvania Press.

Newell, Margaret Ellen. 2003. "The Changing Nature of Indian Slavery in New England, 1670–1720." In *Reinterpreting New England Indians and the Colonial Experience*, edited by Colin G. Calloway and Neal Salisbury, 106–136. Boston: Colonial Society of Massachusetts.

*New York Times*. 1941. "Indian Tribes Hold Powwow in Hotel: 1, 500 Gather Here, Many in Traditional Costumes, for Send-Off for Trainees." March 16.

———. 1953. "Two Powwows Mark American Indian Day." September 27.

Ngũgĩ wa Thiong'o. 1993. *Moving the Center: The Struggle for Cultural Freedoms*. Portsmouth, NH: Heinemann.

———. 1998. *Penpoints, Gunpoints, and Dreams: Towards a Critical Theory of the Arts and the State in Africa*. Oxford: Clarendon Press.

Ortiz, Fernando. (1947) 1995. *Cuban Counterpoint: Tobacco and Sugar*. Translated by Harriet de Onís. Durham, NC: Duke University Press.

Parker, Andrew, and Eve Kosofsky Sedwick. 1995. "Introduction: Performativity and Performance." In *Performativity and Performance*, edited by Andrew Parker and Eve Kosofsky Sedwick, 1–18. New York: Routledge.

Pearse, Roy Harvey. 1988. *Savagism and Civilization: A Study of the Indian and the American Mind*. Berkeley: University of California Press.

Peroff, Nicholas C. 1982. *Menominee Drums: Tribal Termination and Restoration, 1954–74*. Norman: University of Oklahoma Press.

Phelan, Peggy. 1993. *Unmarked: The Politics of Performance*. London: Routledge.

Polhemus, Ted. 1975. "Social Bodies." In *The Body as a Medium of Expression*, edited by J. Benthall and Ted Polhemus, 13–35. New York: E.P. Dutton.

Power, Susan. 1994. *The Grass Dancer*. New York: Berkley Books.

Powers, William K. 1961. "The Sioux Omaha Dance." *American Indian Tradition* 8(1): 23–33.

———. 1962a. "The Rabbit Dance." *American Indian Tradition* 8(3): 113–118.

———. 1962b. "Sneak-Up Dance, Drum, and Flag Eagle Dance." *American Indian Tradition* 8(4): 166–171.

———. 1966. "Feathers Costume." *Powwow Trails* 3(7–8): 4–14, 19.

———. 1968. "Contemporary Oglala Music and Dance: Pan-Indianism versus Pan-Tetonism." *Ethnomusicology* 12(3): 352–372.

———. 1990. *War Dance: Plains Indian Musical Performance*. Tucson: University of Arizona Press.

Pritchard, Evan T. 2002. *Native New Yorkers: The Legacy of the Algonquian People*. San Francisco: Council Oak Books.

Reardon, Christopher. 1998. "Dance: When Collaborators Find Themselves Out of Step." *New York Times*, August 30.

Ridington, Robin, Dennis Hastings, and Tommy Attachie. 2005. "The Songs of Our Elders: Performance and Cultural Survival in Omaha and Dane-zaa Traditions." In *Powwow*, edited by Clyde Ellis, Luke Eric Lassiter, and Gary H. Dunham, 110–129. Lincoln: University of Nebraska Press.

Roach, Joseph. 1996. *Cities of the Dead: Circum-Atlantic Performance*. New York: Columbia University Press.

Roberts, Chris. 1992. *Powwow Country*. Helena, MT: American and World Geographic Publishing.

———. 1998. *Powwow Country: People of the Circle*. Missoula, MT: Meadow Lark Publishers.

Rose, Wendy. 1992. "The Great Pretender: Further Reflections on Whiteshamanism." In *The State of Native America: Genocide, Colonization, and Resistance*, edited by Annette M. Jaimes, 403–421. Boston: South End Press.

Rowlandson, Mary. (1682) 1997. *The Sovereignty and Goodness of God, Together with the Faithfulness of His Promises Displayed*. Edited by Neal Salisbury. Boston: Bedford Books.

Royce, Anya Peterson. 1977. *The Anthropology of Dance*. Bloomington: Indiana University Press.

Rydell, Robert W. 1984. *All the World's a Fair: Visions of Empire at American Expositions, 1876–1916*. Chicago: University of Chicago Press.

Rynkiewich, Michael A. 1980. "Chippewa Powwows." In *Anishanabe: 6 Studies of Modern Chippewa*, edited by Anthony J. Paredes, 31–100. Tallahassee: Florida State University Press.

Said, Edward W. (1978) 1994. *Orientalism*. New York: Vintage Books.

Sanchez, Victoria Eugenie. 1995. "'As Long As We Dance, We Shall Know Who We Are': A Study of Off-Reservation Traditional Intertribal Powwows in Central Ohio." PhD diss., Ohio State University.

Sarris, Greg. 1993. *Keeping Slug Woman Alive: A Holistic Approach to American Texts*. Berkeley: University of California Press.

Sayers, Isabelle S. 1981. *Annie Oakley and Buffalo Bill's Wild West*. New York: Dover Publishers.

Schechner, Richard. (1977) 1994. *Performance Theory*. New York: Routledge.

———. 1985. *Between Theater and Anthropology*. Philadelphia: University of Pennsylvania Press.

———. 1993. *The Future of Ritual: Writings on Culture and Performance*. New York: Routledge.

———. 2002. *Performance Studies: An Introduction*. New York: Routledge.

Scheflen, Albert E. 1974. *How Behavior Means: Exploring the Contexts of Speech and Meaning: Kinesics, Posture, Interaction, Setting, and Culture*. Garden City, NJ: Doubleday.

Seals, David. 1990. *The Powwow Highway*. New York: Plume.

Searle, John R. 1986. "What Is a Speech Act?" In *Critical Theory since 1965*, edited by Hazard Adams and Leroy Searle, 60–69. Tallahassee: Florida State University Press.

Seton, Ernest Thompson. (1910) 2010. *Boy Scouts of America: A Handbook of Woodcraft Scouting, and Life-Craft*. Memphis, TN: General Books.

Shifrin, Ellen. 1979–1980. "Nineteenth-Century Performing Indians: An Annotated Bibliography." *Dance Research Journal* 12(1): 13–23.

Siegel, Marcia. 1991. "Accessing the Non-Verbal—Again." Unpublished manuscript.

Skinner, Alanson. (1915) 1916. "Societies of the Iowa." In *Societies of the Plains Indians*, edited by Clark Wissler, 679–740. New York: The Trustees of the American Museum of Natural History.

Sklar, Diedre. 1994. "Can Bodylore Be Brought to Its Senses?" *Journal of American Folklore* 107(423): 9–22.

Smith, Rex Alan. 1975. *Moon of Popping Trees*. Lincoln: University of Nebraska Press.

Speck, Frank G. (1940) 1998. *Penobscot Man: The Life History of a Forest Tribe in Maine*. Orono: University of Maine Press.

Speck, Frank G., and Leonard Bloom in collaboration with Will West Long. (1951) 1993. *Cherokee Dance and Drama*. Norman: University of Oklahoma Press.

Spitta, Silvia. 1997. "Transculturation, the Caribbean, and the Cuban-American Imaginary." In *Tropicalizations: Transcultural Representations of Latinidad*, edited by Frances R. Aparicio and Susana Chavez-Silverman, 160–182. Hanover: University Press of New England.

Stephenson, Lisa. 1993. *Powwow: Questions and Answers*. Bismarck, ND: United Tribes Technical College.

Sweet, Jill D. 1985. *Dances of the Tewa Pueblo Indians: Expressions of a New Life*. Santa Fe, NM: School of American Research Press.

Takaki, Ronald. 1990. *Iron Cages: Race and Culture in 19th-Century America*. New York: Oxford University Press.

———. 1993. *A Different Mirror: A History of Multicultural America*. Boston: Little, Brown.

Teller, Henry Moore. 1883. Preface Letter. In United States Office of Indian Affairs, *Rules Governing the Court of Indian Defenses*. Washington, DC: Government Printing Office.

Toelken, Barre. 1991. "Ethnic Selection and Intensification in the Native American Powwow." In *Creative Ethnicity: Symbols and Strategies of Contemporary Life*, edited by Stephen Stern and John Allan, 137–156. Logan: Utah State University Press.

Underhill, Ruth M. 1965. *Red Man's Religion: Beliefs and Practices of the Indians of North America*. Chicago: University of Chicago Press.

Urciuoli, Bonnie. 2001. "The Indexical Structure of Visibility." In *Human Action Sign in Cultural Context: The Visible and Invisible in Movement and Dance*, edited by Brenda Farnell, 189–215. Metuchen, NJ: Scarecrow Press.

Utter, Jack. 1992. *Wounded Knee and the Ghost Dance Tragedy*. Memorial Edition. Lake Ann, MI: National Woodlands Publishing.

Varela, Charles. 2001. "Cartesianism Revisited: The Ghost in the Moving Machine or the Lived Body." In *Human Action Sign in Cultural Context: The Visible and Invisible in Movement and Dance*, edited by Brenda Farnell, 216–293. Metuchen, NJ: Scarecrow Press.

Vizenor, Gerald. (1967) 1990. "Socioacupunture: Mythic Reversals and the Striptease in Four Scenes." In Vizenor, *Crossbloods: Bone Courts, Bingo, and Other Reports*, 83–97. Minneapolis: University of Minnesota Press.

———. (1989) 1993. "A Postmodern Introduction." In *Narrative Chance: Postmodern Discourse on Native American Indian Literatures*, edited by Gerald Vizenor, 3–16. Norman: University of Oklahoma Press.

———. 1994. *Manifest Manners*. Hanover, NH: Wesleyan University Press.

Wald, Priscilla. 1994. "Terms of Assimilation: Legislating Subjectivity in the Emerging Nation." In *American Indian Persistence and Resurgence*, edited by Karl Kroeber, 78–105. Durham: Duke University Press.

Watchman, Renae. 2005. "Powwows Overseas: The German Experience." In *Powwow*, edited by Clyde Ellis, Luke Eric Lassiter, and Gary H. Dunham, 241–257. Lincoln: University of Nebraska Press.

Weaver, Jace, Craig S. Womack, and Robert Warrior. 2006. *American Indian Literary Nationalism*. Foreword by Simon J. Ortiz. Afterword by Lisa Brooks. Albuquerque: University of New Mexico Press.

West, W. Richard, Jr. 1992. "Foreword." In *Native American Dance: Ceremonies and Social Traditions*, edited by Charlotte Heth, ix–x. Washington, DC: National Museum of the American Indian, Smithsonian Institution with Starwood Publishing.

Wetmore, Helen Cody, and Zane Grey. (1899) 1918. *Last of the Great Scouts ("Buffalo Bill")*. New York: Grosset & Dunlap.

White, Julia C. 1994. *The Pow Wow Trail*. Summertown, TN: Book Publishing Company.

Whitehorse, David. 1988. *Pow-Wow: The Contemporary Pan-Indian Celebration*. San Diego: San Diego State University Press.

Williams, Drid. 1997. *Anthropology and Human Movement: The Study of Dances*. Lanham, MD: Scarecrow Press.

———. 2000. *Anthropology and Human Movement: Searching for Origins*. Lanham, MD: Scarecrow Press.

———. 2001. "Space, Intersubjectivity, and the Conceptual Imperative: Three Ethnographic Cases." In *Human Action Sign in Cultural Context: The Visible and Invisible in Movement and Dance*, edited by Brenda Farnell, 44–81. Metuchen, NJ: Scarecrow Press.

———. 2004. *Anthropology and the Dance: Ten Lectures*. 2nd ed. Urbana: University of Illinois Press.

Williams, Walter L. (1986) 1992. *The Spirit and the Flesh: Sexual Diversity in American Indian Culture*. Boston: Beacon Press.

Wissler, Clark, ed. 1916a. *Societies of the Plains Indians*. New York: The Trustees of the American Museum of Natural History.

———. 1916b. "General Discussion of Shamanistic and Dancing Societies." In *Societies of the Plains Indians*, edited by Clark Wissler, 853–876. New York: The Trustees of the American Museum of Natural History.

———. 1916c. "Societies and Dance Associations of the Blackfoot Indians." In *Societies of the Plains Indians*, edited by Clark Wissler, 359–460. New York: The Trustees of the American Museum of Natural History.

———. 1916d. "Societies and Ceremonial Associations in the Oglala Division of the Teton-Dakota." In *Societies of the Plains Indians*, edited by Clark Wissler, 1–99. New York: The Trustees of the American Museum of Natural History.

Yost, Nellie Snyder. 1980. *Buffalo Bill: His Family, Friends, Fame, Failures, and Fortunes*. Athens: Ohio University Press.

Young, Gloria Alese. 1981. "Powwow Power: Perspectives on Historic and Contemporary Intertribalism." PhD diss., Indiana University.

———. 1994. "Dance as Communication." In *Native American Expressive Culture*, edited by José Barriero, 9–15. Ithaca, NY: Akwe: kon Press.

Zile, Judy Van. 1999. "Capturing the Dance." In *Dance in the Field: Theory, Methods, and Issues in Dance Ethnography*, edited by Theresa J. Buckland, 85–99. New York: St. Martin's Press.

# Index

*Page numbers in italics refer to illustrations.*

DR. ANN AXTMANN has extensive experience in body, movement, and dance studies. Her primary interest is in the potential of movement to express the personal, the social, and the political within and across cultures.

Ann holds a PhD in Performance Studies from New York University and is a Certified Movement Analysis. Former teaching positions include: the University of Puebla, Mexico, the Gallatin School, NYU, and LIMS, NYC. She has also performed with the Joffrey Ballet, American Ballet Theater, and many other dance companies. As a choreographer, she created over 20 dance-theater works which have been performed throughout Mexico and in the USA. These works deal with themes such as rape, homelessness, *Las Madres de la Plaza de Mayo*, and women's independence.

Dr. Axtmann's publications include numerous journal articles in English and Spanish. Her book *Indians and Wannabes: Native American Powwow Dancing in the Northeast and Beyond* won the 2013 Northeast Popular Cultural Association's (NEPCA) Peter C. Rollins Book Award. She is currently living on Mount Desert Island in Maine and working as an independent scholar and author.

www.ingramcontent.com/pod-product-compliance
Lightning Source LLC
Chambersburg PA
CBHW021619270326
41931CB00008B/767